Japan and Korea

Japan and Korea:
Contemporary Studies

Proceedings of the Fourth Nordic Symposium on
Japanese and Korean Studies

edited by Bjarke Frellesvig and Roy Starrs

AARHUS UNIVERSITY PRESS

Published with the financial support of the Aarhus University Research
Foundation, the Danish Research Council for the Humanities, the Danish
Research Council for the Social Sciences, and the Japan Foundation.

AARHUS UNIVERSITY PRESS
University of Aarhus
DK-8000 Aarhus C
Fax (+ 45) 8619 8433

73 Lime Walk
Headington, Oxford OX3 7AD
Fax (+ 44) 1865 750 079

Box 511
Oakville, CT 06779
Fax (+ 1) 860 945 9468

ANSI/NISO
Z39.48-1992

Table of Contents

Literature

Culture and Society

Introduction

Bjarke Frellesvig and Roy Starrs

The papers in this book are based on presentations given at the *Fourth Nordic Symposium on Japanese and Korean Studies* which was held at the University of Aarhus, 5-8 September 1995, as the official meeting of the Nordic Association for Japanese and Korean Studies (NAJAKS). The majority of the presentations at the symposium appear in this volume (a single contributor, Shimamori, was prevented at the last minute from taking part in the symposium, but the paper is included here).

Topically, the contributions to this volume, as to the original symposium, fall in three categories: linguistics, literature, and culture and society. Within each category a variety of approaches and subject matters are represented. However, it is also conspicuous that the great majority of contributions deal solely with Japan. Surely this to some extent reflects the fact that formal Korea studies are firmly established at only a single university in the Nordic countries (the University of Stockholm, Sweden), whereas Japan studies have a long standing in the curricula of several universities within each of the Nordic countries. One may hope that in the future Korea studies will find its natural place among East Asian studies also in the Nordic countries.

Linguistics

Bramsen addresses the functions of the grammatical morpheme *ga/i* in Korean, in particular pointing out that it is not limited to marking grammatical subject (and that the term 'subject marker' therefore is inappropriate), but also has a number of other functions, for example to mark predicate nominals in certain constructions.

Hagers adduces evidence from a Korean hangul source on the Ryukyuan language from the beginning of the 16th century to support hypotheses about the development of verb and adjective inflection in Ryukyuan, concerning both the formation of the 'conclusive' form and the role played by the suffix *sa*, usually thought to be nominalizing.

Presenting data from her own longitudinal study, supplemented with other published data, *Hayashi* discusses the development in the speech of Japanese children of the expression of spatial relations, concluding that language specific patterns are discernable already in the speech of children under three years.

Irgens discusses how the notion of 'subjectivity' may be used to account for different phenomena in the grammars of Japanese and Norwegian, particularly the differences between *ga* and *wa* marking of subjects in certain sentences in Japanese and the use of the 'modal past' in Norwegian.

Presenting a wide array of data collected at the National Language Research Institute in Tokyo as part of a charting of the grammar of Japanese dialects, *Onishi* explores the possibility of establishing diachronic relationships between Japanese dialects on the basis of mergers of the conjugation classes of verbs.

Incorporating the contrasting notions of 'spontaneity' and 'causativity' (agentivity) in a description of grammatical voice in Japanese, *Shimamori* claims that the grammatical system reflects the Japanese people's traditional sense of values and that Japanese prefers intransitive 'to become' expressions over transitive 'to do' expressions in comparison with for example English.

Working within the framework of Jonathan Kaye's 'government phonology', *Yoshida* addresses the formalisation of accent assignment rules in Japanese, arguing that Japanese 'pitch accent' has more in common with stress accent than with tone in a true tone language. Also discussed is the apparent development in Standard Japanese from mobile towards fixed accent in nouns.

Literature

Although four of the six literary essays here deal with modern Japanese fiction — perhaps a fair indication of the popularity of this field — there is, nonetheless, a wide diversity of themes and approaches even among those four essays.

In a finely ironic and provocative reassessment of the oeuvre of the recent Nobel laureate, Ôe Kenzaburô, *Van Haute* causes us to wonder whether the very political correctness which made Ôe such prime Nobel material did not also long since lose him the popularity he once enjoyed, especially among the younger generation of Japanese readers.

Taking a more comparative literary approach, *Nagashima* and *Thunman* deal with two of the more interesting cases of cross-fertilization between Western and modern Japanese fiction: Mori Ôgai's highly sophisticated adaptation of Hans Christian Andersen's charming romantic tale, *The Improvisator*, and Mishima Yukio's borrowings, both subtle and unsubtle, from Raymond Radiguet in his postwar debut work, *Tôzoku* (*Thieves*), itself as romantic and as fantastic as an Andersen fairy tale.

Looking at modern Japanese fiction from a wider perspective, *Starrs* examines the ways in which some of the major Meiji writers struggled to develop a 'national narrative' as part of the general nation-building project of their age.

Turning our attention to an altogether earlier phase of Japanese fiction, *Takeuchi* draws on a wide scholarship in Tokugawa popular literature and social customs to provide some fascinating insights both into traditional Japanese concepts of marriage, so different from the Western romantic ideal, and into how these changed over time, even in a supposedly unchanging 'feudal' society.

In a welcome reminder that Japanese literature is as rich in poetry as in fiction, *O'Brien* translates and elucidates some haunting lyrics from one of the first major figures in modern Japanese poetry.

Culture and Society

If anything, the essays on society and culture are even more diverse than those on literature.

Bjørn examines the consequences for the relationship between Danish headquarters of multinational companies and their Japanese subsidiaries of the different management strategies employed at the subsidiaries, on the basis of interviews with both Danish and Japanese managers.

Based on his own field work, *Hermansen*'s essay provides an absorbing glimpse into the rarely seen 'underside' of Japan's economic miracle: one of the seedy areas of Osaka where 'day labourers' eke out their hand-to-mouth existence.

With a rare and exemplary lucidity, *Lidin* elucidates the full range of implications which the key Confucian concepts of *ki* and *ri* assumed in Tokugawa thought, and continue to assume in the background of modern Japanese thought.

Merviö analyzes the role played by stereotypes in any nation's, including Japan's, image of itself and of other nations.

Park examines the state of democracy in contemporary Japan, giving due consideration to the various resistances found in the traditional culture to democratic institutions and ways of thought.

Selstad examines and assesses the representation of the 'unique' and the 'ordinary' in Japanese urban life by other researchers in the light of his own field work in an 'urban village' in Tokyo.

Takahashi offers an in-depth analysis of the rhetoric of Japanese social welfare discourse and of how it has reflected the changing political trends of the recent past.

Acknowledgements

The Fourth Nordic Symposium on Japanese and Korean Studies was supported economically by the *Embassy of the Republic of Korea* in Denmark, the *Faculty for the Humanities at the University of Aarhus*, and the *Japan Foundation*. The organizer of the symposium, Bjarke Frellesvig, would like to take this opportunity to reiterate and publicize his thanks for this support without which it would have been impossible to organize the symposium.

The publication of this book has received economic support from *Aarhus University Research Foundation* (Aarhus Universitets Forskningsfond), the *Danish Research Council for the Humanities* (Statens humanistiske Forskningsråd), the *Danish Research Council for the Social Sciences* (Statens samfundsvidenskabelige Forskningsråd), and the *Japan Foundation*. The editors gratefully acknowledge this generous support.

Finally, the editors would like to express their gratitude to Dr Tønnes Bekker-Nielsen, director of Aarhus University Press, for his encouragement and support of this project, and also to our editor, Ms Sanne Lind Hansen, for her patient and painstaking editorial work on what was a bulky, difficult and diverse manuscript.

Transcription and names

Unless specifically noted, Japanese words are transcribed according to the Hepburn system and Korean words according to the McCune-Reischauer system. Words and names with an established English usage are excepted from this.

Following native custom, Japanese and Korean names are given with the family name first. However, in some cases individuals have chosen to write their own name in another order.

Linguistics

Korean Nominal Syntax with Special Regard to Nominative Constructions and the Various Functions of the Morpheme Ga[1]

Jørgen Bramsen

Introduction

The purpose of this paper is to discuss some key features of Korean nominal syntax. First, I want to comment in general on the terminology that traditionally is used in Korean nominal syntax for the nominative case. Second, I will illustrate some of the grammatical functions through examples. Finally, I will discuss the nature of the Korean case-system, and suggest the need for a new terminology for some of the functions in Korean nominal syntax.

My topic is 'Nominal Syntax, with Special Regard to Nominative Constructions and the Various functions of the Morpheme *ga*'. As indicated in the title, I want especially to concentrate on some problems related to the description of the morpheme *ga*. Considering the number of constructions that are possible for the subject in Korean and the number of grammatical functions the morpheme *ga* with the allomorph *i* (Hereafter I will refer to it as *ga* only) is capable of, it is odd that no grammar of the Korean language has, as yet, attempted to make a systematic presentation of the grammar of the nominative case with a complete listing of the grammatical morphemes and their distributions. My interest in the grammatical description of the various functions of the morpheme *ga* was triggered by reading Song, Seok-choong *Explorations in Korean Syntax and Semantics*. In this work, he makes a polemic reference to Samuel Martin's choice of terminology for *ga* as subject marker, and calls it mistaken. Since that time, I began to collect and list all the variations possible for the subject construction and Korean nominative grammar, and list the grammatical distribution of the morphemes

1. I want to offer special thanks to Tedda Rønnenkamp-Holst for reading this paper and giving valuable suggestions.

involved. My intention was to get a full picture of the whole scope of possible nominal constructions. This led me to the conclusion that the way traditional Korean grammar presents Korean nominal syntax is far from satisfactory.

Let me begin with a few observations concerning the classification of the case-morpheme *ga*. As mentioned above, Song points out in his book that Samuel Martin makes a mistake when he calls this morpheme a 'subject marker'. It is, however, not only Martin who makes this mistake. It has become standard terminology in most Korean grammars. Thus, for example, in a paper surveying thirty years of Korean linguistic research, entitled: 'Linguistic Theory and the Study of Korean Grammar', Nam Ki-sim (Nam 1983:153) likewise calls *ga* the subject-marker. My point here is that after 30 years of linguistic research in Korean grammar, a wrong terminology is still current for one of the most central morphemes in the grammatical system. Even though these linguists surely are well aware of the other grammatical functions of *ga*, still a misconceived grammatical terminology is upheld.

In recent years, new grammars have adopted a new term for *ga*, namely nominative marker (e.g. O'Grady 1991). But even this term can be misleading, because it also covers *only some* of the grammatical functions that *ga* performs.

The various ways of stating the subject

Let us begin by examining the various ways the grammatical subject can be represented in the sentence, and make a list of the different grammatical morphemes that can mark the subject. The following morphemes are possible:

1. ø
2. *ga*
3. *nŭn*
4. *kkesŏ*
5. *to, rang, mada, man, ina*, etc.
6. *rŭl*
7. *ŭi*
8. *ege*
9. *esŏ*

Here we have 9 different morphemes, all of which can mark the subject. This clarifies that the grammatical construction of the subject exceeds the boundaries of the morpheme *ga*. Consequently, a definition of the subject based upon the morpheme *ga* is insufficient. The question then is—how can we give a formal definition of the subject? Can it or can it not be linked with a morphological criterion?

If we take a look at the list, we can specify the grammatical function of the morphemes, and thereby reduce the grammar of the subject construction to fewer underlying grammatical structures.

1. First, we have the unmarked subject construction symbolized by ø (zero). When the subject thus is unmarked, only word order is left to constitute the noun or noun phrase as subject. Therefore, we have to conclude that the constituent factor of the subject here is *word order*.

2. Next, we have the morpheme *ga*, and to this group we can add no. 4 *kkesŏ*, since *kkesŏ* functions as an honorific allomorph of *ga*. Here, therefore, the subject noun phrase is marked by a morpheme. We can therefore say that the morpheme becomes the constituent factor of the subject here.

3. Next, we have *nŭn*, and to this group we can add the morphemes from no. 5: *to, rang, mada, man, ina*, etc. These grammatical morphemes are often grouped together and called 'delimiters' (Sohn 1994:29, 106, 225, 378). By delimiters is understood a class of grammatical morphemes, whose function is not to mark case but to delimit the content of the noun phrase in terms of adding a specification to the noun phrase. Thus:

nŭn delimits: topic — contrast
to delimits the noun in the sense — 'even, also'
rang delimits the noun as connective — 'and'
mada delimits the noun as frequentative — 'every'
man delimits the noun as limit — 'only'
ina delimits the noun as disjunction — 'or'

Since the delimiters do not mark case, but can freely be combined with all cases, they do not function to constitute the subject as subject. Hence *word order* again must be considered the constituent factor of the subject function.

One further comment on this group is due. Some linguists might argue that *nŭn* should be grouped by itself as a topic-contrast marker, because this function plays a major role in Korean syntax. Thus, Sohn describes the Korean language as a 'topic prominent language' (Sohn 1994:204). It can be suffixed both to nouns, verbal forms, negations etc., marking the suffixed word or phrase as the sentence theme. The grammatical distribution of *nŭn* is, however, too complex to describe here.

4. Finally, we have the last four grammatical morphemes, nos. 6, 7, 8 and

9. These four can be grouped together because they all are case-markers; no. 6 marks the accusative case, no. 7 the genitive case, no. 8 the dative case and no. 9 marks the locative case. The fact that these four cases, respectively, can function to mark the grammatical subject in a sentence requires a comment.

The *accusative* morpheme *rŭl* marking the subject is the result of the subject to object raising process that takes place in indirect discourse and causative constructions. The following two sentences give examples of this.[2]

First an example of the subject marked by *rŭl* in indirect discourse:

John-i kyosunim-ŭl ap'ŭsidako midŏtta
'John believed the professor to be sick'. (O'Gr.: 142)

and next, in a causative construction:

abŏji-ga adŭr-ŭl oge haetta
'The father made his son come'. (H.S.L.: 164)

A noun suffixed with the *genitive* case marker *ŭi* can function as the grammatical subject in an adnominalized sentence. This usage of the genitive case dates back to Late Middle Korean (approx. 16th century), but is, however, quite rare. Let me cite an example from Skillend 1979, to illustrate this use:

syojang-ŭi wŏnhaomnan pa ...
'what this general wishes' ... (Sk.: 124)

The *dative* morpheme *ege* can function as the subject of a verb when it expresses the agent of an action. Thus, for example:

ŏmŏni-ga adŭr-ege halmŏni-rŭl tari-rŭl chumurŭge handa
'the mother makes her son massage his granny on the leg'. (H.S.L.: 168)

Finally, we shall examine two examples of the *locative* morpheme *esŏ, e* functioning as the subject. This usually turns up in 'covered' double subject constructions, where a noun marked by the locative marker can replace one of the subjects. It is, however, quite rare:

---

2. See O'Grady 1991, chapter 9, and Lee Hansol 1989:155-77 for further explanation about the subject to object raising process.

i hakkyo-e sŏnsaeng-i p'iryohada
'This school needs teachers'. (S.H-m.: 236)

or, as in the following example—where the locative marked noun functions as the subject, and the accusative marked noun as object:

uri tim-esŏ chŏ tim-ŭl igiŏtta
'Our team defeated that team' (Ibid.: 236)

Since nos. 6, 7, 8 and 9 are marginal in the marking of the subject and re-stricted to very specific areas, they do not contribute significantly to the overall framework of the grammar of the subject.[3] We can thus summarize the foregoing by saying that we have two ways of formalizing the subject:

i. by word order constituency;
ii. by morphological constituency, i.e. by *ga*.

When we analyze the function of *ga* in more detail, however, we will find that the more fundamental function of the morpheme *ga* is to bring out em-phasis. Thus we will have to conclude that the most fundamental constituent for the subject is word order. I shall return to both *ga*'s function to bring out emphasis and word order as subject constituent later.

We shall leave the question of the underlying constituency of the subject and look at the distribution of *ga*, while bearing in mind that this gram-matical morpheme traditionally has been described as the subject marker.

The distribution of *ga*

1. Let's first illustrate *ga* in its function as *subject marker*. Sentence 1.a con-veys such an example.

(1.a)   Kyongsu-ga sagwa-rŭl ta mŏgŏ pŏriŏtta.
         'Kyongsu ate all the apples up'. (S.H-m: 180)

2. Next we shall illustrate *ga* in the function of *predicate nominal or com-plement* marker. The sentences 2.a and b illustrate this function. We have two instances, where the predicative position or complement is marked by *ga*:

3. For further examples of the locative functioning as subject, see Sohn 1994:236.

i.   when the copula is negated;
ii. with the verb *toeda*

Sentence 2.a illustrates it with a negated copula:

(2.a)   I gŏs-i ch'aeg-i ani-eyo
         'This is not a book'. (F.L.: 12)

Sentence 2.b illustrates it with *toeda*:

(2.b)   nŏ-nŭn hullyunghan munp'ilka-ga toel p'iryo-ga ŏpta
         'you don't have to be a famous writer'. (Chik'u: 132)

When we discuss the function of *ga* as subject-marker and *ga* as complement
marker, there are two features of Korean grammatical construction of which
we have to be aware.

The first is simply the very common tendency in Korean to drop the
subject altogether when it can be deduced from the context. This results in
a sentence construction with only the complement marked by *ga* if followed
by the negated copula, or *toeda*. The complement marked by *ga* should, of
course, not be confused with the lacking subject. However, if we have a
definition of *ga* as subject marker, we will have a problem with explaining
such a sentence. 2.c and 2.d are examples of this:

(2.c)   sige-ga ani-eyo
         '(this) is not a watch'. (F.L.: 12)

(2.d)   sigi-rŭl ssŭgi wihaesŏ-nŭn hullyunghan munjangga-ga toe-ŏ-ya hal
         piryo-nŭn ŏpta
         'In order to write a diary (you) don't have to be a famous writer'. (Chik'u:
         129)

We would be forced to conclude that *sige-ga* in 2.c and *munjangga-ga* in 2.d
were subjects, which they are not. They are complements.

Another important feature related to the function of *ga* as complement
marker is the fact that Korean, unlike most Indo-european languages, does
not have a grammatical rule that requires case agreement for nouns in the
predicative relationship. The result is that an object of a transitive verb which
is marked by the accusative marker *rŭl* can have its complement marked by
the nominative marker. 2.e is an example of this.

(2.e)   sŏnsaeng-ŭn cheja-rŭl ingan-i toe-ge haetta
           'The teacher made his pupil to become a man'. (L.H.: 166)

Like the aforementioned sentence, this sentence also cannot be explained if
we define *ga* as subject marker.[4]

3.   Next, we have the so-called *'double subject construction'*. The double subject construction is possible with two types of verbs:

i.   with the verbs of existence *itta* and *opta*;
ii. with adjective-verbs.

3.a, b and c are examples of these 'double subject constructions':

(3.a)   kŭ saram-i ch'aeg-i issŏyo?
           'Has he a book?' (S.M.: 29)

(3.b)   nae-ga igŏs-i choh-a-yo
           'I like this thing'. (S.M.: 96)

(3.c)   kŭ-nŭn na-rŭl/nae-ga par-ŭl/par-i ap'ŭge haetta.
           'He caused my foot to be painful.' (H.S.L.: 166)

Some grammarians have attempted to explain this type of construction as a
result of an underlying object-function, and named the second *ga* the 'objective *ga*'. This explanation is, however, refuted by other grammarians, on
the ground that neither the existence verb nor the adjective verb can take an
object (Oh 1971:48).
   Before leaving the double subject construction, we shall take a look at a
double subject construction with a topicalized subject, which is the logical,
but not formal subject.

---

4. It is possible also to find cases of reversed incongruency, i.e. where the complement to
   an unstated subject is given in accusative. Thus, for example, nal/inga pankisilga
   (nal<narŭl) (Does it make you happy that it is I?) Kasa poem *sa mi in gok* line 35/36.

(3.d)   John-ŭn sur-i masigi-ga sirhaetta
         'Concerning John, alcohol drinking was unlikeable'.[5] (O., C-k: 153)
         or: 'John didn't feel like drinking'.

Here we have three subjects; two, i.e. *sur-i masigi-ga* in a double subject construction with the verb *sirhada* —'to be unlikeable', and one marked by *nŭn*,
which is the subject for the nominalized verb *masigi*. The nominalized sentence, *John-ŭn sur-ŭl masigi-ga* then functions as subject for *sirhaetta*. Notice
that *sul-i* then appears as an underlying object.

4.   Ga and *nŭn*. The distribution of *ga* and *nŭn* is quite complex, as mentioned earlier, and I shall not attempt to discuss it in detail. One important
rule that regulates the distribution of *ga* and *nŭn* is, however, appropriate
here. In conditional subclauses, the distribution of *ga* and *nŭn* is determined
by whether the main clause and the subordinate clause have the same or different subjects. The rule reads as follows: If the subject of a conditional
clause is different from the subject of the main clause, the subject of the conditional clause is always marked by *ga*; if the main clause and the conditional
clause have the same subject, the subject of the conditional clause is marked
by *nŭn*.

(4.a)   Kŭbun-i kamyŏn kagessŏyo
         'If he goes, I'll go too'. (P.F.Y.T.: 188)

(4.b)   Na-nŭn kŭ gŏs-ŭl mach'imyŏn kagessŏyo
         'If I finish that, I'll go'. (P.F.Y.T.: 189)

Another common distribution of *ga* and *nŭn* turns up in embedded sentence
constructions. A noun marked by *nŭn* can be lined up with a following noun
marked by *ga* in an embedded construction, each being subject for a following verb:

$$S_1 + nun\ S_2 + ga\ ...\ V_2\ V_1$$

4.c and 4.d give examples of this:

5. Oh, Choon-kyo explicates the grammatical construction of the sentence in the following
   way: John - T(opic), liquor - S(ubject), drink - Nom-S (nominalizer-subject) unlikeable.
   Like many Korean grammatical constructions, this does not lend itself to a direct translation into English.

(4.c)   Kinami-nŭn isanghan harabŏji-ga che saenggag-ŭl ŏttŏk'e alkka amman
         saenggak-hae-pwado (morŭr-ir-imnida)
         'No matter how much Kinami would try to think it over, he will not be
         able to understand how the strange old man knew his thinking'. (B.L.: 86)

Here we have *Kinami-nŭn ... harabŏji-ga* and *alkka saenggakhae pwado* in an
embedded $S_1 S_2 - V_1 V_2$ construction.

A variation of the embedded sentence construction appears when the
second subject consists of a double subject construction, thus producing:

$$S_1+nŭn \; S_{2a}+ga + S_{2b}+ga \; ... \; V_1 V_2$$

Example 4.d gives such a sentence, here in a causative sentence construction:[6]

(4.d)   kŭdŭr-ŭn nae-ga kae-ga silk'e mandŭrŏtta
         'They made me dislike dogs'. (H.S.L.: 167)

We likewise find it in embedded relative clauses with the quasi-free (verbal)
noun *kŏt* that functions as head in participle constructions. 4.e gives such an
example:

(4.e)   Yongho-nŭn Mincha-ga onŭn kŏs-ŭl poatta
         'Yongho saw Mincha coming'.

It should be mentioned that in embedded sentence constructions, S_1 and S_2
can both be suffixed by *ga* as in 4.f or both suffixed by *nŭn* as in 4.g:

(4.f)   John-i Yongmi-ga ap'ŭdako midŏtta
         'John believed that Yongmi is sick' (O'Grady: 139)

(4.g)   Mary-nŭn John-ŭn ŏje hakkyo-e kan kŏt kattago marhaetta
         'Mary said that John appeared to have attended school yesterday
         (although Tom did not)'. (O. C-k: 140)

As a final example of the *nŭn-ga* distribution within the same period, but not
related to embedded constructions, I will cite an example from Sohn 1981:

---

6. Notice that *nae-ga kae-ga* as well could have been stated as the object for *mandŭrŏtta*,
resulting in a double object construction: *kŭdŭr-ŭn na-rŭl kae-rŭl silk'e mandŭrŏtta*.

Na-nŭn kŭ ŭmsig-i mas-i choh-ta
'I like the taste of the food'. (Sohn: 677)

Here we have a double subject construction *kŭ ŭmsigi-i mas-i* with a 'logical',
not formal, subject placed ahead of the double subject construction.[7]

5.   In example no. 5, we find another use of *ga*. This illustrates the so-called
multiple subject construction.

(5.a)   nae-ga ch'a-ga tire-ga kŭmŏng-i natta
            'I have a hole in a tire of my car'. (S.H.m.: 204)

The grammatical function of *ga* in 5.a is usually explained as an underlying
genitive and is named *cumulative genitivization*.[8] Like the double subject construction, this function of *ga* is very productive.[9]

Ga with word-classes other than nouns

6.   Next, we shall observe how *ga* can be suffixed to *word classes other than
nouns*. It is a common phenomenon for both the case markers and grammatical number markers that their distribution is not limited only to the
noun class of words. They can be suffixed also to adjectives, adverbs, post-
positions and verb forms. The result is that case markers and grammatical
number-markers can be suffixed to a word to which they formally do not
belong.
     Let's first look at an example with the plural marker. 6.a is an example
of this:

---

7. Sohn 1981 points out that the tradtional description of *nŭn*, as used with an already
    stated subject, and *ga*, as used to introduce new subjects does not account for all the
    various usages of *nŭn* and *ga*. When a generic term, or a thing done habitually, or a
    commonly known thing is the subject, it will mostly be suffixed by *nŭn*.
8. According to S. Martin 1992:284 'Each of the subjects successively narrows the
    specification down'.
9. The multiple subject construction has a 'cousin' in the multiple topic construction (Sohn
    1994:203). We have such a construction in 5.b:

    (5.b) sungmo-nŭn na-nŭn ajik-ŭn poepchi-nŭn anhaetta
            'I haven't seen my aunt yet'. (S.H.m. 1994:203)

    Since this construction, however, is restricted neither to the nominative case nor to
    nouns or verbal nouns, it does not necessarily add to our understanding of the gram-
    mar of the subject construction.

(6.a)   kŭrŏm chal-tŭl kage
          'Well, so-long, fellows'. (F.L.: 362)

Here we have the plural marker *tŭl* attached to the adverb *chal*, while it grammatically belongs to the unexpressed plural subject - 'you'. In the same way, the morphemes *ga* and *rŭl* can be suffixed to word classes different from nouns.

Example no. 6.b shows how the morpheme *ga* is suffixed to an adverb of place: ŏdi 'where'.[10]

6.b)   chongsimi[11] abŏji-nŭn ŏdi-ga ap'ŭsyŏssŏyo?
          'Where was Chongshim's father hurting?' (F.L.: 219)

Here we have a double subject construction *abŏji-nŭn ŏdi-ga* with an adjective verb. The second part of the double subject construction is made up by the interrogative adverb *ŏdi* to which the case marker *ga* has been suffixed, thus forming a double subject construction together with *abŏji-nŭn*.

Example 6.c shows how *ga* can be suffixed to a *postposition*. Here we find it with the preposition *kkaji*:

(6.c)   irwŏlbut'o iwŏlkkaji-ga cheil ch'uptaeyo
          'they say that it is most cold from January to February'. (F.L.: 221)

In this example, the time specification *ilwŏlbut'o iwŏlkkaji* appears to be treated as the subject of the sentence, put in indirect discourse.

So far, we have examined how *ga* can mark the subject, the predicative position, form a double subject with certain verbs, function as a genitivization when a string of nouns marked by *ga* are juxtaposed and even raise an adverbial specification of place or time into the grammatical functions of subject. Now we shall see how *ga* can perform a function totally unrelated to its function as case marker.

---

10. Most Korean grammars classify *ŏdi* as a noun. I am, however, not convinced that this is the case. It is just as reasonable to assume that the Korean language possesses a small class of original time and place adverbs, which share a common class of case marking suffixes. It is a characteristic of the agglutinative type of morphology that its grammatical suffixes are not restricted according to word classes as in the inflectional type of morphology.

11. Notice that the *i* added to Chongsim's name is not the grammatical morpheme *i*, but a euphonic vowel.

Functions of *ga* unrelated to case marking

We can divide this into 3 categories:

i.   *ga* with *negation*
ii. *ga* with *conjunctional forms*
iii. *ga* with *other case morphemes*

7.i Let us first look at *ga* suffixed to, or rather infixed into, the *negation*: example no. 7.a is such an example.

(7.a)   Toriŏ kyolgwa-ga choch'i-ga mot haetta
          'on the contrary, the results were not good at all'. (S.M.: 316)

Here we see that *ga* can be inserted into the longer negative formation. S. Martin calls this phenomenon 'negative preemphasis', and explains that *ga* here merely functions to give emphasis to the negation. *Ga*, or *rŭl*, is inserted into the negation of adjective verbs, whereas *rŭl* is inserted into the negation of action verbs.[12] The longer form of the negation can also be themasized by *nŭn*.[13]

7.ii Next we have *ga* suffixed to *conjunctional forms*. In 7.b we have an example with the conjunctional morpheme *taga*, which indicates transference of one verbal action to another.

(7.b)   Kogi-rŭl chabada-ga nŏhŏdo kot chugŏ-bŏrimnida
          'Even when you put a fish away, which you have just caught, it dies right away'. (B.L.: 218)

Ga can likewise be suffixed to the conjunctional form -*sŏ*, when this is constructed with *anida* in the meaning 'not so, that'. Example no. 7.c illustrates this:

(7.c)   kŭ marŭi ttŭs-ŭl arasŏ-ga anira ...
          'It was not so, that I understood the meaning of that word ...' (B.L.: 207)

---

12. S. Martin 1992:317 gives a listing of several categories of verbs that can add the negative preemphasis to the longer form of the negation.
13. For further explanation, see S. Martin, 1992:316, 338, and Cho 1975:69.

Here we might add the construction with the post-adnominal noun *chi*, that is constructed with a statement of time period and the verb *toeda*. Example no. 7.d shows how *ga* can be suffixed to this:

(7.d)   Kyongsu-rŭl an chi-ga han sam nyŏn-i toemnida.
         'I've known Kyongsu about three years'. (F.L.: 232)

This could also be explained as a nominalized clause *Kyongsu-rŭl an chi-ga* that is the formal subject with *ham sam nyŏn-i* in the predicative position.

7.iii Finally we shall observe what is probably the most surprising distribution of the morpheme *ga*. This distribution allows *ga* to be suffixed to *an already stated case morpheme*. Example 7.e shows this:

(7.e)   kŭ ch'aeg-ŭn chib-e-*ga* innŭndeyo
         'I have that book at home' (S.H-m: 184)

Yang In-sok explains this function of *ga* as 'the nominative intruder' (Yang, 1972:196), while Sohn, Ho-min (Sohn 1994:107, 184) explains this function of *ga* as a kind of delimiter, that only serves to bring focus.

The different types of distribution of *ga*

Now we can sum up the different types of distribution of *ga* in the following way.

A. It can mark the subject
B. It can function as the predicative/complement marker
C. It can function as a genitivization
D. It can add emphasis
E. It can function as a delimiter of focus

We can sum up this discussion by saying:

that: i. the subject position can formally be marked in several other ways than just by the morpheme ga and that: ii. the morpheme *ga* performs several other grammatical functions than just to mark the subject or (even wider) the nominative case.

This can be illustrated in the following way:[14]

Morphemes that all can   Functions of *ga*
be suffixed to the formal
subject

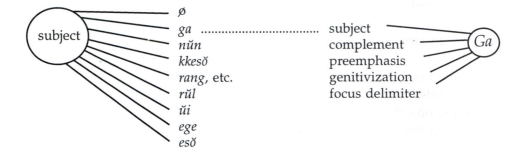

Thus we may conclude that neither the term 'subject marker' nor 'nominative marker' offers an adequate terminology for *ga*.

This brings us, therefore, on to the following questions. First: what, then, can be the formal definition of the subject in Korean? Secondly: how can we formulate a rule that can account for all the functions of *ga*?

Let us begin with the subject. What is it that constitutes the subject as subject in Korean? If we simplify the system of the morphological formalized marking of the subject, we can reduce it to two basic formalizations:

i. morphologically unmarked
ii. morphologically marked

If we have a morphologically unmarked subject, how then is its grammatical function as subject indicated to us? The answer must be: by word order.

Korean is a so-called SOV language. This means that in an ordinary sentence, we will find first a subject, then an object and finally the verb. This word order regulates the grammatical function of the nominals in the sentence, so that if case-markers are not suffixed to the nouns, word order itself adds the grammatical coding of the nominals in the sentence. Hence a sentence like:

14. The dotted line indicates the 'traditional' explanation of the subject function, i.e. as noun + *ga* = subject.

kae mǔl mŏkko sip'o handa
'The dog wants to drink water'.

is understandable. Furthermore, the following sentence:

sagwa mŏgŏyo
'He eats an apple'.

is understandable by a combination of 3 rules:

i.   the previously mentioned rule that the subject is not stated if the
     context clearly indicates it.
ii. that the object takes the second position in the sentence
iii. and then the verb follows.

This results in: $\emptyset$. (+) noun - case marker. (+) V. > SOV

Thus we see that word order regulates the grammatical coding process
(unlike English, where the phrase 'eats apple' is unacceptable). Word order
thus plays the underlying syntactic function, if case-marking is not employed.[15]

Then the next question follows: what, then is the function of *ga*, when it
is added to the subject?

According to Sohn, Ho-min in his recent grammar on the Korean
language, it depends on whether *ga* is suffixed to a noun that is the subject

---

15. However, if case-markers *are* employed, the word-order of nominals becomes flexible.
    Thus, for example, it is possible to say *ton-ǔl na-eke ŏnniga kir-esŏ onǔl chuŏtta*, 'Today
    my older sister gave me money on the street' (Sohn 1994:210).
       We may add here that this also helps to explain the various multiple nominal
    constructions, such as double subject constructions, multiple subject constructions, topic
    + double subject constructions, etc. Sohn 1981, explains that these constructions are
    allowable because of the multiple slots that are available before the verb in the SOV
    type languages. It occurs to me that the particular case of Korean as a SOV type
    language can be further explicated by expanding the SOV structure into a
    S.S. – V. structure   (ex 3.b)
    T.S.S. – V. structure   (ex 3.d)
    T.T.T. – V. structure   (ex 5.b)
    S. X_n – V. structure   (ex 5.a)
    This description allows better for the concept of multiple nominal spaces before the
    verb, because it makes room for four positions in front of the verb. The hyphen marks
    the absence of O (= object).

of an adjective verb or subject of an action verb. When it is suffixed to a noun that is the subject of an adjective verb, it brings emphasis.

8.   He gives the following examples (Sohn:183).

(8.a)   Mincha-ga yeppŏyo
          'It is Mincha, who is pretty.'

Here *ga* is suffixed to a noun that is the subject of an adjective verb, and hence it brings out emphasis to the noun phrase, while the corresponding sentence *Mincha yeppŏyo* would mean: 'Mincha is pretty'. But when a subject of an action verb is marked by *ga*, the situation is ambiguous. Example no. 8.b illustrates this with two possible translations:

(8.b)   chŏgi Kyongsu-ga onda.
          'there comes Kyongsu'; 'It is Kyongsu, who is coming there'. (S., H-m: 183)

Thus, it would seem that it is possible to conclude that the more fundamental function of *ga* is to bring emphasis, especially considering its function as preemphasizer in example 7.a and its function to give emphasis in 8.b. That means that we have to conclude that the real constituent of the subject function is *word order.*

The Korean Case System

To conclude, let us consider the nature of the Korean case system. First, I would like to point out one interesting fact. In the grammatical functions of *ga* that we have surveyed, only one function can be considered obligatory. That is its function to mark the complement, when followed by *anida* or *toeda*. This is the only obligatory rule in the constructions mentioned so far. Contrary to this, it appears that case marking in the nominative (and accusative) case(s) is a matter of choice. One can choose to mark the grammatical function or not. It is optional.

     In this presentation, I have concentrated on the nominative case. However, almost all the types of functions that the nominative can perform can likewise be performed by the accusative case. It, too, can make double object constructions. It can make multiple object constructions, where the accusative functions as a genitivization. It can be suffixed to other word classes. It can drop the function of case altogether and function as preemphasizer and be inserted in the longer form of the negation, and it can be dropped or replaced by the topic marker *nŭn* or delimiters.[16] Thus like the morpheme *ga*, the morpheme *rŭl* functions, to a large extent, as an optional, non-obligatory marker. Option seems to be the core of the case marking system for the subject and object. When you choose to mark a grammatical function, you do it to bring out emphasis. Case marking is therefore not a matter of rule or routine.

S. Martin, 1992, in his discussion of the Korean case system, quotes a French grammarian, Félix-Clair Ridel, from the last century. He confirms the aforementioned conclusion, and says that always adding the case morphemes to the nouns is considered 'clumsy, awkward and even bad taste by Koreans'. Cases are more often used just as variations of speech (S. Martin 1992:287).

This seems to be a prominent feature of the Korean case system that sets it apart from the Indo-European. The Indo-European case marking system, in its original form, was a matter of necessity. The Korean is not. This gives rise to the feature of flexibility in the grammar of Korean nominal syntax, both concerning the (±)case-marking of nominals and, when marked, the flexibility of word order (see footnote 14). The underlying structure of word order is what secures the grammatical function of each word. If and when this is not clear, a case morpheme can always be added to clarify the grammatical function — and, if not needed, it can still be added just for emphasis.

Conclusion

In the introduction to this paper I mentioned that the terminology for the case markers in certain areas seems unsuited or incorrect. Thus we have seen that the morpheme *ga* performs several other syntactic functions than just marking the subject. If the terminology gives a faulty representation of the actual function and distribution of grammatical morphemes, it does not serve the language description well. A description of the Korean case system and its accompanying terminology should give a systematic description of the distribution and function of all its syntactic morphemes, as well as provide a suitable terminology. It should, it would seem, also describe the interaction between the case system and word order, and incorporate a rule of option and replacement of the grammatical morphemes.

---

16. In addition, it performs a number of specific grammatical functions, such as: a) stating time duration; b) the purpose of a movement; c) the goal or direction of a verb of movement; etc.

In the case of the morpheme *ga*, it should describe its function to bring emphasis to the noun, adverb, negation or verbal form to which it is suffixed. Emphasis seems, as I have tried to demonstrate, to be the only *one* feature common to all the different usages of *ga* (Notice that only in its function to mark the complement is this not the case). One could therefore suggest that the word *emphasizer* could serve as a part of the general terminology to define *ga*. However, since the function of *ga* to bring emphasis is applied to otherwise quite diverse syntactic constructions, it will hardly be possible to coin just *one* term that can cover all the different usages of *ga*. What is needed is a terminological system that can handle all the various functions of *ga*. One could perhaps extract a terminology from the existing description of the different functions of *ga* and name them accordingly. Hence we would have: the subject-(emphasizer)-*ga*; the complement-*ga*; the double-subject-*ga*; the genitivization-*ga*; the conjunctional form-emphasizer-*ga*; the negation-emphasizer-*ga*; and the case-intruder-*ga*. This would seem to be the most natural solution.

Abbreviations used in the grammatical examples

Chik'ŭ	Chik'ŭ yongŏ
F.L.	Lukoff, Fred, 1989
L., B.	Lewin, Bruno, 1970
L.H.	Lee, Hansol, 1989
O, C-k	Oh, Choon-kyu, 1971
O'Gr.	O'Grady, 1991
P.F.Y.T.	Park, Francis Y.T., 1984
S., H-m	Sohn, Ho-min, 1981
Sk.	Skillend, W.E., 1979
S.M.	Martin, Samuel, 1992
Y., I-s	Yang, In-seok, 1972

References

Ch'ik'ŭ yongŏ. Pocket size English study course for Korean highschool students. Seoul.

Cho, Choon-kuk. 1975. The Scope of Negation in Korean. *The Korean Language, Its Structure and Social Projection*, ed. Sohn Ho-min. Honolulu: University of Hawaii Press.

Hong, Chai-song. 1985. *Syntaxe des Verbes de Mouvement en Coréen Contemporain*. Amsterdam: John Benjamins.

Lee, Hansol H.B. 1989. *Korean Grammar*. New York: Oxford University Press.

Lewin, Bruno. 1970. *Morphologie des koreanischen Verbs*. Wiesbaden: Harrassowitz.

Lukoff, Fred. 1989. *An Introductory Course in Korean*. Seoul: Yonsei University Press.

Martin, Samuel E. 1992. *A Reference Grammar of Korean*. Tokyo: Tuttle.

Nam, Ki-sim. 1983. Linguistic Theory and the Study of Korean Grammar. *The Korean Language*, ed. The Korean National Commission for UNESCO, 137-48. Seoul: The Si-sa-yong-o-sa Publishers, Inc.

O'Grady, W. 1991. *Categories and Case: the Sentence Structure of Korean*. Amsterdam: John Benjamins.

Oh, Choon-kyu. 1971. *Aspects of Korean Syntax: Quantification, Relativization, Topicalization and Negation*. Seoul: Pan Korea Book Corp.

Park, Francis Y.T. 1984. *Speaking Korean*, vol. I. Elisabeth N.J.: Hollym International.

Skillend, W.E. 1979. The Expression of the Subject in 'Imjin nok'. *Memoires du Centre d'études Coréennes*, no. 1. Melanges de coreanologie offerts à M. Charles Hagenauer, 119-38.

Sohn, Ho-min. 1981. Multiple Topic constructions in Korean. *Hangeul*, vol. 173/174, 669–89.

Sohn, Ho-min. 1994. *Korean*. London: T.J. Press.

Song, Seok-chong. 1988. *Explorations in Korean Syntax and Semantics*. Berkeley, University of California: Institute of East Asian Studies.

Yang, In-seok. 1972. *Korean Syntax: Case Markers, Delimiters, Complementation and Relativization*. Seoul: Paek hap ch'ulp'ansa.

The Importance of a Korean Source on the Ryukyuan Language

Steven Hagers

In the year 1501 a glossary was attached to one of the works of Sin Sukchu, the *Haedong cheguk ki (Annals of the different countries in the eastern sea)*.[1] The title of this glossary is 'Ŏŭmbŏnyak', which means 'Translation of speech sounds'. Ledyard comments that (1966:419, n. 65):

Sin himself never visited the Ryukyus; the glossary in his book was compiled after his death on the occasion of a Ryukyu embassy to Seoul in 1501. The glossary itself consists of about 40 short sentences and some 130 words in Mandarin, with Ryu-kyuan equivalents transcribed in the Korean alphabet. The transcriptions are not always consistent with each other, and there are other slips due to copyists and block carvers. Nonetheless the material is very interesting, as useful for the study of old Ryukyuan as it is for Korean sound values.

There are two main fields in which the source is important: firstly, in the study of phonology and secondly, in the reconstruction of the development of the inflectional forms of verbs and adjectives. In this paper I will focus on the reconstruction of the development of the inflectional forms of verbs and adjectives.

Shibatani (1990) mentions that the Ryukyuan dialects preserve the distinction between the conclusive form and the attributive form of verbs and

---

1. The systems of transcription employed in this paper are the following: Korean, McCune-Reischauer; Classical and Modern Japanese, Hepburn; Old Japanese, the system employed by Martin (1987). For the Shuri-Naha dialect of Ryukyuan I have developed my own system which is largely based on *Okinawa-go jiten* (1983). My aim, however, was to use one sign for one phoneme, so I adopted some characters from the phonetic alphabet. For the transcriptions of other Ryukyuan dialects I have used the spellings found in the literature. Citations of Ryukyuan are in **bold** print and those of Japanese are in *italic* type.

adjectives. It is true that the verbs in the dialect of Shuri and Naha possess this distinction between the conclusive and attributive forms, but even verbs, which do not possess this distinction in Old Japanese, do show this pattern in their paradigms. In Old Japanese there is a morphological distinction between conclusive and attributive in most classes of vowel stem verbs. Thus the verb *uku* 'to receive' (modern Japanese *ukeru*) differed in its conclusive and attributive forms: *fyito̲ uku* meaning 'the man receives', and: *ukuru fyito̲* meaning 'the man who receives' or 'the receiving man'. A consonant stem verb like *kaku* 'to write', however, didn't have such a morphological distinction between conclusive and attributive: *fyito̲ kaku* meaning 'the man writes', and: *kaku fyito̲* meaning 'the man who writes' or 'the writing man'. In the modern dialect of Shuri and Naha these four forms are:

qcu nu ʔukijuŋ	'the man receives'
ʔukijuru qcu	'the man who receives, the receiving man'
qcu nu kacuŋ	'the man writes'
kacuru qcu	'the man who writes, the writing man'

There is a clear distinction between conclusive and attributive in both **ʔukijuŋ** and **kacuŋ**.

The exceptions to the rule that consonant stem verbs in Old Japanese do not show any distinction between conclusive and attributive forms, are the two verbs for 'to be' *wori* and *ari* and all verbs which are compounds with *ari* (for example, the auxiliary *faberi* and the copula *nari* and *tari*, and the like). These verbs form a subclass of the regular verbs with a *r*-stem. The attributive forms of both verbs are regular compared with the regular *r*-stem verbs, being *aru* and *woru*, but the conclusive forms of these verbs are highly irregular, being *ari* and *wori*, which are formally the same as the infinitive forms. It is tempting to state that the distinction between the conclusive and attributive forms in Ryukyuan is a relic of Proto Japanese, and that Japanese is much more innovative than Ryukyuan, as indeed many scholars have believed, but it is a regrettable error since this development is rather new.

Hattori (1959) came to the conclusion that the conclusive form, the attributive form, and some other forms in the verbal paradigm of regular verbs as well as most of the irregular verbs are compounds of the infinitive form and the verb **uŋ** 'to be', which is cognate with Japanese *wori*. Two very important verbs, which belong to the group of irregular verbs, and are not compounds of the infinitive and the verb **uŋ**, are the verbs **uŋ** and **ʔaŋ** them selves. Since the conclusive and attributive forms of all verbs are compounds with either **uŋ** or **ʔaŋ**, one can easily conclude that the distinction between conclusive and attributive is a feature of these two verbs only.

The Ryukyuan verbs **uŋ** and **ʔaŋ** exhibit, like their Old Japanese cognates, a distinction between the attributive and conclusive forms. However, the forms are quite different from that of Japanese. The attributive forms have an ending in **-ru**, but the conclusive forms have an ending in *-ŋ*, where the Japanese forms have *-ri*. Thus the conclusive form of both verbs is, unlike in Japanese, distinguished not only from the attributive, but also from the infinitive forms, which are **ui** and **ʔai**.

The origin of the conclusive ending *-ŋ* is still subject to discussion. This point is not relevant since the development took place after the source was compiled. From the modern forms in the dialect of Shuri and Naha, one can conclude that the development of the verbal forms in the conclusive must have been as follows. I have postulated five steps. I use the verb for 'to write' as example.

1. Originally there was a conclusive form, which was more or less an equivalent for the Japanese conclusive form. ***kaku**.
2. At some time this old conclusive was replaced by a form which was a compound of the infinitive form and the verb for 'to be'. ***kaki wo(ri)**.
3. The original conclusive ending wore off; ***o** became **u** and ***k** before i became palatalized. ***kaci u**.
4. The compound of the infinitive and the verb for 'to be' was contracted and assimilated. ***kacu**.
5. A new conclusive ending was attached. **kacuŋ**.

For some steps it was only possible to postulate them by examining the Korean source. For example, the fact that first the old ending of the conclusive form wore off can only be found in the source.

The examples as I present them consist of four lines. The first line is an exact transliteration of the hangŭl; all syllables are separated by a period. The second line gives my interpretation of how it actually sounded in the 16th century. The third line indicates the form as it would be in Modern Shuri-Naha dialect. Finally, the fourth line gives an English translation. You may notice in the given examples some strange characters are sometimes used in the hangŭl representation. The most striking one is that **n** and **r** are often interchanged. Further, there is often a **n**, **m** or **ng** used merely as a device to voice a subsequent voiceless consonant, especially with **k** and **p**.

item 9

> woan.ku.co.syo.ong.koa.că.t'at.cyŏi
> **wan kudzo ʃoogwaҫɯ taqcee**
> *waŋ kuzuʃoogwaҫi taqceeŋ*
> I left last year at New Year.

item 11

> woan.ku.tu.si.sya.ong.koa.că.c'ui.t'a.ci.kit.cyŏi
> **wan kutuʃi ʃaogwaҫɯ ҫuitaci kicee**
> *waŋ kutuʃi ʃoogwaҫi ҫiitaci (q)ceeŋ*
> I arrived this year on the first day.

Verb forms as **taqcee** (item 9) and **kicee** (item 11) are compounds with the verb for 'to be' **ʔaŋ**, while there is no trace of either the modern ending **-ŋ** or the old conclusive ending. So one can only conclude that the old conclusive ending had worn off by the time of the recording of the Korean source.

There is a variant form of the conclusive in the modern dialect, which appears when sentence particles are attached. It was called the 'apocopated form' by Chamberlain (1895) because this form lacks the modern ending **-ŋ**. But since I have previously stated that the modern conclusive form is an extension of an 'original' endingless conclusive form rather than that the 'apocopated' form is an apocopation of the modern conclusive, I prefer to use the term 'conclusive stem' for this variant form.

The assimilated forms that replaced the original conclusive forms have their origin in the original progressive form, which existed in the infinitive form plus the verb for 'to be'. The same construction was also the progressive form in Old Japanese before the modern *-te iru* forms replaced it. That the progressive form took over the function of the conclusive can still be seen in the different meanings of the form. This form embodies both meanings: conclusive and progressive.

In Ryukyuan palatalization is a feature which occurs under the influence of front vowels. It is therefore certain that the modern assimilated compounds which build the conclusive and attributive forms were formed after the stem consonants were palatalized under the influence of the infinitive suffix **i**, to account for such forms as **kaci** and **kacuŋ** from the verb for 'to write' alongside the form **kakaŋ** 'not to write', where the original consonant is preserved. So the existence of assimilated forms must date after the appearance of the source even before the beginnings of the palatalizations.

The above forms **taqcee** and **kicee** are past tenses with a perfective aspect, which originated in a compound of the gerund or *-te* form plus the verb for 'to be' **ʔaŋ**. These forms are conclusive forms, albeit of the past tense. There are two facts, however, worthy of attention. First, those forms which are clearly conclusive forms, possess no conclusive ending, as they do in the modern dialect. Second, there are no examples of conclusive forms in the present tense although there are sentences which are meant to be sentences in the present tense. But the form which appears in those sentences is the infinitive form, or an equivalent form. There are at least seven infinitive forms where we would expect a conclusive form.

item 18

sa.kŭi.oa.ka.si
sakï wakaʃi
saki wakaʃuŋ
To heat the wine.

item 36

yu.ki.p'u.ri
juki Φuri
juci φujuŋ
It snows.

item 51

p'i.ru.ku.mi
Φi nukumi
φii nukunuŋ
To warm oneself at the fire.

item 73

nu.mi
numi
nunuŋ
To drink (wine).

item 74

sa.kŭi.a.ri
sakï ari
saki ʔaŋ
There is wine.

item 78

ang.kŭi.ri
agïri
ʔagijuŋ
To eat (lit. 'to raise').

item 100

c'a.oa.ka.si
ca(a) wakaʃi
caa wakaʃuŋ
To make (heat) tea.

In the same way we find some so-called '*-te* forms' which are really meant to be simple past tense forms, '-*ta* forms' in Japanese, which are to be held strictly apart from the perfective forms which we found earlier.

item 23   item 76

    sa.kŭi.mi.na.rat.ti   sa.kŭi.i.u.ti
    sakï mina naqti   **sakï wiuti**
    sakï ɲna nataŋ   *saki (nudi) wiitaŋ*
    The wine was all finished.   He was drunk.

What we can conclude from the fact that there is no real conclusive form appearing where this form would be necessary is:

1   that the old conclusive ending was lost at the time of the source;
2   that it was not yet replaced by the original progressive form, but by the infinitive form;
3   likewise that the *-te* form served as and instead of the *-ta* form.

The reason why the infinitive form served as the conclusive form is probably due to the influence of the progressive form, which after all contained the infinitive form. Therefore, it is not unreasonable to assume that the form containing the verb **uŋ** served as the progressive, while the form without the verb **uŋ** served as the simple conclusive at the time of the source. The same applies to the past tenses, which are represented by the **-te** forms. Again, this is not an unreasonable notion, since the *-te* form itself is originally the infinitive form of an auxiliary of the past tense. Even up until today this **-te** form serves as the question form for the past tense, whereas the present tense has a construction built on the so-called conclusive stem and thus is also a relatively new development.

Let us now look at the adjectival forms in the Korean source in which sixteen adjectives in their conclusive form appear. I present only a few of them here.

item 14   item 27

    o.pu.si   că.ra.ru.si.ru.sa
    opusa   **çɯra nu ʃirusa**
    ʔufusaŋ   *çira nu ʃirusaŋ*
    There is much.   The face is white.

item 29

ko.no.p'i.cyo.ki.mo.ro.yo.ta.sya
kono Φico kimo no jotaʃa
kunu qcu cimu nu jutaʃaŋ
This man has a good temper.

item 30

ko.no.p'i.cyo.ki.mo.ro.yo.oar.sa
kono Φico kimo no jowasa
kunu qcu cimu nu jutaʃaŋ
This man has a bad temper.

item 50

săn.ta.sa
sɯdasa
sidasaŋ
It's chilly.

item 101

a.mi.sa
amasa
ʔamasaŋ
It's sweet.

All of these examples are in the so-called **-sa** form. It is said that the adjectives in the dialect of Shuri and Naha, among most other dialects, are compounds of the **-sa** form and the verb for 'to be' **ʔaŋ**. In Japanese the *-sa* form builds an abstract noun, but in Ryukyuan it is the base for the inflectional forms, somewhat like the *-kari* forms in Classical Japanese.

The adjective in item 14 has the written form **o.pu.si**, presumably a carver's mistake, which I have interpreted as a **-sa** form. Since the difference in hangŭl between the **i** and the **a** is only a tiny stroke to the right of a vertical bar, this is very well possible.

Most of these **-sa** forms are instances of adjectives standing alone, and it would be very reasonable to state that these forms are abstract nouns. So **sɯdasa** in item 50 could mean 'chilliness', and so on. In four entries the **-sa** form is also used, but clearly in a form which is to be interpreted as a conclusive form. Here only the items 27, 29 and 30. This is paralleled by the verbs in the source which use the infinitive form as the conclusive form.

Uchima (1984) offers a large survey of the Ryukyuan adjectival inflectional forms. These can be ordered in three groups. Of each group I will quote at least one dialect always with the adjective *takai* 'is high', 'is expensive':

1   Amami, Okinawa, Yaeyama, Yonaguni:
     taasaʔaamu (Tamina), **takasaʔan** (Kunigami), **takasaŋ** (Shuri-Naha), **ta-
     kasan** (Nishime);
2   Northern Okinawa:
     takaʃeen (Sesoko);
3   Miyako:
     takakam (Nishizato).

For each of these groups Uchima reconstructs a hypothetical historical form:

1   **sa+ari+mu**
2   **sa+ari+wori+mu**
3   **ku+ari+mu**

From the part **-mu** in these forms stems the form from which the modern
ending **-ŋ** should have originated.

   I think that the reconstruction for group three is correct; it completely
parallels the *-kari* forms of Old Japanese. The reconstruction for group two,
however, is a monstrosity, not only phonetically, but also semantically. I
think that this form should be reconstructed as **-ʃi+ari**, where **-ʃi** probably
is identical to the Old Japanese conclusive suffix. There is only one dialect
in this group.

   The reconstruction for group one is in essence correct. Although I believe
it should be further divided into two sub-groups: one sub-group in which it
is really a compound of the suffix **-sa** and the verb **ʔaŋ**, as it is shown here,
and another sub-group where it is not a compound with the verb **ʔaŋ**, but
in which the adjective only attaches the inflectional forms of the verb **ʔaŋ** to
the suffix **-sa**. This difference may seem trivial but is very important because
it implicates a totally different point of view. In the first sub-group we are
dealing with a compound, but in the second group we are dealing with an
analogical reform of the adjectival inflection. That we should reconstruct two
sub-groups is justified by the fact that there are some dialects which except
for their forms with a long **a**, have forms with a short **a** where we would expect a long **a**. For example, the dialect of Kunigami, which alongside the
conclusive **takasaʔan** has the attributive **takasanu** from *__takasaru__ where we
would expect *__takasaʔanu__.

   When we then form two sub-groups from group one, we should put the
dialects which have long **a**'s in their adjectival forms, in sub-group 1, and the
dialects with short **a**'s in sub-group 2. In that case the dialect of Shuri and

Naha belongs to sub-group 2 and thus has analogical reformed forms for the adjectival inflections.

In the modern dialect the suffix **-sa** still represents a kind of conclusive form, much like the 'direct predication' of Old Japanese. According to Martin (1987) almost all Old Japanese examples of *-sa* are direct predications; he offers two examples which I will cite here together with their translation in Modern Japanese and in the modern dialect of Shuri and Naha.

> *imwo ga kanasisa* 'the dear girl [is] so adorable!'
>   (ModJ: *joshi ga kawaii koto yo*; S-N: **wakawinagu nu kanaʃa**)
> *fyito no tomosisa* 'the people [are] so few!'
>   (ModJ: *hito ga toboshii koto yo*; S-N: **qcu nu ʔikirasa**)

This fact together with the striking similarity with modern Ryukyuan prompt me to believe that this *-sa* is more than just a nominalizer at least in Old Japanese and in the modern dialect of Shuri and Naha. Since in Ryukyuan this form is a kind of conclusive form, also completely paralleled in Old Japanese, I think it is strange to judge this form as a 'direct predication' and thus a nominal form, owing to the fact that this suffix *-sa* in Modern Japanese is a nominal suffix. In Ryukyuan the suffix even spread its influence to verbs, which now have an alternative conclusive form in **-sa**. In verbs this suffix is attached to the conclusive stem; for example, **kacusa** 'he writes indeed'. Of course this suffix is used in the verb **ʔaŋ** too: **ʔasa** 'it is indeed', but in the adjectives it is not used; for example, not *takasasa, but **takasa**, 'it is high indeed.'

These facts lead me to suppose a verbal origin for this suffix rather than the nominal origin which it is generally said to possess. In that case in Japanese the suffix lost its verbal load which it still had in the Nara period and developed to be completely nominal. In Ryukyuan this suffix retained its verbal origin and moreover developed to be the main suffix for the conclusive form until the suffix analogically attached the inflectional endings of the verb **ʔaŋ**. At that point the suffix returned to its original meaning of a less direct conclusive form. Beside this development, like in Japanese the suffix developed a nominal meaning, but it might be that this nominal meaning was already present in Proto Japanese. It is also possible to suppose cognacy with the Korean suffix **-ta**.

In summary the importance of the Korean source is that it tells us about when the major sound changes in the Ryukyuan language took place. It also offers a glimpse into the way in which verbal and adjectival inflections developed. In this connection it shows that around the year 1500 the verbal and adjectival conclusive forms were forms which in Japanese are considered as nominal forms.

References

Chamberlain, Basil Hall. 1895. *Essay in aid of a grammar and dictionary of the Luchuan Language*. Transactions of the Asian Society of Japan, vol. 23, supplement. Tôkyô.

Hattori, Shirô. 1959. *Nihongo no keitô*. Tôkyô: Iwanami-shoten.

Ledyard, Gari K. 1966. *The Korean language reform of 1446: the origin, background, and early history of the Korean alphabet*. University of California, Berkeley, Dissertation.

Martin, Samuel E. 1987. *The Japanese language through time*. New Haven and London: Yale University Press.

Okinawago jiten. 1983. Kokuritsu koku-go kenkyû-jo (ed.). 2nd print. Tôkyô: Ôkurashô insatsukyoku.

Shibatani, Masayoshi. 1990. *The languages of Japan*. Cambridge: Cambridge University Press.

Uchima, Chokujin. 1984. *Ryûkyû hôgen bunpô no kenkyû*. Tôkyô: Kasama shoin.

The Acquisition of Spatial Expressions by Japanese-Speaking Children[1]

Mariko Hayashi

1. Introduction

1.1 Spatial language

Understanding space and spatial relations is fundamental for human cognition, and any language seems to have both lexical and grammatical means to encode it. However, it does not mean that spatial cognition and language is universal across cultures and across languages. On the contrary, what is encoded and how seems to differ considerably from culture to culture, and from language to language.

As for grammatical means for expressing space, for example, Talmy (1985, 1991) shows that there is a systematic difference among languages with respect to Path notions, i.e. movement into, out of, up, down, on, off, and so on. In some languages including English, Path of motion is typically expressed by prepositions and verb particles such as *on*, *in*, *up*, and *down*. In other languages including Japanese, it is typically conflated with motion in the verb such as *hairu* (*go in*[2]), *deru* (*go out*), *agaru* (*go up*), and *oriru* (*go down*) (see also Kita preprint).

There are also considerable crosslinguistic differences on the lexical level as to how to structure space. This is the main concern of the present paper, and we will discuss about it in detail later.

---

1. The present study is part of a joint crosslinguistic project which deals with spatial cognition and language. I would like to express many thanks to my colleagues, C. Sinha, K.J. de Lopez, and L.A. Thorseng, for their cooperation.
2. In the present paper, approximate English translation is given in parentheses. The purpose is not to give a complete translation, but just to give non-Japanese speaking readers a rough idea of what each Japanese expression is about.

1.2 Spatial language acquisition

In the field of child language, most researchers seem to assume that young children construct certain non-linguistic space concepts to begin with, and they learn early spatial terms by mapping them onto these already constructed concepts (Clark 1973, Sinha 1988).

No doubt, young children know considerably about space before they begin to talk about it. However, even if we assume that children rely on their early non-linguistic cognition, which is assumed to be more or less universal, to the extent that languages differ, children have to learn, sometime in the course of their development, spatial categories which are appropriate to their target languages. The wide-spread universalist-cognitivist view on the acquisition of spatial language has been challenged recently. By comparing children acquiring respectively Korean and English (Choi & Bowerman 1991) and Korean, English, and Dutch (Bowerman 1996), Choi and Bowerman found, already in the beginning phase of language development, clear differences in the children's ways of encoding space, which are in accordance with each target language.

Our project, which the present study is part of, is in line with Choi and Bowerman's studies. That is, by relying on crosslinguistic, and also cross-cultural comparison, we aim at discussing what could be universal and what could be specific with respect to spatial cognition and language.

1.3 Earlier results

I will briefly summarize part of the earlier results from our project (Sinha et al. 1994, Hayashi 1994b); the part which concerns the Japanese language and its acquisition. In our project, we limit ourselves to spatial relations, which would typically be expressed in English by prepositions and verb particles such as *in* and *on*. In order to encode such spatial relations, Japanese makes use of postpositional locative particles such as *ni* (*at*) and de (*at*). As a form-class, they can be compared to prepositions in English. However, the number of these locative particles is significantly limited. There are only 6 of them, i.e. *ni* (*at*), *de* (*at*), *kara* (*from*), *e* (*to*), *o* (*through*), and *made* (*as far as*). Consequently, some of them bear much more general meanings than English prepositions do. Japanese also relies on verbs such as *ireru* (*put in*) and *noseru* (*put on*), and nouns such as *naka* (*inside*) and *ue* (*upper part*) in order to realize spatial relational meaning. Furthermore, as locative meaning is distributed to more than one form-class, some of the locative particles and nouns can be and often are omitted from the surface structure, especially in colloquial form.

We explored the consequences of these characteristics of the Japanese language in terms of acquisition patterns and strategies. We analyzed data from one Japanese-speaking child in the age range of 11-36 months. We found that locative verbs appear considerably earlier than locative nouns and particles. The child relied heavily on locative verbs in the whole period studied in order to express spatial relations.[3]

1.4 Crosslinguistic spatial semantics

In the present paper, I will draw on our earlier work mentioned above, and extend it by making a preliminary semantic analysis of data from two Japanese-speaking children. We are concerned with what young Japanese-speaking children talk about with respect to space, and how early they arrive at language-appropriate spatial semantic categories.

Japanese carves up space into semantic categories in a way which is interestingly different from English. To my knowledge, however, there is no systematic description of spatial semantic categories of the Japanese language so far. The following is thus a very preliminary step towards such description. There have been two main sources of inspiration to this step. One is Choi and Bowerman's work on Korean (Choi & Bowerman 1991, Bowerman 1996), as Korean and Japanese are closely related to each other.

The other source of inspiration has been a coding system which we have developed in order to analyze spatial relational references (Sinha et al. 1995). In this system, each spatial reference is valued with respect to contact, support and containment relations, orientation of objects, movement of objects, and so on. Paying attention to such perceptual and functional features has helped us realize certain differences between English and Japanese spatial semantic categories.

Now, let us look at English *on*. Roughly speaking, English on encodes, with respect to space, contact and support between two objects. Japanese sometimes makes finer distinctions as to the nature of two objects and contact/support in question which English *on* is indifferent to. One such example is clothing verbs. Japanese uses different verbs such as *kiru, haku,*

---

3. Later on, we analyzed data from another Japanese-speaking child in the age range of 18-36 months, and found the same pattern of development. That is, early appearance of and heavy reliance on locative verbs on the one hand and late appearance of locative nouns and particles on the other.

and *kaburu* for putting clothing onto different parts of the body whereas English uses *put on* across the whole range.

Another example of finer division of *on* category is the manipulation of putting something onto the surface of another thing. The following manipulations in space are all categorized as the same in English.

a1. *put* book *on* table
a2. *put* picture *on* wall
a3. *put* sticker *on* table/wall

Japanese seems to be sensitive with respect to the nature of objects and contact/support as can be seen in the following examples. When it concerns loose horizontal contact, the verb *oku/noseru* is used as shown in b1. When it concerns loose vertical contact, with the object in focus being supported by a hook, the verb *kakeru* is used as shown in b2. For tight contact, for example, with glue, the verb *haru* is used as shown in b3. regardless of the orientation of contact.

b1. têburu ni hon o *oku/noseru*   Loose horizontal contact and support
    (put book on table)

b2. kabe ni e o *kakeru*[4]   Loose vertical contact and support
    (put picture on wall)   (Picture is supported by hook)

b3. Têburu/kabe ni shiiru o *haru*   Tight horizontal/vertical contact (put sticker
    on table/wall)   and support

Furthermore, Japanese distinguishes between location of events and location of existence by using respectively *de* and *ni*. In c1. and c2. below, the referential situations may be identical. However, in c1. the kitchen is categorized as a place for event whereas in c2. it is categorized as a place of existence. On the other hand, English does not make such a distinction as can be seen in the translation.

c1. okâsan wa daidokoro *de* ryôri o tsukutte-iru.
    (Mammy is cooking *in* the kitchen.)

c2. okâsan wa daidokoro *ni* iru.
    (Mammy is *in* the kitchen.)

---

4. 'Kakeru' need not always encode contact/support between two objects as can be seen in the following example: *kawa ni hashi o kakeru (build bridge over river)*.

Generally speaking, spatial relational categories seem to be smaller in Japanese than those in English. That is, Japanese makes finer distinctions which English is indifferent to. As Bowerman (1996) also points out, this is partly related to the means which each language relies on to express them, i.e. Japanese heavily relies on verbs which are open-class morphemes, and English heavily relies on prepositions which are closed-class morphemes.

In the following, I will present the results from a preliminary semantic analysis of data obtained from two Japanese-speaking children.

2. Method

2.1 Data

The data analyzed come from two children, Adam and Aki. Aki's data were collected in Japan, whereas Adam's in Denmark. In fact, Adam was bilingual in Danish and Japanese. But Japanese was much more dominant than Danish in the period in which many of the spatial expressions we are concerned with in the present paper appeared. Adam was video-taped monthly by myself (Hayashi 1993, 1994a). 30 min. of each session is transcribed. Aki was video-taped weekly by Miyata (Miyata 1995, MacWhinney 1994). Approximately 60 min. of each session is transcribed. For the present analysis, one session a month is selected from the Aki corpus. The data analyzed cover the children's age range of 18-36 months.

2.2 Coding

As mentioned before, we focus in our project on a spatial relation obtaining between two entities. We call these entities as Trajector (TR) and Landmark (LM) respectively. Trajector is an object (or event) whose location or motion is in focus. Landmark is an object or region in space, in relation to which Trajector is located. In *The book is on the table*, the location of the book is specified in relation to the table. Thus, the *book* is Trajector, and the table is Landmark. *On* specifies the spatial relation obtaining between the book and the table.

The unit of the present analysis is each spatial relational reference by Adam and Aki. In order to be coded, at least one of the three components, i.e. Trajector, Landmark, and their spatial relation, should be lexically expressed. Furthermore, all three components should be identifiable from the context. Repetition and imitation are excluded from coding.[5]

3. Results and discussion

3.1 Spatial relational references

Some of the children's spatial utterances are given below. The session numbers are given in italics. The children's age in each session is given in the tables to follow. TR stands for Trajector, LM for Landmark, and Rel. for Relational Morpheme/s. My interpretation of each utterance is given in parentheses. For example, in the first utterance, Adam just says, 'Ada kuma-chan'. A spatial relational morpheme is missing. My interpretation of this utterance is 'Adam is sitting on Teddy bear'. That is, Adam specifies his location in relation to Teddy. Thus, Adam himself is Trajector and Teddy Landmark.

ada14

TR+LM	ada kuma-chan. (Adam is sitting on Teddy bear).
LM	usa-chan. (Adam is sitting on the rabbit).

ada21

TR+LM+Rel.	far mo hikôki ni noru. (Daddy too gets on a plane).

ada22

TR+Rel.	kuruma mo haitchau. (The car too enters the play-ground).

aki25

TR	futa. (I put a lid on the pot).
Rel.	tôtta. (The bike ran through the tunnel).

aki32

LM+Rel.	obon ni nosete. (Put the melon on the tray.)

Tables 1 and 2 below give an overview of the spatial relational references coded according to our criteria. The children's age in each session is pro-

---

5. These criteria are more strict than those applied in our earlier analysis.

vided in months and days in the first column. The total number of instances
coded is given in the second column. The columns 3 through 5 indicate
which of the three components is/are overtly expressed. TR stands for Trajector, LM for Landmark, and Rel. for Relational Morpheme/s.

As mentioned above, each transcript of Adam data is 30 min. of duration
whereas that of Aki data is 60 min. Thus, the apparent difference between
Adam and Aki as to the total number of instances coded may be due to the
length of transcripts.

Ses. No.	Age in months days	Total	TR and/or LM	Rel.	TR and/or LM+Rel.
ada8	17.25	1	1		
ada9	18.17	3	3		
ada10	19.14	1	1		
ada11	20.12	0			
ada12	21.16	1	1		
ada13	22.18	2	2		
ada14	24.14	8	7		1
ada15	25.11	2		1	1
ada16	26.20	4	3		1
ada17	27.27	8	5		3
ada18	29.00	9	5		4
ada19	29.28	2			2
ada20	30.27	3		1	2
ada21	31.26	10	2		8
ada22	33.06	21	3	3	15
ada23	34.18	2		1	1
ada24	35.28	4	2		2

Table 1. Spatial relational references by Adam.

Adam begins relatively stably to talk about spatial relations at 24 months,
and Aki at 28 months. In the beginning, both children tend to express Trajector and/or Landmark alone without relational morpheme/s. In the later
period, such tendency decreases significantly. Both Adam and Aki produce
a considerable number of relational morphemes. Most of them are verbs such
as *dasu* (*take out*), *noboru* (*go up*), *noru* (*get on*), *ireru* (*put in*). Locative particles
ni (*at*), *de* (*at*), *kara* (*from*), *made* (*as far as*), and *e* (*to*) also appear. In Aki,

relational morphemes frequently appear alone whereas in Adam they tend to be combined with TR/LM.

Ses. No.	Age in months days	Total	TR and/or LM	Rel.	TR and/or LM+Rel.
aki02	18.10	0			
aki03	19.04	0			
aki04	20.23	0			
aki06	22.00	0			
aki08	24.05	0			
aki12	25.03	2	1	1	
aki16	26.00	1	1		
aki21	27.04	4	3	1	
aki25	28.04	22	7	4	11
aki28	28.29	6	1	2	3
aki32	30.15	14	4	8	2
aki35	31.05	20	1	10	9
aki39	32.03	17	7	1	9
aki43	33.00	8	1	3	4
aki47	33.29	10		6	4
aki52	35.00	7	1	3	3
aki56	36.00	21	1	11	9

Table 2. Spatial relational references by Aki.

Expressing Trajector and/or Landmark alone is also observed in young English-speaking children. Bowerman (1996) refers to earlier studies in which young children combine two nouns, such as *towel bed*, without using the relational morpheme *on*. Tomasello (1987), studying a child in her second year, reports that the child sometimes omitted spatial prepositions *on* (e.g. Bug monkey-bars) and *in* (e.g. Ball garbage). All these instances suggest certain primacy of non-linguistic conceptualization of spatial relations in young children. That is, children to begin with construct certain non-linguistic spatial relational concepts, and then they look for linguistic expressions for them.

What do Adam and Aki talk about? They talk about manipulations of things, such as putting things onto other things, taking them off, putting things into containers, taking them out. They talk about attaching things like stickers. They talk about the direction or goal of their own movement as well as movement of other people and objects. They talk about location of events, things and people. The spatial relations which Japanese children talk about seem to be similar to those which English-, Danish-, Korean-, and Dutch-speaking children are reported to do in the literature (Sinha et al. 1994, Tomasello 1992, Bowerman 1996). This may be related to the cognitive primacy in earlier periods of development just mentioned above.

3.2 Spatial semantic categories

If early strategies which Japanese-speaking children apply in order to learn spatial relational terms are similar to those applied by English-speaking children, and if the spatial relations which Japanese-speaking children talk about are similar to those English-speaking children talk about, can we also expect that Japanese children's early spatial semantic categories are similar to English children's? In the first section of the present paper (1.4), we pointed out, very preliminarily, that Japanese makes certain semantic distinctions which English is indifferent to. Do Adam and Aki apply similar semantic distinctions as English-speaking children do, and consequently produce certain errors? Or, are they already sensitive to these distinctions?

First, we look at the subdivision of the English *on* category. Adam and Aki seem to appropriately subdivide *on* category by using different verbs depending on the nature of contact/support. Tables 3 and 4 show the verbs[6]

Verb	TR	LM	Loose horizontal contact	Loose vertical contact	Tight contact
noru	daddy Adam penguin rabbit	plane plane swing horse	+ + + +		
noseru	horse	rabbit	+		
tsukeru	cream	Adam			+

Table 3. Subdivision of on *category by Adam.*

---

6. The approximate translations of these verbs are as follows; *noru* (*get on*), *noseru* (*put on*), *tsukeru* (*put on*), *oku* (*put on*), *kakeru* (*put on*), *tsuku* (*stick to*), *haru* (*put on*).

Verb	TR	LM	Loose horizontal contact	Loose vertical contact	Tight contact
noru	toy	car (2)	+		
	crayon	car	+		
	fruit	tray	+		
	Aki	play-vehicle (6)	+		
	daddy	play-vehicle	+		
	Aki	trampoline (2)	+		
	mammy	train (2)	+		
noseru	car	truck	+		
	melon	tray (2)			
oku	tissue	diaper	+		
	ticket	lap	+		
	*sticker	wall			+
kakeru	insect-catcher	wall (by hook)		+	
tsuku	plasticine	toy			+
haru	sticker	table (2)			+

Table 4. Subdivision of on category by Aki.

which Adam and Aki use to express the *on* relation between TR and LM. If a combination of the same TR and LM appears more than once, the number of instances is given in parentheses.

An instance of erroneous use is found in Aki data which is marked by * in table 4. In aki47, Aki talks about putting stickers on various objects. It is appropriate to use the verb *haru* (*put on*) regardless of the direction of contact/support, and Aki correctly uses it twice when he puts a sticker on a table. However, when he puts a sticker on a wall, he uses *oku* (*put on*). Although one single instance does not allow us a reliable interpretation, Aki might be trying to make distinction, by using two different verbs, between horizontal and vertical contact, which is sometimes relevant in Japanese.

In the first section (1.4), we pointed out that Japanese distinguishes be-

tween a place of event and a place of existence by using *de* (*at*) and *ni* (*at*) respectively. Do Adam and Aki correctly use *de* and *ni*? A couple of utterances
by each child are given below. My interpretation of each utterance is given
in parentheses.

ada21   mizuumi *ni* ita.
          (Baby ducks were on the lake.)

ada22   Kitty-chan no yûenchi *ni* iru yo.
          (The horse is in Kitty's play-ground.)

ada22   ada toire *de*.
          (Ada pees in the bathroom.)

aki47   ki *ni*.
          (Cicadas are in a tree.)

aki25   koko *de* chokkin.
          (I cut it here.)

aki39   koko *de* miru.
          (I look at the book here on the balcony.)

Table 5 below shows the total number of instances counted. Both *ni* and *de*
are polysemous. Only the instances in which these particles are used in order
to mark a place of event or a place of existence are counted. No apparent
errors are found. Adam and Aki seem to be using *ni* and *de* appropriately.
However, as the number of instances is limited, no reliable interpretation of
the results is possible.

Child	ni	de
Adam	11	1
Aki	1	3

Table 5. Use of ni *and* de

As mentioned in 1.4. the use of clothing verbs would give us an excellent opportunity to discuss the spatial semantic categories which seem to be
characteristic of Japanese. It is often reported in the literature that young

children talk about putting on and taking off clothing. However, only one such instance is found in the present Japanese data. It might be due to the contexts in which these data were collected. That is, these data were mainly collected in playing situations and eating situations in which clothing is not the main focus of conversation.

To summarize, the spatial relations which young Japanese children talk about seem to be similar to those which English-speaking children talk about. But, already before the age of three, Japanese children seem to make certain semantic distinctions which are appropriate to the language they are learning.

References

Bowerman, M. 1996. Learning how to structure space for language. A cross-linguistic perspective. *Language and Space*, (eds.) P. Bloom, M. Peterson, L. Nadel & M. Garret. Cambridge, Mass: MIT Press.

Choi, S. & Bowerman, M. 1991. Learning to express motion events in English and Korean: The influence of language-specific lexicalization patterns. *Cognition* 41, 83-121.

Clark, E.V. 1973. Non-linguistic strategies and the acquisition of word meanings. *Cognition* 2, 161-82.

Hayashi, M. 1993. Adam data. CHILDES database.

Hayashi, M. 1994a. A Longitudinal Investigation of Language Development in Bilingual Children. Unpublished Ph.D. dissertation. University of Aarhus.

Hayashi, M. 1994b. The acquisition of spatial expressions by a Japanese-speaking child. Paper presented at The 7th International Conference of the European Association of Japanese Studies, Copenhagen.

Kita, S. preprint 1995. *Japanese 'motion verbs' without motion semantics*.

MacWhinney, B. 1994. *The CHILDES project: tools for analyzing talk*. Hillsdale, N.J.: Erlbaum.

Miyata, S. 1995. The Aki corpus. Longitudinal speech data of a Japanese boy aged 1.6-2.12. *Bulletin of Aichi Shukutoku Junior College* 34.

Sinha, C. 1988. *Language and Representation: A Socio-naturalistic Approach to Human Development*. London: Harvester-Weatsheaf.

Sinha, C. & Thorseng, L.A. 1995. A coding system for spatial relational reference. *Cognitive Linguistics*, 6-273, 261-309.

Sinha, C., Thorseng, L.A., Hayashi, M. & Plunkett, K. 1994. Comparative spatial semantics and language acquisition: evidence from Danish, English, and Japanese. *Journal of Semantics* 11, 253-87.

Talmy, L. 1983. How language structures space. *Spatial Orientation: Theory, Research, and Application*, (eds.) H.L. Pick & L.P. Acredolo. Plenum Press.

Talmy, L. 1985. Lexicalization patterns: Semantic structure in lexical forms. *Language Typology and Syntactic Description*, vol. 3 (Grammatical Categories and the Lexicon), (ed.) T. Shopen. Cambridge: Cambridge University Press.

Talmy, L. 1991. Path to realization: A typology of event conflation. In: *Proceedings of the Berkeley Linguistics Society*, vol. 17.

Tomasello, M. 1987. Learning to use prepositions: A case study. *Journal of Child Language* 14, 79-98.

Tomasello, M. 1992. *First Verbs: A case study of early grammatical development*. Cambridge: Cambridge University Press.

Subjective or Objective?

A Comparison of Utterance Types in Japanese and Norwegian

Benedicte M. Irgens

There are certain phenomena in grammar that can not be accounted for without reference to context. These phenomena belong to the domain of pragmatics, given a definition of the kind proposed in Levinson (1983:9): 'Pragmatics is the study of those relations between language and context that are grammaticalized, or encoded in the structure of a language'. My paper concerns some problems to be discussed in my doctoral dissertation in linguistics at the University of Bergen. The working title of the dissertation is 'Subjectivity and View point in Japanese and Norwegian', and involves a discussion of the notion of *subjectivity* and how this is manifested in the linguistic form of the two languages. The main problem with a concept like subjectivity is that it is not easily definable, but I think it might prove fruitful when accounting for certain pragmatic phenomena, such as the difference between what Kuno (1973) calls *neutral descriptions* (or *ga*-sentences that are *not* exhaustive listings) and *wa*-sentences:

(1)   Tarô-ga gohan-o tabete iru.
        Taro-SUBJ food-OBJ eat(GER) be(AUX)
        Taro is eating (food).

(2)   Tarô-wa gohan-o tabete iru.
        Taro-TOP food-OBJ eat(GER) be(AUX)
        Taro is eating (food).

Formally, the sentences differ in that the underlying subject in neutral descriptions is marked with the subject particle *ga*, while in *wa*-sentences it is marked with the pragmatic topic particle *wa*. Semantically, however, there seems to be a modal difference which make them interesting for my own study. Since the two sentence types express the same propositional content, the difference is extra-propositional (Shibatani 1990).

The exact difference between sentences such as these is difficult to pinpoint, but in certain cases, *wa*-sentences are predications about a topic and can be true/false *independent of the moment of utterance*, while neutral descriptions express actions and states as observed by the speaker and have truth conditions which vary *depending on the moment of utterance*. Thus, (3) is a generic statement about the sky, whereas (4) is a specific statement about the way the sky looks at the moment of utterance:

(3)   Sora-wa aoi.
      sky-TOP blue
      The sky is blue.

(4)   Sora-ga aoi.
      sky-SUBJ blue
      The sky is blue (right now).

(The difference between (1) and (2), however, is not as clear, since they both are specific statements and not generic. One reason for this may lie in the aspectual form of the verb.) Since the difference between (3) and (4) is more obvious, I will start by looking at them in the following.

There is a tendency in the literature to characterize descriptions as somewhat more *objective* than *wa*-sentences. Both Masuoka (1991) and Nitta (1989) claim that these sentences express an objective description of a state or event, and Iwasaki (1993) classifies sentences like (4) as having Zero-perspective, meaning that the speaker is not a participant in the situation described and that the sentence does not describe any experience of a sentient being. Kuno (1973:51) also says: 'Sentences of neutral description present an objectively observable action, existence, or temporary state as a new event'.

What is actually meant by objective here is not clear, but if we take objective to mean 'shared by both the speaker and the hearer', this is problematic for a number of reasons. One is the existence of examples such as (5), which is found among Kuno's own examples of neutral description:

(5)   Atama-ga itai.
      head-SUBJ aches.
      (Lit.) Head aches. I have a headache.

(6)   Kutsu-ga chiisai.
      shoe-SUBJ small
      These shoes feel small (for me).

The adjective *itai* belongs to a class of Japanese words that, when in the indicative mood, can only denote the speaker's own internal feeling or psychological state. Formally, (5) and (6) are *ga*-sentences, but since they can not be used to report about other people than the speaker, they can reasonably be called subjective.[1]

Another argument for considering *ga*-sentences more subjective than their *wa*-counterparts is that they are generally more context-bound — among other things, they cannot be used to denote a non-temporary state or action (Kuno 1973), like generic statements, for example. *Ga*-sentences express what the speaker is perceiving in the moment of utterance and imply that that state of affairs might change through time. Hence the unacceptability of (10):

(10)   *Tôkyô-ga ookii.
Tokyo-SUBJ big
(Look!) Tokyo is big.

Still another characteristic of descriptions is that the *ga*-constituent cannot be a 1st person noun.

(11)   *Boku-ga hashitte iru.
I-SUBJ run(GER) AUX
(I am running).

This fact has been pointed out by a number of scholars, though some do

1. One obvious problem that arises with this kind of analysis, is how to deal with sentences with an explicit first person noun as topic:
(7)   Watashi-wa atama-ga itai.
I-TOP head-SUBJ hurts
I have a headache.
The naturalness of such a sentence (except with a contrastive reading) is debatable. In spontaneous speech, there is a tendency for the topic particle to be omitted, like in (8):
(8)   Watashi atama-ga itai.
I head-SUBJ hurts
I have a headache.
The topic constituent can not be added to any description, however, so that (9) is not acceptable:
(9)   *Watashi-wa Tarô-ga gohan-o tabete iru.
I-TOP Taro-SUBJ food-OBJ eat(GER) be(AUX)
I will not discuss these problems any further here, but they are undoubtedly relevant.

mention specialized contexts where sentences like these are felicitous, e.g. when watching a video-taped recording of oneself running etc. (Nitta 1989).

Kuno (1973:55) notes this apparent restriction, and says:

> It also seems that the speaker is not allowed to look at his own action or existence objectively and to describe it as if it were a new event. This seems to be why it is next to impossible to interpret sentences with the first person subject (...) as sentences of neutral description.

If we consider sentences like (11) not as objective statements but rather as a report about what the speaker senses at the moment of utterance, regardless of whether this sensation can be shared by other people or not, the oddity of these sentences explains itself. The speaker's existence is signalized by the *ga*-sentence as such, and need not be explicitly mentioned.

A linguistic fact in one language can by no means be used as evidence that the same holds for another, but such facts still may be of some help in a discussion like the one above. Norwegian has no formal distinction of the kind mentioned, but it is possible to mark the *subjectivity* in a sentence by giving the predicate verb past tense (a modal function of the inflectional category PAST). The subjective version presents an observable action or a temporary state the way it is percieved by the speaker in the moment of utterance, (without the speaker being explicitly mentioned with a pronoun). Just like the Japanese descriptions, their grammatical subject must always have specific reference, and can never be generic, as can be seen from example (14).

(12)   Disse blomstene var pene.   (13)   Disse blomstene er pene.
       these flowers be(PAST) beautiful   these flowers be(PRES) beautiful
       These flowers are beautiful (I think).   These flowers are beautiful.

(14)   Blomster er/*var pene.
       flowers be(PAST) beautiful
       Flowers are beautiful.

(15)   Hana-ga kirei desu. (only specific reading)
       flower-SUBJ beautiful COP
       (Those) flowers are beautiful.

As can be seen, these sentence types in Japanese and Norwegian have the generic/specific distinction in common. What about the other previously mentioned characteristics of Japanese descriptions? 1) they can be used to express the inner feelings of the speaker (such as pain) and 2) that they can not have the first person noun in subject position.

Since the Norwegian modal past is not formally distinguishable from temporal past, it is not always possible to decide which of the two we are dealing with. Still, the deictic expressions in (16) and (17) help to give the sentences a modal interpretation:

(16)   Dette gjorde ondt.
       this do(PAST) painful
       This is painful!

(17)   Nå var det kaldt her.   (18) Nå er det kaldt i Japan.
       now be(PAST) it cold here   now be(PRES) it cold in Japan
       How cold it is in here now.   Japan is cold now.

Norwegian modal past may very well have a first person subject, as in (19):

(19)   Så fin jeg var nå!
       how nice I be(PAST) now
       How nice I look!

However, the most natural context for an utterance of this type is when the speaker is looking at him/herself in the mirror and stating his/her own opinion about his/her looks. Japanese descriptions with a first person subject are described as unacceptable by Kuno, but as I have already mentioned, they are possible in certain contexts, and their status as unacceptable is highly arguable.

Japanese descriptions and Norwegian modal past sentences naturally do not behave in exactly the same way. However, the characteristics they share may serve as an indication that they both are inherently subjective.

The concept of subjectivity is frequently used in linguistic literature concerning semantics and pragmatics, usually in a vague and intuitive way. This is the case for very many pragmatic concepts, since the field of study itself is relatively new and not too well-defined. Since Japanese seems to have relatively more pragmatic information coded in the grammar, there is a tradition in Japanese linguistics to use the notion of subjectivity or *shukansei* to account for certain phenomena in Japanese — maybe more so than in literature on English and definitely on Norwegian. The Japanese literature on this topic still seems to take the meaning of the concept somewhat for granted. Among more recent work, we have Iwasaki (1993:4), for example, who, as far as I can see, proposes no definition, but just states that 'The speaker, who is present for all utterances of colloquial discourse, inevitably influences the utterance form in various ways'.

Maynard (1993:12) also uses a wide interpretation of the word, and says as follows:

Here I use 'subjectivity' in a restricted way primarily as it relates to the language producer's subjectivity as reflected in the expression of his or her personal attitude and feelings.

Others, such as Makino (1987), prefer using a functional concept of communication orientation, either speaker or hearer orientation, and argue that descriptive *ga* is speaker-oriented.

References

Iwasaki, Shôichi. 1993. *Subjectivity in Grammar and Discourse*. Amsterdam: John Benjamins.

Kuno, Susumu. 1973. *The Structure of the Japanese language*. Cambridge, Mass: MIT Press.

Levinson, Stephen C. 1983. *Pragmatics*. Cambridge University Press.

Makino, Seiichi. 1987. How Relevant Is a Functional Notion of Communicative Orientation to Ga and Wa? *Perspectives on Topicalization — the Case of Japanese WA*, ed. by John Hinds et al. Amsterdam: John Benjamins.

Masuoka, Takashi. 1991. *Modaritii no bunpoo*. Tokyo: Kuroshio shuppan.

Maynard, Senko. 1993. *Discourse Modality — Subjectivity, Emotion and Voice in the Japanese Language*. Amsterdam: John Benjamins.

Nitta, Yoshio. 1989. *Gendai nihongo-bun no modaritii no taikei to kôzô. Nihongo no Modaritii*. Tokyo: Kuroshio shuppan.

Shibatani, Masayoshi. 1990. *The Languages of Japan*. Cambridge: Cambridge University Press.

Diachronic Correspondence in the Conjugations of the Verbs of the Japanese Dialects[1]

Onishi Takuichiro

1. Introduction

The purpose of this paper is threefold.

Firstly, I wish to propose the notion of conjugation class, which is a particularly effective tool for historical comparative research on the conjugation of verbs in the Japanese dialects. Secondly, I wish to provide an outline of what can concretely be attained through the application of this notion. Thirdly, I wish to show cartographically on various levels how the merger of the conjugation classes is distributed in all the Japanese dialects.

My conclusion is that by looking at the conjugation classes and their subseuent mergers, one can set up a basic model for considering the historical relationships of the verbal conjugations in the Japanese dialects.

2. What are conjugation classes?

In this section I shall explain what conjugation classes are.

They are a way of dividing words into groups which then form the base for the historical comparison of the verbal conjugations in the Japanese dialects.

I shall set up the classes based on the way groups of words correspond to the oldest conjugation framework we have available, and we have then the following nine types of conjugation classes: *kami ichidan rui* 'upper mono-grade class', *kami nidan rui* 'upper bi-grade class', *shimo ichidan rui* 'lower

1. I would like to thank Peter Hendriks of the University of Wisconsin for help with my English. I am also deeply grateful to my colleague Ms Shirasawa for hand-drawing map 1, 2 and 3. Cited linguistic forms are in this paper transcribed phonemically.

mono-grade class', *shimo nidan rui* 'lower bi-grade class', *yodan rui* 'quadri-grade class', *kahen rui* 'irregular k class', *sahen rui* 'irregular s class', *nahen rui* 'irregular n class', and *rahen rui* 'irregular r class'. I consider it unnecessary, however, to posit the category 'lower mono- grade' and shall return to this point later.

The names of the classes correspond to the names of the conjugations in classical grammar. Note, however, that while the names of the various classes are based on the classical conjugation forms, these conjugation classes are, as I mentioned, but groups of words, and the names themselves do not say anything directly about the current forms of the conjugations in the dialects.

(1) shows some examples for each of the conjugation classes. The verbs are presented in their classical sentence-final form, and in some cases I have also included, in parentheses, the modern sentence-final forms for ease of recognition. The abbreviated name for each class is also listed on *(1)*.

(1)   *rui* = 'class'
Kami ichidan rui 'Upper Mono-grade class': [UM]
    kiru 'to put on', *niru* 'to boil', *miru* 'to see', *iru* 'to shoot',
    wiru 'to exist', ...
Kami nidan rui 'Upper Bi-grade class': [UB]
    oku (*okiru*) 'to get up', *sugu* (*sugiru*) 'to pass', *otu* (*otiru*) 'to fall',
    todu (*toziru*) 'to close', *nobu* (*nobiru*) 'to extend',
    kuju (*kuiru*) 'to regret', *oru* (*oriru*) 'to descend', ...
Shimo ichidan rui 'Lower Mono-grade class': [LM]
    keru 'to kick'
Shimo nidan rui 'Lower Bi-grade class': [LB]
    u (*eru*) 'to get', *aku* (*akeru*) 'to open', *agu* (*ageru*) 'to raise',
    atu (*ateru*) 'to hit', *du* (*deru*) 'to go out', *nu* (*neru*) 'to sleep',
    tabu (*taberu*) 'to eat', *iru* (*ireru*) 'to put in', *uwu* (*ueru*) 'to plant', ...
Yodan rui 'Quadri-grade class': [Q]
    kaku 'to write', *kagu* 'to smell', *sasu* 'to pierce', *tatu* 'to stand up',
    kahu 'to buy', *tobu* 'to fly', *kamu* 'to bite', *waru* 'to devide', ...
Kahen rui 'Irregular K class': [IK]
    ku (*kuru*) 'to come', ... (compound verbs)
Sahen rui 'Irregular S class': [IS]
    su (*suru*) 'to do', ... (compound verbs)
Nahen rui 'Irregular N class': [IN]
    sinu 'to die', *inu* 'to leave'
Rahen rui 'Irregular R class': [IR]
    ari (*aru*) 'to exist', *wori* (*oru*) 'to exist'

If one compares the conjugation classes across all the dialects, it is evident that each dialect has different forms and systems for its conjugations. However, if one pays attention to conjugation classes as an arrangement of word groupings, then one can see clear correspondences between the various dialects, and also with the central language — that is, the Kyoto dialect of the classical period.

In other words, depending on the conjugation system of each dialect, in some cases two or more conjugation classes have come together as one, while in other cases a single conjugation class has tenaciously maintained its independence.

Furthermore, this leads one to predict that these correspondences have a diachronic relationship underlying them.

This diachronic prediction can be substantiated in the following way. If it were the case that the current state of the conjugations in the dialects were the result of a totally random flow, then one would not be able to explain the actual fact that there are correspondences between the conjugation classes. That is to say, because one can see correspondences, this means that there must be a diachronic relationship between the conjugations of the various dialects.

Based on these correspondences, then, what sort of diachronic changes are possible?

One is that the group of words which belong to a conjugation class undergo changes together as a unified group. This is a natural conclusion to the explanation that a group of words acts together as one type.

Secondly, there is the fact that one cannot explain the history of the dialects by comparing them to the process of historical change undergone by the central dialect.

The argument can not arise that the dialects do nothing but reflect a certain stage of the central language due to the fact that even if the classes do correspond it is only because the dialects have a phonological correspondence to the central language.

The situation in each area, when viewed from the point of view of conjugation class, does not necessarily reflect the history of the central dialect as we know it. Even if their origins were the same as that of the central language (and this is but one possibility), there should be differences in the way the classes developed towards their current state in each dialect.

Based on this, then, it should be possible to trace the lineage — that is to say the historical relationships — of the conjugations in the dialects through a comparison of the correspondences of the conjugation classes.

In other words, we have here the hypothesis that if one proceeds by comparing the conjugation classes in the various present-day dialects, one can
close in on the history of conjugation in the whole of the Japanese language.

Furthermore, I would like to again make it clear that this hypothesis does
not just boil down to how the dialects branched off from the central
language.

Using this as a point of departure, I shall continue to look at the conjugation classes, taking them to be one tool with which to investigate the history of the language.

3. The merger and independence of the conjugation classes

When words which belong to different classes come to have the same type
of conjugation, I call this 'merger of classes'. On the other hand, in cases in
which one presumes that a class has not merged with others, I shall call this
class 'independent'. Furthermore, whether classes are independent or not, if
there is a demarcation between classes, I shall say that these classes are 'distinguished' from one another. I will show the distinctions with slash mark
in the following.

Again, I am not taking up the point at the moment of what the actual
forms of the conjugations are in the merged situation, but shall explain concretely in what way one should consider the state of affairs.

(2) shows the general form of the conjugation for the Tokyo dialect
(which is more or less the same as that of the modern standard language).
I have just shown representatives from each of the conjugation classes, but
for the most part the words which belong to each category have the same
conjugation.

I use a hyphen to separate the verb from the particles and the inflectional
suffixes. The conjugation form is that part of the word separated from the
particles and suffixes.

The stem is that part which takes various conjugation forms but which
hardly changes itself. The remaining part of the conjugation form is the conjugational suffix.

Differing conjugations are thus to be seen in the differing suffixes.

(2) Tokyo Dialect

	negative	nonpast	conditional	imperative	volitional		stem
1.							
UM (*to see*)	mi-nai	miru	mire-ba	miro	mijoo	→	mi
UB (*to get up*)	oki-nai	okiru	okire-ba	okiro	okijoo	→	oki
LB (*to open*)	ake-nai	akeru	akere-ba	akero	akejoo	→	ake
2.							
LM (*to kick*)	kera-nai	keru	kere-ba	kere	keroo	→	ker
Q (*to write*)	kaka-nai	kaku	kake-ba	kake	kakoo	→	kak
IN (*to die*)	sina-nai	sinu	sine-ba	sine	sinoo	→	sin
IR (*to exist*)	aru		are-ba			→	ar
3.							
IK (*to come*)	ko-nai	kuru	kure-ba	koi	kojoo	→	k
4.							
IS (*to do*)	si-nai	suru	sure-ba	siro	sijoo	→	s

State of the mergers of the conjugation classes UM UB LB/LM Q IN IR/IK/IS.

From this one can see the following; 1st point: The upper mono-grade, upper bi-grade, and lower bi-grade classes do not differ from one another in conjugation. 2nd point: The lower mono-grade, quadri-grade, irregular n, and irregular r classes do not differ in conjugation from one another, but they do differ from those in 1st. 3rd point: The irregular k and irregular s classes differ from each other, and also from those in 1st and 2nd.

The situation that can be deduced from these conjugation classes as far as mergers is concerned is the following: upper mono-grade, upper bi-grade, lower bi-grade/lower mono-grade, quadri-grade, irregular n, irregular r/irregular k/irregular s.

(3) is that of my own dialect. I was born in Yao City in Osaka Prefecture, grew up in Nara Prefecture, and commuted to both middle and high school

in Osaka Prefecture. I call my dialect the Hanna dialect, and I do not expect that it differs too greatly from others in the central part of the Kinki District.

(3) Hanna (Osaka-Nara) Dialect

		negative	nonpast	conditional	weak-imperative	volitional		stem
1.								
UM	(to see)	mii-heN	miru	mi-tara	mii	mijo	→	mi(i)
UB	(to get up)	oki-heN	okiru	oki-tara	oki	okijo	→	oki
LB	(to open)	ake-heN	akeru	ake-tara	ake	akejo	→	ake
2.								
LM	(to kick)	kera-heN	keru	ket-tara	keri	kero	→	ker
Q	(to write)	kaka-heN	kaku	kai-tara	kaki	kako	→	kak
IN	(to die)	sina-heN	sinu	siN-dara	sini	sino	→	sin
IR	(to exist)	ora-heN	oru	ot-tara	ori	oro	→	or
3.								
IK	(to come)	kee-heN	kuru	ki-tara	kii	kojo	→	k
4.								
IS	(to do)	see-heN	suru	si-tara	sii	sijo	→	s

State of the mergers of the conjugation classes UM UB LB/LM Q IN IR/ IK/IS

The actual forms of the verbs do differ from those of the Tokyo dialect, but the situation as to the mergers of the conjugation classes is the same as that of Tokyo: upper mono-grade, upper bi-grade, lower bi-grade/lower mono-grade, quadri-grade, irregular n, irregular r/irregular k/irregular s.

4. Dimensions to the mergers

On the basis of the mergers undergone by the conjugation classes, one can divide them further into dimensions. The lower the number of dimensions, the more differences between the classes, and the higher the number of dimensions, the more merged the classes, as can be seen on *(4)*. As it is the case that as mergers progress the number of dimensions increase, then the lower the number of dimensions, the more differences there are between the classes and the older one can think them to be.

(4)
1 dimensional conjugation
UM/UB/LM/LB/Q/IK/IS/IN/IR

2 dimensional conjugation
UM UB/LM/LB/Q/IK/IS/IN/IR
UM/UB LM/LB/Q/IK/IS/IN/IR
UM/UB/LM LB/Q/IK/IS/IN/IR etc. 36 possible combinations

3 dimensional conjugation
UM UB LM/LB/Q/IK/IS/IN/IR
UM/UB LM LB/Q/IK/IS/IN/IR
UM/UB/LM LB Q/IK/IS/IN/IR etc. 462 possible combinations

4 dimensional conjugation
UM UB LM LB/Q/IK/IS/IN/IR
UM/UB LM LB Q/IK/IS/IN/IR
UM/UB/LM LB Q IK/IS/IN/IR etc. 2646 possible combinations

5 dimensional conjuagtion
UM UB LM LB Q/IK/IS/IN/IR
UM/UB LM LB Q IK/IS/IN/IR
UM/UB/LM LB Q IK IS/IN/IR etc. 8211 possible combinations

6 dimensional conjugation
UM UB LM LB Q IK/IS/IN/IR
UM/UB LM LB Q IK IS/IN/IR
UM/UB/LM LB Q IK IS IN/IR etc. 7770 possible combinations

7 dimensional conjugation
UM UB LM LB Q IK IS/IN/IR
UM/UB LM LB Q IK IS IN/IR
UM/UB/LM LB Q IK IS IN IR etc. 3025 possible combinations

8 dimensional conjugation
UM/UB LM LB Q IK IS IN IR
UM UB/LM LB Q IK IS IN IR
UM UB LM/ LB Q IK IS IN IR etc. 255 possible combinations

9 dimensional conjugation
UM UB LM LB Q IK IS IN IR

Taking this point into consideration, I will now go on to a discussion of the lineal relationships.

5. Lineage based on conjugation classes

In considering lineal relationships, I shall basically adhere to the following principle: 'Classes, once merged, will not separate again along the lines of their previous distinctions'. This means, for example, that if the conjugations upper mono-grade, upper bi-grade, and lower bi-grade merge, then it will in principle not be the case that words belonging to the former upper bi-grade class separate off all at once from the rest, resulting in the state: upper mono-grade, lower bi- grade/upper bi-grade.

6. Application to the various dialects

Based on an investigation of the state of the mergers as gleaned from relatively detailed synchronic data, I shall now lay out a method for looking at the diachronic relationships of the dialects. The state of the merger of the conjugation classes of several dialects is as is shown on (5).

(5)
Tokyo:	UM UB LB/LM Q IN IR/IK/IS	6 dim.
Bungotakada City:	UM/UB/LB/LM Q IR/IK/IS/IN	3 dim.
Oita City-Motomachi:	UM/UB LB/LM Q IR/IK/IS/IN	4 dim.
Nagasaki City:	UM UB/LB/LM Q IN IR/IK/IS	5 dim.
Kagoshima City:	UM UB LM Q IN IR/LB/IK/IS	6 dim.
Tsuruoka City-Oyama:	UM UB LB/LM Q IN IR/IK/IS	6 dim.
Taneichi-Hiranai:	UM UB LB/LM Q IN IR/IK/IS	6 dim.
Suwa (Nagano):	UM UB LB/LM Q IN IR/IK/IS	6 dim.
Shizuoka City:	UM UB LB IS/LM Q IN IR/IK	7 dim.
Akiyamago (Nagano):	UM UB LM LB IS/Q IN (IR)/IK	7 dim.

I shall not present here a detailed conjugation chart, but shall just make a comment about the Suwa dialect. If one excludes the passive and causative forms, the irregular s verbs (such as *suru*, 'to do') can be classified synchronically as being of the same type as the upper mono-grade, upper bi-grade, lower bi-grade group. In which case the merger of the classes would be a seven dimensional one just like that of Shizuoka. Thus one has here a different view of the merger depending on the way one takes the framework of the conjugation table. I shall return to this point later.

If one compares even the above ten dialects, one can still make certain comments about their diachronic relationships. For example, if one compares Bungotakada, having three dimensions, with Oita City-Motomachi, having four, it is possible that there be a lineal relationship between them. This is because the merger in the Bungotakada dialect of the upper bi-grade and lower bi-grade classes results in the situation we find in the Oita City-Motomachi dialect.

On the other hand, if one compares the four-dimensional Oita City-Motomachi with the five-dimensional Nagasaki, they do differ in having but one dimension more or less, but there is no possible lineal relationship between them. The reason being that while in Oita City-Motomachi the upper bi-grade and lower bi-grade classes have merged, they remain distinguished in the Nagasaki dialect.

7. National distribution

At the National Language Research Institute we are compiling a *Grammar Atlas of Japanese Dialects* — the *GAJ* — which, while not focussing on conjugation classes, is still quite useful in this regard, as various conditions have been standardized, and the data are taken from throughout Japan. I will show here some maps presenting the distribution of the mergers which have taken place in the mainland dialects, and which are based on data I have arranged from the volumes of the GAJ which deal with conjugation — Volumes Two and Three.

Note that from looking at various data for the mainland dialects one comes to understand that the irregular r class has merged with the quadri-grade, and I shall take that as a premiss for what follows.

First of all, I shall show *map 1* laying out the state of the mergers for all nine classes, from upper mono-grade to irregular r. I shall refer to this level of treatment as Level 1.

In actual fact, there are problems with dealing with all the dialects at this level, and those are the problems that arise from giving the lower mono-grade class the same weight as the other classes.

For one, there were unusual circumstances in the origin of this class in the central language, in that it arose at first in the Heian Period, and was not to be found previous to that. It also only contains the one verb *keru*, 'to kick'.

If one closes one's eyes to these circumstances in the central language, there are still problems looking at it from the point of view of the dialects,

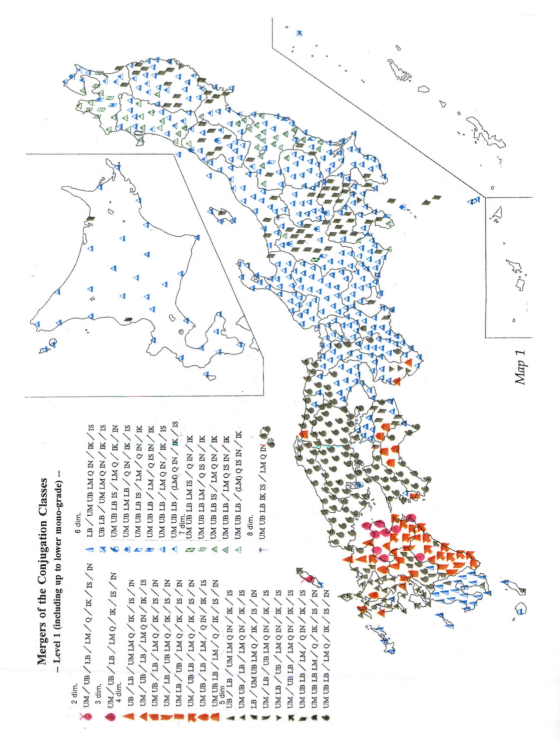

Mergers of the Conjugation Classes
— Level 1 (including up to lower mono-grade) —

Map 1

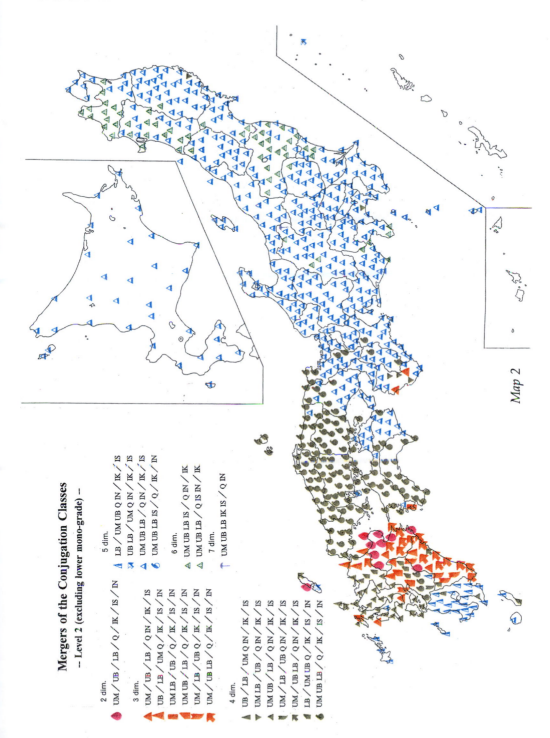

Map 2

Mergers of the Conjugation Classes
-- Level 2 (excluding lower mono-grade) --

and that is that there are many dialects which do not use the word *keru* it-self. In the GAJ, in cases when we have received replies using a different vo-cabulary item, we have distinguished these replies from those dealing with the grammar, and have treated them solely from the point of view of vo-cabulary items. That this type of reply has been particularly frequent in this case is clearly shown in the section for *keru*.

Next, there is the problem of analysis. There are cases where the lower mono-grade class is independent, but for the most part if one looks at their actual forms, one can see that they are wavering between the vowel-base forms and the consonant-base forms. On the basis of this it would be pos-sible to come to the conclusion that it is but a transient form, and that it is a separate phenomenon which should be dealt with in terms of the history of the word itself — quite apart from the point of view of conjugation clas-ses.

There is also a problem from the point of view of the theory of con-jugation classes, and that is, as I just mentioned, there is only the one verb *keru* which belongs to the lower mono-grade class in the first place. One is working from the principle that it is precisely because the connection be-tween classes and verbs is arbitrary that one can consider the lineage of the classes, and the lower mono-grade class has problems from the point of view of this all-important arbitrariness.

As one can see, many questions arise if one allows the lower mono-grade class to have independence as a class. As a result, I shall not be considering it a class, and shall continue by excluding from consideration the verb *keru*.

Map 2 is a map of the mergers based on the eight verb classes: upper mono-grade, upper bi-grade, lower bi-grade, quadri-grade, irregular k, irregular s, irregular n, (and irregular r). I shall refer to this level of treatment as Level 2. If one takes into consideration the problems with lower mono-grade in the Level 1 treatment, then it would seem that this level shows a situation some-what closer to the historical truth.

What I am about to say may seem irrelevant, but if one puts a filter on the lens of one's camera when taking a photograph, it often happens that a cer-tain aspect of the subject comes more clearly into view compared to when one does not use such a filter.

I would like to take this into consideration now. A little while ago I illustrated the state of the mergers based on data gathered from all the dia-lects, and noted that in the case of the Suwa dialect if one excluded the pas-sive and causative verbs forms, then it would be possible to see the irregular s class as merged with the upper mono-grade, upper bi-grade, lower bi-grade class. It would appear that such a consideration is possible for dialects other than that of Suwa as well.

On *map 3*, I shall try, then, to look at the state of the mergers excluding the passive and causative forms, and shall refer to this level of treatment as Level 3.

Comparing *map 3* of Level 3 to the map of Level 2, one might call it a view of the subject through a filter which blocks out the causative and the passive.

What is noteworthy about the Level 3 view are the movements of the irregular k, and the irregular s classes. Compared to Level 2 one can see that many areas appear where the irregular s, in particular, has merged with the upper mono-grade, upper bi-grade, lower bi-grade class. Also — although less widespread — there are areas where the irregular k and the irregular s have merged.

By the way, the question of what kind of conjugation form should be screened out with a filter is still an area for further debate. For example, one would predict that the application of a filter to hide the imperative form would give yet another view. I would imagine that in the Kanto region there would appear areas where the irregular k class would merge with the upper mono- grade, upper bi-grade, lower bi-grade class.

However I think that the screening out of the causative and passive forms means something quite different, grammatically speaking, from screening out the imperative form. Of course, as the conjugational form differs, the grammatical meaning also differs. However, more than this, it is a problem of the position or relative weight of the passive and causative versus the imperative in the conjugation system as taken in a wider grammatical and semantic sense. While the causative and passive forms are derivational, the imperative is inflectional. It is important that one pay attention to the question of what sort of grammatical meaning is distinctive to each sort of filter.

8. Conclusion

In this paper I have explained what the idea of conjugation class is, and have laid out some basic pointers in the direction of what sorts of enquiries one can pursue through its concrete application. Subsequently, we saw that it is

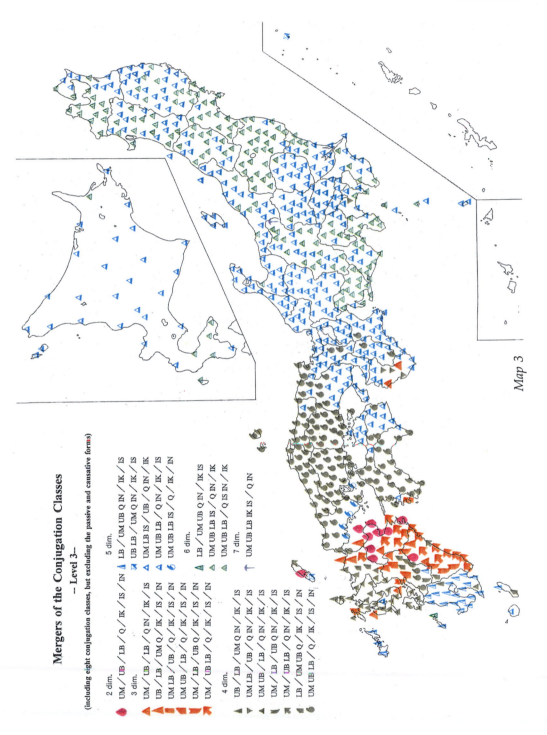

Mergers of the Conjugation Classes
– Level 3 –
(including eight conjugation classes, but excluding the passive and causative forms)

2 dim.

UM / UB / LB / Q / IK / IS / IN

3 dim.

UM / UB / LB / Q IN / IK / IS
UB / LB / UM Q / IK / IS / IN
UM LB / UB / Q / IK / IS / IN
UM UB / LB / Q / IK / IS / IN
UM / LB / UB Q / IK / IS / IN
UM / UB LB / Q / IK / IS / IN

4 dim.

UB / LB / UM Q IN / IK / IS
UM LB / UB / Q IN / IK / IS
UM UB / LB / Q IN / IK / IS
UM UB / LB / UB Q IN / IK / IS
LB / UM UB Q / IK / IS / IN
UM UB LB / Q / IK / IS / IN

5 dim.

LB / UM UB Q IN / IK / IS
UB LB / UM Q IN / IK / IS
UM LB IS / UB / Q IN / IK
UM UB LB / Q IN / IK / IS
UM LB IS / Q / IK / IN

6 dim.

LB / UM UB Q IN / IK IS
UM UB LB IS / Q IN / IK
UM UB LB / Q IS IN / IK

7 dim.

UM UB LB IK IS / Q IN

Map 3

possible to concretely investigate diachronic relationships by looking at conjugation classes and their mergers. In this sense, one might well say that the notion of conjugation class is valuable as a diachronic measure.

Furthermore, by applying this measure to all the dialects we saw that when setting up the classes, there was no need to establish the class of lower mono-grade, and that if one limited one's view of the conjugational forms somewhat, then hidden aspects of the merger came forth.

Before I finish, I would just like to say a few words about further applications.

One wonders whether this kind of model would only be useful for Japanese.

Might it not also be a valuable tool for other languages, such as Korean or the Altaic languages, for example, or perhaps even the Indo-European languages.

Further, would it be possible, as what one might call 'classology', to use this method in areas other than conjugation, and if so, in what areas?

I would think that in principle it would be applicable in any situation where there is an arbitrary relationship between a framework and groups of words. If that were the case, would it perhaps be applicable in investigating gender in Indo-European languages? To the best of my knowledge, in the Scandinavian languages the relationships between each gender and the words which take that gender are to be considered arbitrary.

One expects the idea to broaden out even from here. At least as far as Japanese is concerned, it has been used quite productively in studies of accent.

Spontaneity and Causativity

Reïko Shimamori

Introduction

Voice has generally been studied as an opposition between passive voice and active voice. However, passive voice, emphasizing the passivity of the sentence subject, can include a notion of 'spontaneity'; and active voice, because of an active attitude of the sentence subject towards an object, can be compared with causative sentences. In fact, in Japanese, passive sentences can often be confused with sentences with an intransitive verb implying a notion of spontaneity; for instance, we generally say:

(1-a) kono hen   ni   mo takai biru   ga   takusan tachi-
       this neighborhood loc also high building NOM   many   be built
       mashi- ta   ne.
       POLITE PAST   CONSENT
       'Many high buildings have also been built in this neighborhood, haven't they?'

rather than:

(1-b) kono hen   ni   mo takai biru   ga   takusan tate-
       this neighborhood LOC also high building nom   many   build
       rare-   mashi- ta   ne.
       PASSIVE   POLITE PAST   CONSENT

It is also sometimes difficult to draw a clear distinction between a causative sentence and an active sentence with a transitive verb. Thus, we say:

(2-a) hata wo tateru   'to haul up a flag'
       flag ACC haul up (vt)

but

(2-b)   seito wo   tat-   aseru   'to make a pupil stand'
        pupil ACC   stand CAUS

This paper will deal with these two contrasted notions, i.e. spontaneity and causativity, on both syntactic and semantic levels. Concretely, I will study different expressions of passive voice, intransitive and transitive structures, causative sentences, and comparing their syntactic and semantic characteristics, I will refer to fundamental differences between languages which emphasize the agent of an action, like English, and Japanese which tends to apprehend a situation comprehensively, without reference to a person as agent. Finally, this paper will point out some differences in the way of thinking of speakers of these two kinds of languages.

1. Passive voice in Japanese

1.1 Definition

Passive voice is a contrasted notion of active voice, or more precisely it must be considered as the opposite of transitive expressions. It is usually employed in order to denote an action viewed from the patient's vantage point. The opposition between passivity and transitivity can be clearly described as follows by the elements which constitute the 'prototype' of each conception:

1) *Prototype of transitivity*
   Semantically:
   i)   There are two participants: agent and patient
   ii) The subject (= agent) acts intentionally (an agentive subject)
   iii) The object (= patient) undergoes a change

   Syntactically:
   i)   A sentence has the following pattern: A *ga* P *wo* V
   ii) A sentence can be transformed into a passive one

   Morphologically:
   i)   A verb is in its basic form (non-marked)

2) *Prototype of passivity*
    Semantically:
    i)   There are two participants: agent and patient;
    ii) The subject (= patient) undergoes a change
    iii) The subject is non-agentive

    Syntactically:
    i)   A sentence patterns as follows: P *ga* A *ni* V-*(r)areru*
    ii) A sentence has a corresponding active sentence

    Morphologically:
    i)   A verb is marked by the passive suffix -*(r)areru*

However, it is common knowledge that in Japanese, both transitive and in-transitive verbs can be used in the passive. Compare the following sentences:

(3-a)   watashi   wa   sensei   ni   home-   rare-   ta.
        I   TOPIC   teacher   DAT   praise   PASSIVE PAST
        'I was praised by the teacher'.

(3-b)   watashi   wa   sensei   ni   e   wo   home- rare-   ta
        I   TOPIC   teacher   DAT   picture OBJ   praise PASSIVE past
        'I was praised for my picture by the teacher'.

(3-c)   watashi   wa   shiken no   aida- jû sensei ni   soba   ni   i -
        I   TOPIC   exam   GEN   while all teacher DAT beside LOC   be
        rare   ta.
        PASSIVE   PAST
        'The teacher had been staying beside me during the examination'.

Such sentences are all passive sentences, but the semantic functions of the subjects are different in each case; in (3-a), the subject *watashi* 'I' is the patient of the action of *homeru* 'to praise'; in (3-b), the action aims at the picture *e* (syntactic object and patient), and the subject *watashi* 'I' is the possessor; in (3-c), the action of 'staying' *iru* has no aim, but psychologically the subject *watashi* 'I' feels himself a victim of the action.

What these passive sentences have in common is that the sentence subject directly or indirectly undergoes an action; in other words, non-agentive subject characterizes passive sentences, while active sentences are characterized by agentive subjects.

Besides, we can observe that the principal role of a passive construction is to promote an item which is not the agent to the rank of the sentence subject, the most important function of a sentence, and to demote the agent from that of subject to an optional noun phrase argument. Thus, the structure enables the speaker to form an utterance without an agent, when the latter is unknown or indefinite 'they', 'one', etc.

1.2 Grammatical passive and lexical passive

Passive voice with a verb marked by the suffix *-(r)areru* is often used when the agent is unknown or indefinite.

In Japanese, on the other hand, there are many verbal pairs such as *kowasu* 'to break (vt)/*kowareru* 'to break (vi)', *tateru* 'to build'/*tatsu* 'to be built', etc., which form transitive vs intransitive verb oppositions. They have a common stem, and may be marked by one of the suffixes of intransitivity (e.g. *-ru, -aru, -eru*), or of transitivity (e.g. *-su, -asu, -osu, -eru*). The transitive verbs describe actions which effect a change in an entity presented as the object of sentences (patient), while the intransitive verbs express the same action from the patient's vantage point (the patient which undergoes a change). Now, let us compare the following examples:

(4-a)   otôto   ga   kamera wo   naoshi-   ta.
        brother NOM camera ACC repair   PAST
        'My brother has repaired the camera'.

(4-b)   kamera ga   naot-   ta.
        camera NOM   be repaired   PAST
        'The camera has been repaired'.

These two examples represent only one and the same fact; the camera was repaired, but with the difference that (4-a) focusses on the agent *otôto* 'younger brother' and on the process of the action, while example (4-b) stresses its result, regardless of the agent. In this context, the use of intransitive verbs is much more natural than that of the passive voice which implies an agent (4-c).

(4-c)   kamera ga   naos- are-   ta.
        camera NOM   repair PASSIVE   PAST
        'The camera has been repaired'.

Similarly, when the agent is irrelevant and the speaker is only interested in the result of an action, he generally employs an intransitive verb (5-a) rather than a passive construction (5-b).

(5-a)   kono hen   ni mo takai biru   ga   takusan tachi-
        this neighborhood LOC also high building   NOM   many   be built
        mashi- ta-   ne.
        POLITE PAST CONSENT
        'Many high buildings have also been built in this neighborhood, haven't they?'

(5-b)   kono hen   ni mo takai biru   ga   takusan tate-
        this neighborhood LOC also high   building NOM many   build
        rare-   mashi- ta   ne.
        PASSIVE POLITE   PAST CONSENT
        'Many high buildings have also been built in this neighborhood, haven't they?'

We can thus consider certain intransitive verbs which have a corresponding transitive verb as lexical realizations of the passive voice, because of the close affinity, from the semantic point of view, to the grammatical realization of the passive voice marked by the suffix -(r)areru. 'Lexical passive' may be very close to (or corresponds to) 'unaccusative intransitives'. However, I will use in this paper the term of 'lexical passive' contrasting with 'grammatical passive'. In the next section, I will examine the question of the semantic features which link these two different realizations of passive.

1.3 Semantic features of two types of passive sentences

As we have seen above, in Japanese a lexical passive can be used instead of a grammatical passive, in spite of some semantic differences, and the former is an agentless expression which is, in most cases, incompatible with an agentive noun phrase, while the latter generally implies the existence of an agent (often a definite one) even if it is not mentioned.

In order to compare lexical and grammatical passive expressions, it would be useful to study the prototype of lexical passive. Here are some examples of lexical passive sentences:

(6)   senjitsu   no arashi de   furui sakura no ki ga taore- ta.
      the other day GEN storm CAUSE old   cherry GEN tree NOM fall   PAST
      'The storm of the other day brought down an old cherry tree'.

(7)   doa   ga   ai-   te, shiroi kao ga   yami   ni   ukabiagat- ta.
         door NOM   open GER white face NOM darkness LOC loom up   PAST
         'The door opened, and a white face loomed up in the darkness'.

(8-a)   kabin ga   tana kara   ochi-   te   koware- te   shimat- ta.
         vase NOM   shelf SOURCE fall down GER break(Vi) GER finish   PAST
         'The vase fell down from the shelf and broke'.

(8-b)   kabin wo tana   kara   otoshi- te   kowashi- te   shimat- ta.
         vase ACC shelf SOURCE let fall GER break(Vt) GER finish   PAST
         '(I) let a vase fall from the shelf and broke it'.

In (6), the event ('an old cherry tree fell down') was caused by a natural force ('a storm'); in (7), there is an active person (a human agent) who acts intentionally; the speaker remains an observer and describes comprehensively the scene. This is also true in (8-a), in which the speaker makes no reference to the question of whether the event was caused by an outside force or not, while in (8-b), it is obvious that an agent (a human being) is the cause of this situation. We can notice that (6,7,8-a), structured on an intransitive verb, give a comprehensive view of a situation without discriminating between agent and patient. In these kinds of expressions, only one entity is concerned, the object which undergoes a change, and the sentences mainly express its results.

The prototype of lexical passive is as follows:

Semantically:
i)   There is one entity: the patient
ii) The subject undergoes a change
iii) The subject is non-agentive

Syntactically:
i)   Sentences have the following pattern: P *ga* V *-ru, -aru, -eru, -reru**

Morphologically:
ii)   The verb is marked by the suffix *-ru, -aru, -eru, -reru**

**-ru, -aru, -eru, -reru* are suffixes of intransitivity (unaccusative intransitive)

Comparing the above prototype of a lexical passive with that of a grammatical passive (cf. 1.1), the similarity between the two prototypes is striking. Removing the reference to an agent, we can obtain the near prototype of lexical passive.

The very characteristic of passive expressions (whether it is a grammatical or a lexical passive) precisely consists in the absence of agent, and also in the non-agentive subject. These types of sentences present an event as taking place apart from any intentional involvement on the part of the subject; besides, they do not indicate whether another entity is responsible for triggering off the event. The traditional Japanese grammar defined the characteristic of these sentences *jihatsu* 'spontaneous'. Lexical and grammatical passives have this nuclear 'spontaneous' meaning.

2. Active voice

2.1 The Transitive structure and its meaning

Unlike passive sentences, active ones have an agentive subject, i.e., the subject of sentences acts intentionally to cause a certain result to the object. The subject is an animate noun in the typical transitive structure, and the object is completely dominated by the subject. This dominant position of the subject is the very characteristic of a transitive structure.

(9)   Akechi Mitsuhide ga   Oda Nobunaga wo koroshi- ta.
        (proper noun)   NOM (p.n.)   ACC kill   PAST
        'Akechi Mitsuhide killed Oda Nobunaga'.

(10)   akambô ga   miruku wo   non- de   iru.
        baby   NOM milk   ACC drink GER PROG
        'A baby is drinking (some) milk'.

(11)   kare   wa   tsuma   wo aishi- te   iru.
        he   TOPIC wife   ACC love   GER STATE
        'He loves his wife'.

(12)   mikan wa   bitamin B wo fukun- de   iru.
        orange TOPIC vitamine B ACC contain GER STATE
        'Oranges contain vitamine B'.

(9) is a typical transitive sentence with an agentive subject (Akechi M.) and the object (Oda N.) which undergoes a change (= death). (10) also has an agentive subject (= baby), but the object (= milk) does not undergo any obvious change. Nevertheless, the action comes from the subject to the object. In (11), it is difficult to say that an action takes place, but a feeling (= love) emanating from the subject (= he) reaches the object (= his wife). (12), finally,

is a static sentence which does not express any action or event, but it is also considered as a transitive sentence just because of the dominant role of the subject (= orange).

So we can conclude that the major characteristic of transitive sentences consists in the subject's complete domination over the object, and in the sentence pattern: A *ga* P *wo* V. Here, the use of the particle *wo* indicates a complete submission of the preceeding noun phrase to the subject, and the *wo* marked noun phrase is considered as a non-agentive argument. Now, let us compare the following pair:

(13-a) garasu ga   koware-   ta.
        glass   NOM break (vi)   PAST
        'The glass is broken/broke'.

(13-b) kodomo   ga   garasu wo   kowashi- ta.
        child(ren) NOM glass   ACC break (vt) PAST
        'Children broke the glass'.

If we are merely interested in an event which happened, we generally utter (13-a) (with an unaccusative intransitive verb) without any reference to an agent. On the contrary, if we want to insist on the person who caused the same event, we naturally opt for a transitive structure (13-b). Transitive sentences clearly express a participation of an outside force in the realization of an action or a given event. The comparison between the prototype of transitivity (cf. 1.1) and that of lexical passive (cf. 1.3) clarifies the difference between the two types of sentences. We can say that the transitive structure has the effect of focussing on an agent in a comprehensive process, or of introducing an agentive subject. The shift from the intransitive to the transitive structure is thus the first step of causativity.

2.2 The Causative structure and its meaning

Certain transitive verbs are syntactically linked as causatives to their corresponding intransitive verbs, such as *kowasu* (vt) 'to break (vt)/*kowareru* (vi) 'to break (vi)', *tateru* (vt) 'to build'/*tatsu* (vi) 'to be built', from which they are derived by addition of one of causative suffixes: *-su*, *-asu*, *-osu* or *-eru*. Others have no corresponding intransitive verbs with the same stem for both transitive and intransitive verbs. In such instances, if we want to emphasize the influence of an outside force in an event, we generally resort to a grammatical means consisting in the use of the causative suffix: *-(s)aseru*.

(14-a)   akambô ga   miruku wo   non- de   iru.
         baby   NOM milk   ACC drink GER   PROG
         'A baby is drinking (some) milk'.

(14-b)   okâsan ga   akambô ni   miruku wo   nom- ase-   te   iru
         mother NOM baby   DAT milk   ACC drink CAUS GER   PROG
         'A mother is giving some milk to (her) baby.'

When an action (here, 'to drink (some) milk') is realized because of the influence of an external power (here, 'the mother'), this additional item takes
the place of the sentence subject as the initiator of an action, and the actor
(the subject in 14-a) is demoted to an agentive oblique case (that of indirect
object, or the 'goal' aimed at by an outside entity).

As for transitive verbs with two nuclear noun phrases, such as *nomu* 'to
drink', after a causative transformation, the subject of the basic sentences is
necessarily *ni* -marked (which generally is considered as a mark of an
agentive noun phrase), whether it is really an agentive or non-agentive noun
phrase. The causative sentences pattern is the following: A_1 *ga* A_2 *ni* P *wo* V
-(s)aseru where A_1 is the causative sentence subject which acts intentionally
so that the action expressed by the verb should be performed by another person (A_2); it is necessarily an animate being, and in most cases a human noun
phrase. A_2 is the agent of the action expressed by a verb, and at the same
time, the goal of a causative action, receiving an order or an invitation
coming from A_1. A_2 also is an animate noun phrase. P is the object of the action, and is generally an inanimate item.

With intransitive verbs which structurally require only one noun phrase,
two causative sentence patterns are possible. Let us compare the following
pair of sentences:

(15-a)   ato de kodomo *ni*   ik- ase-   masu.
         later   child   DAT go   CAUS POLITE
         'I will have my child go (there) later'.

(15-b)   ato de kodomo *wo*   ik- ase-   masu.
         later   child   ACC go   CAUS POLITE
         'I will send my child (there) later'.

In (15-a), *kodomo* 'child' is *ni*- marked, which means that the agent acts on his
own will, following an instruction given by the sentence subject (here, an implied subject 'I'). It is a consenting agent, and this type of sentence can be

called 'indirect causative' because of the indirect effect of the subject on the result. In (15-b), on the other hand, the same agent is marked by *wo*, which means, as shown in the previous section, the total submission of the preceding noun phrase (the sentence object) to the sentence subject. The will of the agent *kodomo* 'child', if any, is not taken into account; he acts mechanically, handled by the sentence subject ('I'). In this case, the noun phrase marked by *wo*, whether it is an animate or inanimate being, is considered as non- agentive, and the sentence is a 'direct causative sentence', because the action ('to go') is directly caused by the sentence subject will. This type of sentence thus connects with transitive sentences.

It is obvious that if the 'agent' is an inanimate item, it must be marked by *wo* to the exclusion of *ni*.

(16)   kodomo- tachi wa   me   *wo* kagayak- ase-   te   o-
        child   PLUR TOPIC eye(s) ACC sparkle   CAUS   GER   POLITE
        hanashi ni   kikiit-   te   i-   ta.
        DAT   story listen attentively   GER   STATE   PAST
        'The children were listening attentively to the story with sparkling eyes'.

2.3 Semantic features of two types of active voice.

In the previous section, we have shown that both transitive and causative structures highlight the influence of an outside force in order to produce a certain action or result. The sentence subject is in both cases agentive, and an animate (and human) noun phrase in canonical transitive and causative structures.

The two notions thus merge and can alternate with each other, in some cases, without any significant change in meaning.

(17-a) kodomo wo   jitensha no   ushiro ni   nose-   ta.
        child   ACC   bicycle   GEN back   LOC take on PAST
        '(I) took (my/a) child on the seat of my bicycle'.

(17-b) kodomo wo   jitensha no   ushiro ni   nor-   ase-   ta.
        child   ACC   bicycle   GEN back   LOC ride   CAUS   PAST
        '(I) took (my/a) child on the seat of my bicycle'.

However, in other cases, transitive and causative sentences have their own uses, and consequently one cannot be used instead of the other.

(18-a)   sensei   ga   kôtei   ni   hata wo   tate-   ta.   (*tat- ase- ta)
         teacher NOM   schoolyard LOC   flag ACC   hoist   PAST   (stand CAUS PAST)
         'A teacher hoisted up a flag at a schoolyard'.

(18-b)   sensei   ga   kôtei   ni   seito wo   tat-   ase-   ta.   (*tate- ta)
         teacher NOM   schoolyard LOC   pupil ACC stand CAUS PAST   (hoist PAST)
         'A teacher kept a pupil standing in the schoolyard'.

In (18-a), *hata* 'flag', the object of the transitive verb *tateru* 'to hoist (up)', is
an inanimate item which cannot act by itself, and is completely submitted to
the subject. The object is the patient of the action. This is also true in the corresponding intransitive verb *tatsu* 'to stand' which highlights a result.

(18-a') kôtei   ni   hata   ga   tat-   ta.
         schoolyard   LOC   flag   NOM   stand PAST
         'A flag stood erect in the schoolyard'.

To sum up, in transitive structures, an outside force (= the sentence subject)
acts directly on the object, to change it. The object is considered as *non-
agentive*, whether it is an inanimate noun or not. The following scheme illustrates a canonical transitive construction: Agent ---- (action) ----> Patient.

In (18-b), on the other hand, the sentence object, *seito* 'pupil', is an
animate noun and can act by itself. The causative suffix: *-(s)aseru* expresses
an indirect intervention of an outside force for a realization of an action.
Causative structures can be analysed as follows: A_1 *ga* A_2 *wo* (/ *ni* P *wo*) V
-(s)aseru where *-(s)aseru* means that A_1 acts intentionally so that the action
expressed by the verb will be realized by another person (A_2). Unlike transitive structures, A_1 does not directly influence over A_2; his action is limited
to a simple order or suggestion. A canonical causative structure can be
schematized as follows: A_1 ---- (s)aseru ----> (A_2 ----(action) ----> (P))

From this comparison it follows that transitive and causative structures
have in common an agentive subject which acts with a determined purpose,
but they differ from one another in the sentence object which is non-agentive
in transitive structures and agentive in causative ones. The intentional participation of an agent which brings out an event is the very characteristic of
'causality', binding together transitive and causative structures into a unified
concept, that of *active voice*.

3. Conclusion

In Classical Japanese, verbs were quite commonly marked by one of the suffixes: -*su* or -*ru*. The former, coming from the verb *su* 'to do', indicated that an action originated in an outside force: it remains in Modern Japanese in certain transitive verbs with a causative meaning, such as *kowasu* 'to break (vt)', *naosu* 'to repair', and has also produced the causative suffix -*(s)aseru*. The latter, whose origin certainly is the verb *aru* 'to be' expressed an action realized 'of itself', as part of a natural course of events. The suffix is not only the origin of the passive suffix -*(r)areru* in Modern Japanese, but also it is left as the passive or spontaneous suffix in some intransitive verbs, like *naru* 'to become' (opp. *nasu* 'to do'), *naoru* 'to be repaired', and *kawaru* 'to change (vi)'.

Classical Japanese thus clearly indicated whether an outside entity caused an event 'intentionally' or whether one viewed an event comprehensively without reference to a possible agent.

The opposition between passivity and transitivity, or more generally between spontaneity and causativity, was thus essential for the Japanese mind. The same event can be perceived as a result of a human action or of a natural change. In the first case, one stresses an action resulting from the intention of an agent. In this frame of mind, there are two distinct entities belonging to two separate groups, and one of them (an agent) acts on the other (a patient). This type of sentence can be characterized by *suru* ('to do')-type expressions (as termed by Ikegami (1981)). Sentences are focussed on the human being who is the centre of interest.

In the second case, the speaker is interested in an event comprehensively without analyzing it into its different elements such as agent, patient, ... Here, an event is perceived as occurring of its own will, and the speaker comprehensively recognizes a change in the surrounding world. We can characterize this type of sentence as a *naru* ('to become') expression, according to Ikegami. In these expressions, there is only one entity, in the speaker's mind, which undergoes a change, and another entity, if any, which causes this change, merges into nature; the change is considered as part of a natural course of events.

The clear distinction between the notions of spontaneity and causativity reflects the Japanese people's sense of value; traditional Japanese society was mostly composed of farmers whose life largely depended on nature. Therefore, they attributed a great value to the consequences of natural phenomena, and prefered spontaneous actions rather than intentional actions realized by man. A number of linguists have pointed out that Japanese prefers *naru*-type expressions, and tends to use them even to denote clearly intentional act. For instance:

(19) rainen   no   haru   kekkon suru   koto ni   *nari-*   mashi-   t a .
      next year GEN   spring get   married fact DAT   become POLITE   PAST
      'I *will* get married next spring'.

In English, on the contrary, the general tendency is to extend the use of transitive structures to an inanimate subject which cannot act intentionally.

(20)   *Despair* drove him to commit suicide.

The predominance of transitive structures in English, and more generally in Western languages, can be explained by the fact that Western society has developed through the continuous domestication of nature, thus placing man at the core of the western mind.

Consequently, natural languages can be assigned to one of two major groups, *naru* 'to become' languages and *suru* 'to do' languages, according to whether an event in its entirety or an agent is focussed.

Because a given language pattern reflects the frame of mind of its speakers, and because it is determined by the development of a society, Japanese, which now belongs among *naru*-languages, might in the future change into a *suru*-language as the Japanese become more self-confident. We can already find some indications of this evolution in the following sentence.

(21) tabi-kasanaru   fukô   ga   Kinuko   wo osot-   ta.
      repeated   misfortune NOM   (p.n.)   ACC fall on   PAST
      'Repeated misfortunes fell on Kinuko'.

References

Andô, Sadao. 1986. *Eigo no ronri, nihongo no ronri* (English logic, Japanese logic). Tôkyô: Taishûkan shoten.
Ikegami, Yoshihiko. 1981. *Suru to naru no gengogaku* (Linguistic of do-languages and become-languages). Tôkyô: Taishûkan shoten.
Itasaka, Gen. 1971. *Nihongo no ronri-kôzô* (The Japanese logic structure), 68-88. Tôkyô: Kôdansha.

Jacobsen, Wesley M. 1989. Tadôsei to purototaipu-ron (Transitivity and Prototype). *Nihongogaku no shin-tenkai* (New development of Japanese Linguistics), 213-48. Tôkyô: Kuroshio Shuppan.

Jacobsen, Wesley M. 1991. *The Transitive Structure of Events in Japanese.* Tôkyô: Kuroshio Shuppan.

Kudô, Mayumi. 1990. Gendai nihongo no judôbun (Modern Japanese passive sentences). *Kotoba no kagaku* (Language science) 4, 47-100. Tôkyô: Mugi Shobô.

Kuno, Susumu. 1983. *Shin nihon bunpô kenkyu* (New study of Japanese Grammar). 192-219. Tôkyô: Taishûkan shoten.

Lyons, John. 1968. *General Linguistics.* Cambridge: Cambridge University Press. (Translation into French. 1970. *Linguistique Générale*, 268-97. Paris: Larousse.)

Ôno, Susumu. 1978. *Nihongo no bunpô wo kangaeru* (Reflection on Japanese Grammar). Tôkyô: Iwanami shoten.

Teramura, Hideo. 1982. *Nihongo no shintakusu to imi* (Japanese Syntax and Semantics). 205-21. Tôkyô: Kuroshio shuppan.

Teramura, Hideo. 1978. *Naru*-hyôgen to *Suru*-hyôgen-Nichi-ei tai-hyôgen no hikaku (*Naru*-expressions and *suru*-expressions. A comparative study of Voice in English and Japanese). *Teramura Hideo ronbunshû*, vol. II (Selected Teramura Hideo's articles), 213-32. Tôkyô: Kuroshio Shuppan.

Tsunoda, Tasaku. 1991. *Sekai no gengo to nihongo* (Various Languages in the world and Japanese), 63-116. Tôkyô: Kuroshio Shuppan.

Lexical Accent Assignment in Standard Japanese — The Benefits of a Single-Pitch Analysis

Yuko Yoshida

Introduction

This paper discusses how accent assignment, which characterises a stress accent language, can be introduced in a pitch accent language, Standard Japanese (henceforth Japanese), which has generally been regarded as a tone language rather than a stress language.

1. Typological consideration and a single pitch analysis for Japanese

The starting point is to consider language typology in terms of what aspects of pitch accent phenomena lead to a tone-language analysis on the one hand, and to a stress-language analysis, on the other. First of all, a set of data is provided comprising trisyllabic, morphologically simplex *Yamato* (native) words to show why Japanese can be claimed to be a tone language, and then I shall illuminate why tone analysis is not suitable for Japanese.

(1) Data (NB: * denotes an accent; a bar over segments shows that the relevant part is high-pitched).

a.	b.	c.	d.
*	*	*	
‾‾	‾‾	‾‾	‾‾‾‾‾
na mi da (ga)	ta ma go (ga)	wa ra bi (ga)	ka su mi (ga)
'tear (nom.)'	'egg (nom.)'	'bracken (nom.)'	'haze (nom.)'

The paradigm shows: 1) Some parts are high-pitched while other parts are not high-pitched, 2) The initial syllables are always realised with lower pitch, unless the syllable itself is accented, 3) Accented syllables and syllables to the left (except for the initial syllable) are high-pitched.

From the observation in (1), that some parts are high-pitched while some other parts are not, one could interpret this by assuming that the parts which are high-pitched carry a high-tone, whereas the parts with no high-pitch carry a low tone. This interpretation leads to the claim that Japanese has two tones, a high tone and a low tone (Clark 1983, Haraguchi 1977, 1991, Poser 1984, Pulleyblank 1986) (see also Inkelas & Zec (1988) for a similar analysis of Serbo-Croatian pitch accent).

The observations in 2) and 3) above, however, demonstrate that the pitch pattern in a given Japanese phonological sequence (e.g. in (1)) is predictable, unlike the case of a true tone language such as Chinese. In Chinese, for example, tone information is encoded in each syllable (see McCawley 1968, 1978 for details on tone languages). In Japanese, however, once the accent location is identified, the pitch pattern of the given phonological string is predictable; the initial syllable is always realised with lower pitch, unless the syllable itself is accented, and accented syllables and syllables to the left (except for the initial syllable) are high-pitched.

Tone harmony analysis is derived from the predictable 'tone' pattern. From the fact that accented syllables and syllables to the left (except for the initial syllables) are high-pitched, tone harmony analyses exemplified by that of Haraguchi (1977) claim that the high 'tone' spreads from the accented unit[1] to other units to the left, and other units without a high 'tone' receive low 'tone' by default.

A question arises here as to whether there really should be two tones. There is a source for a high pitch, i.e. the accent. But although the accented syllable is high pitched, there is no apparent source for a 'low' tone.

In fact, there is only one pitch, high-pitch, in Japanese, which finds a parallel in the fact that, in a stress language, only the notion of 'stressing (fortifying)' is relevant, and not 'weakening'. Consider the following two examples, which illustrate how a pitch accent system and a stress accent system may be compared.

---

1. The unit where a pitch is realised varies depending on the framework of the analysis: some employ a syllable and/or a mora (see Poser 1984, Haraguchi 1991). For convenience, I use the term 'syllable' in this paper, and I define a syllable as follows: a syllable consists of a rhyme (whose head is the nucleus) preceded by an optional onset (see Kaye, Lowenstamm & Vergnaud (1990) for more on 'syllables').

(2)   a. English primary stress   b. Japanese pitch

          stress   high-pitched
            | |
          a me ri ca   ta ma go
          | | | | |
          not stressed   pitchless

In a stress accent language such as English, all syllables other than stressed
ones may be considered 'not stressed', but not 'weakened'. The same thing
applies to a pitch accent system: there is a high-pitched syllable and pitchless
syllables (Yoshida 1995).

2. The Licensing Principle (Kaye 1990) and accent assignment

The Licensing Principle should be introduced here to capture the common
ground between a pitch accent and a stress accent, namely, the fact that one
and only one pitch accent/primary stress accent is permitted in one given
domain of the language in question.

(3) The Licensing Principle (Kaye 1990)
All phonological positions save one must be licensed within a domain. The
unlicensed position is the head of the domain.

In other words, a domain has to have one head. The phonetic interpretation
of the head is diverse, depending on each language's option. For convenience, let me assume here a domain as a noun or a phrase (e.g. a noun
plus a case marker). For example, English opts to interpret headship in terms
of the stressed syllable of the domain. In Japanese, on the other hand, headship manifests itself as to be high pitch.
     Another point that should be considered is why a well formed Japanese
sequence is permitted to bear more than one high-pitched syllable in its domain. To have more than one high-pitched syllable per domain contradicts
the assumption that the accented syllable is high-pitched as a consequence
of headship, which is symptomatic of domainhood.
     The initial syllable, which is always pitchless unless the syllable itself is
accented, provides the clue to the question above. To demonstrate how the

pitchless status of the initial syllable helps us to understand why more than one syllable may bear a high-pitch in a Japanese noun, I shall examine some expanded domains, i.e. those of more than one phrase. When in isolation, each phrase in (4) has a pitchless syllable.

(4)   a.   b.

                                      *
       ‾‾‾‾‾‾‾   ‾‾
       sa ka na -o   ta be ru
       'fish-acc.'   'eat-nonpast'

In connected speech, however, the initial syllable of the second phrase is interpreted with high-pitch.

(5)   *
        ‾‾‾‾‾‾‾‾‾‾‾
        sa ka na -o ta be ru

In other words, the initial syllable of the phrase (4b), is the domain initial syllable in isolation, but is no longer the domain initial in the connected speech form in (5). Yoshida (1995) claims that the two phrases form a single domain of pitch accent, thus the domain should follow the convention that has been observed in a smaller domain, i.e. that of a noun or a phrase. Indeed, in the domain of connected speech, as well as that of a single phrase, the observations are identical. There is only one pitch accented syllable and all the syllables to the left, except for the domain initial one, are high-pitched. To recapitulate, the pitch pattern of any domains are predictable: there is a head syllable in a domain, and the head syllable and the syllables to the left are high-pitched, except for the domain initial one. It seems appropriate that the interpretation of the head is a high pitch not only on the head syllable, but also on the neighbouring syllables to the left.

The interpretation of the head is parameterised — fortification to the head in a stress language, and heightening in a pitch accent language. Another difference is that the stress accent is polar and only the head displays prominence, whereas a pitch accent system like Japanese chooses to share the high-pitch between the head and the neighbouring syllables.

So far I have demonstrated that stress accent and pitch accent are similar, in the sense that they are both the interpretation of head status in a given domain, and parametric choice dictates the interpretation of the head as either a stress or pitch. I have thus prepared the ground for discussing the

formalism of Japanese pitch accent assignment, which should be the same as
that of primary stress, given that, in the majority of cases, Japanese pitch accent location is lexically determined. In fact, Haraguchi (1991) claims that a
long (four syllables long or more) Japanese noun is assigned an antepenult
accent .

(6)   a.   b.   c.

         ___   ___   ___
          *   *   *
         u gu i su (ga)   mu ra sa ki (ga)   ho to to gi su (ga)
         'bush warbler (nom.)'   'purple (nom.)'   'mountain cuckoo (nom.)'

Haraguchi only treats shorter words containing lexical marking. Note, however, 'shorter' in his terms, includes trisyllabic words. That is, even in a trisyllabic word, an accent can be assigned to the antepenultimate syllable. If
the words need to be divided into two groups, depending on their length,
then a suitable explanation for this must be sought.

3. Evidence for accent assignment — Diachronic change of accent location

The final issue to be addressed in this paper is the matter of evidence for the
fact that even the trisyllabic words, which were formerly assumed to have
inherently determined accent location, are subject to 'lexical' accent assignment. The factual evidence is two-fold: first, synchronic distributional statistics, and second, the diachronic change of accent location within about
three decades.

The following table gives the distribution of trisyllabic and disyllabic native nouns (Yoshida 1995) taken from the word list with pitch pattern in
Hirayama (1957). Note that I omit any discussion of accentless class of
nouns.[2] In contrast to the fact that the distribution of disyllabic words
depending on accent location is fairly even, that of the trisyllabic words is
not: there is only a single medially accented noun, despite the fact there are
about the same number of initially and finally accented words.

---

2. See Yoshida (1995) for a detailed account of the reason accentless nouns turn out to be
   accentless. In fact, this mechanism provides further evidence for the formalism
   discussed in this paper; however, I shall avoid any extensive theoretical argument in
   this direction.

(7) Count of the nouns depending on accent location (Yoshida 1995) —
taken from the pitch pattern list of Hirayama (1957).

	Disyllabic		Trisyllabic	
	Numbers	Examples	Numbers	Examples
Initial	49	* ka mi (ga) 'god (nom.)'	24	* ma ku ra (ga) 'pillow (nom.)'
Medial	--	n/a	1	* ko ko ro (ga) 'heart (nom.)'
Final	26	* ka mi (ga) 'paper (nom.)'	26	* wa ra bi (ga) 'bracken (nom.)'

The second piece of evidence comes from the change in pitch accent location
(Yoshida 1995). Checking all the nouns counted above, consulting the NHK
accent dictionary (1985) and also 5 informants in 1994, I found that the final
accents of the trisyllabic nouns were unstable. NHK (1984) listed 10 out of
26 finally accented nouns which had lost their accent, and the informants
showed that another word, in addition to the 10 from NHK (1985), has completely lost its accent. Also, the only medially accented word in the table had
started to show an alternative pitch pattern in 1984. Initially accented words
had experienced no change in accent location. The reason is now clear as to
why initial accent is stable — it is the default location for accent assignment
in Japanese.

References

Clark, Mary M. 1983. Japanese as a Tone Language. *Issues in Japanese Linguistics*,
(eds.) T. Imai & M.Saito. Dordrecht: Foris.

Haraguchi, Shosuke. 1977. *The Tone Pattern of Japanese: An Autosegmental Theory of
Tonology*. Tokyo: Kaitakusha.

Haraguchi, Shosuke. 1991. *A Theory of Stress and Accent*. Dordrecht: Foris.

Hirayama, Teruo. 1957. *Nihongo Onchô-no Kenkyû* (A Study of Japanese Accent).
Tokyo: Meiji Shoin.

Inkelas, Sharon & Draga Zec. 1988. Serbo-Croatian Pitch Accent: The Interaction of Tones, Stress and Intonation. *Language* 64:2, 227-48.

Kaye, Jonathan. 1990. 'Coda' Licensing. *Phonology* 7:2, 301-30.

Kaye, Jonathan, Jean Lowenstamm, & Jean Roger Vergnaud. 1990. Constituent structure and Government in Phonology. *Phonology* 7.2, 193-232.

McCawley, James D. 1968. *The Phonological Component of a Grammar of Japanese.* Hague: Mouton.

McCawley, James D. 1978. What is a Tone Language? *Tone: a Linguistic Survey,* (ed.) by Victoria Fromkin. New York: Academic Press.

Nihon Hôsô Kyôkai (NHK). 1985. *Nihongo Hatsuon Akusento Jiten* (Dictionary of Pronunciation and Accent of Japanese), fourth edition. Tokyo: NHK.

Poser, William J. 1984. *The Phonetics and Phonology of Tone and Intonation in Japanese.* Ph.D. dissertation. Cambridge, Mass.: MIT Press.

Pulleyblank, Douglas. 1986. *Tone in Lexical Phonology.* Dordrecht: Reidel.

Yoshida, Yuko. 1995. *On Pitch Accent Phenomena in Standard Japanese.* Ph.D. dissertation, School of Oriental and African Studies, University of London.

Literature

Young and Politically Incorrect: Ôe Kenzaburô's Early Marginal Heroes

Luk Van Haute

When Ôe Kenzaburô (born 1935) was awarded the Nobel Prize for literature in October 1994, it caused a so-called 'Ôe-boom' in Japan. Major bookstores like Kinokuniya and Maruzen put up special 'Ôe-corners' displaying not only Ôe's own works, but also hastily compiled special issues of literary magazines, books on Ôe, and even the Japanese translation of Selma Lagerløf's *The Wonderful Adventures of Nils*, since Ôe happened to mention this Swedish story in his acceptance speech, 'Japan, the Ambiguous and Myself'. Nobel Prize winners have commercial value.

The boom, however, was short-lived. It had been inspired more by curiosity than by genuine interest. The prize did not grant Ôe a long-lasting status as best-selling author, and even his short post-Nobel popularity boost did not match the one he had enjoyed more than thirty years earlier when, as an up-and-coming author, he had been praised as 'the voice of a new generation'. This paper aims at tracing some of the reasons behind the popularity of Ôe's early works and the lack of it in his more recent writings. The load of material on Ôe which appeared in the Japanese media after he was awarded the Nobel Prize, ranging from popular magazines like *Focus*, *Friday*, and *Spa*! to serious academic studies, offers a welcome source of information on this matter.

The main point of this paper is that Ôe's popularity started to dwindle around 1964, not primarily because his literature was becoming 'too difficult', as is often stated, but rather because his heroes became what would now be termed 'politically correct'.[1] There is a clear discrepancy between what academics and prominent literary critics perceive as Ôe's best or most important works and those that are most popular with the public, in

---

1. I use the term 'politically correct' in the meaning of 'not discriminatory towards minorities (sexually or racially) and thereby complying with the prevailing moral standards'.

particular young people. As we will see, the latter are such works as *Sevuntiin* (*Seventeen*, 1961)[2] and *Seiteki ningen* (*Sexual Beings*, translated into English as '*J*', after the protagonist's name, 1963), with rightist assassins and sexual perverts as heroes. The 1964 novel *Kojinteki na taiken* (*A Personal Matter*) is generally considered to signify the start of a new phase in Ôe's oeuvre, mainly because it is his first novel after the birth of Hikari, his brain-damaged son (who, by the way, gathered at least as much attention during the Ôe-boom as the author himself) in June 1963. Undoubtedly Hikari's birth meant a big change in the author's life and work. Ôe never hesitates to point that out himself. But often this novel is considered to be the first in which Ôe explores the 'theme' of the handicapped child instead of the theme of young people in post-war Japan. The change is however not really 'thematic'. The baby is not a 'theme' in *Kojinteki na taiken*, nor is he in Ôe's next novel *Man'en gannen no futtobôru* (*The Silent Cry*, 1967). He is not even a character. He is a mere presence in the background which the protagonist is forced to deal with. Later, for example in *Pinchi rannâ chôsho* (*The Pinch Runner's Memorandum*, 1976) the child will be an actual character, but there too he is not really a 'theme' but rather a new type of the 'active hero' who used to appear in Ôe's oeuvre before, as a counterpart to a passive one, as we will discuss below. It is only from around 1983 with works like *Atarashii hito yo mezameyo* (*O Rouse up, New Men*, 1983) that Ôe writes directly about 'the handicapped child and life with it' as the theme of the story.

The hero of *Kojinteki na taiken*, Bird, is at the outset and through most of the novel no different from previous passive Ôe-heroes. The birth of the baby has not changed the 'problems' (the theme) the hero is confronted with: just like before, he is trying to deal with the social pressure of 'growing up'. Similarly to earlier works, in which the protagonist is confronted with a scholarship, a new relationship, a job opportunity, etc., here it is the birth of a handicapped baby which forces him to make fundamental decisions in life. The main difference actually lies in the final pages, in which Bird solves his predicament by making the 'politically correct' choice, whereas his predecessors tended to do the opposite. Therein lies the actual change. To state that only the birth of Hikari brought this about is a bit too simplistic. For one thing, post-Hikari Ôe-literature still has quite a few examples of politically incorrect heroes: a well known one is the father who allows his handicapped

---

2. Throughout this paper works by Ôe Kenzaburô are given in their original Japanese title. On first occurence there is an English translation (when the work has been translated and published into English I use that title; other translations of titles are my own), and the year in which the work was originally published between brackets.

baby to die in the short story *Sora no kaibutsu Aguii* (*Aghwee the Sky Monster*, 1964), which was actually written and published just before *Kojinteki na taiken*. And there are examples of politically correct endings before *Kojinteki na taiken*, albeit few, in stories which have hardly received any attention from the critics.

I will first give a brief overview of the development of young Ôe heroes from his debut in 1957 up to *Kojinteki na taiken* in 1964 and beyond, and point out elements of both continuity and change. Secondly, by looking at some recent publications on Ôe-literature in Japan, we will see how there seems to be a clear correlation between Ôe's diminishing popularity and his tendency towards political correctness. As a point in case, we will look especially at the reception of *Sevuntiin*.

Young and politically incorrect

Basically, Ôe's early works can be divided into those about young urban heroes (the majority) and those about children in an isolated village in the forest.[3] In this paper we will mainly consider the former. From his debut in 1957 with the short story *Kimyô na shigoto* (*An Odd Job*) up until the novel *Kojinteki na taiken* in 1964, there is in general no such thing as a 'happy end' to be found in Ôe's prose. Toward the end of the story the hero is, if not worse (for example dead), then at least 'not better' off than at the outset.

The heroes of the earliest stories find themselves trapped within walls (often quite literally) from which no escape is possible. Often a chance to escape the impasse presents itself, in the form of a chance to go to the war front in Vietnam (*Miru mae ni tobe*, *Leap Before You Look*, 1958), a scholarship to study abroad (*Warera no jidai*, *Our Times*, 1959), or a relationship with a girl (*Kassai*, *Applause*, 1958) but that chance is invariably aborted through circumstances or, more often, through the hero's inability to act.

Warera no jidai also introduces a new type of hero, which will become more prominent in the early 1960's: the one who chooses a course of action. In *Warera no jidai* this is the passive hero's younger brother. But the active hero's action invariably leads only to self-destruction (for example in *Warera no jidai*, *Sevuntiin*, *Seiteki ningen*). Still, the surviving passive hero feels envy towards the dead active one, since at least he was able to find some (be it politically incorrect) cause to believe in, which allowed him to die 'heroically'. Suicide plays a particular role as an option. The most passive

---

3. Though there are works, like *Okurete kita seinen* (*The Youth Who Came Too Late*, 1960-62), which are a combination of both.

heroes, like Yasuo in *Warera no jidai*, lack even the ability to perform that one act to end their status quo.

While the passive heroes most clearly represent Ôe himself, the active ones (often a younger brother, considered to be Ôe's alter ego) seem to receive most sympathy from the author. Dead though they may end up, at least they tried, at least they found some purpose to dedicate their lives to. This purpose is exactly what the passive post-war youth in 'pseudo-democratic' Japan lacks. Since society does not seem to offer such purpose to young people, some of them go and look for it in anti-social (politically incorrect) behaviour. Ôe often found his inspiration and models in the reality around him.

We will briefly look here at two of those anti-social, politically obviously incorrect young heroes in Ôe's work: the seventeen-year-old right-winger of *Sevuntiin* and J, the sexual pervert of *Seiteki ningen*. Ôe did the actual writing of *Sevuntiin* in November-December 1960, in an immediate reaction to the assassination of Asanuma Inejirô, chairman of the Socialist Party, by the seventeen-year-old Yamaguchi Otoya and the youth's subsequent suicide. *Seiteki ningen* (1963) was conceived after Ôe read a newspaper clipping about a pervert being arrested among the crowd of demonstrators during the so-called ANPO riots of 1960.

Sevuntiin is a particularly interesting case because it is not only inspired by and based on actual facts but follows these facts so closely that the author got into a lot of trouble over the publication of the story. The murder, which took place in October 1960, was covered widely in the media, and when *Sevuntiin* was published in two parts in the literary magazine *Bungakukai* in January/February 1961, it was full of particulars about Yamaguchi, his case and his suicide in jail three weeks after the murder. Especially the second part, entitled *Seiji shônen shisu* (*Political Youth Dies*) left no room for doubt. As a result Ôe was harassed and received death threats from the extreme right, especially from the Dai Nippon Aikokutô leader Akao Bin, who had been Yamaguchi's mentor, and more than vaguely resembles the party leader Sakakibara in *Sevuntiin*.[4]

The interesting thing in *Sevuntiin*, however, is to see which elements of

---

4. Up until today this right-wing pressure still has effect. *Seiji shônen shisu* has never been republished in Japan after its controversial appearance in *Bungakukai*, and for foreign publishers it is not possible to get the rights to the translation, as both Meulenhoff in Holland and Blue Moon Books in New York have found. Besides, Ôe once more received death threats in 1994 after he refused the Bunka Kunshô, a state award which he would have received directly from the emperor.

reality Ôe did not copy (i.e. changed or left out) and which fictional elements he added. If we look at Yamaguchi's family situation, for example, we see that his elder brother had connections with a right-wing organisation (Akao Bin's Aikokutô), and that his father was a member of the Self-Defence Forces. But in *Sevuntiin* the father is a liberal teacher (though there is a sister who works as an SDF nurse), and the one who introduces Seventeen to the Imperial Way Party is not his brother but a friend from school (whose father is an SDF officer). As a result of this fictionalisation of the boy's family background Ôe diminishes the element of 'pre-determination' that may have played with Yamaguchi. It makes Seventeen a much more 'average teenager', with the usual puberty problems such as identity crisis and inferiority complex, and consequently his conversion to emperor-worship and right-wing terrorism seems more coincidental, and at the same time enables more empathy.

Empathy is the key issue in Ôe's descriptions of juvenile delinquents. It is also the case for the Korean boy in *Sakebigoe* (*Outcries*, 1962), an outcast who rapes and murders a high school girl just to give himself an identity,[5] and the same goes for J in *Seiteki ningen*.

Seiteki ningen is divided into two clearly separate parts, which have only the main character in common, a twenty-nine-year-old nouveau riche called J. In Part Two J has become a so-called *chikan*, i.e. someone who rubs himself to orgasm against female bodies on crowded trains, busses, etc. This kind of activity is clearly politically incorrect, but again the author's empathy is amazing: J has a whole philosophy about his activities and just like Seventeen he is portrayed as one who in the end is pure and follows his 'ideals', instead of giving in to the temptations of conformism, which would be a 'self-deception'.

What all heroes have in common is that in the end they are alone. Belonging to a group doesn't work. The jazz-band 'The Unlucky Young Men' of *Warera no jidai*, 'Les Amis' of *Sakebigoe*, J's chikan-club of *Seiteki ningen*, they all fall apart. And also the boy in *Sevuntiin* who joins the Imperial Way Party, eventually leaves that party and remains the loner he always was.

Some have called works like *Sevuntiin* a failed *roman à thèse* (Napier 1991:148-60) or a *roman contre thèse* (Ryan 1993:449-57), but in fact the text itself contains no 'thèse' at all. Of course it is quite common knowledge what Ôe's political views were at the time; he propagated them extensively in his essays. But in this novella Ôe neither advocates nor condemns what his hero

5. This story is also inspired by facts, the so-called Komatsugawakôkô-jiken of 1958.

does. I do not agree with Napier's statement that the boy's suicide is depicted grotesquely and is therefore an attack on the right (Napier 1991: 148). The depiction of the suicide is no more grotesque than Takeyama's in Mishima Yukio's *Yûkoku* (*Patriotism*, 1961). The political views of the two writers may tempt one to suspect overt ideological messages in both texts, pro and contra emperor-worship. But the text of *Sevuntiin* states no message. Though it may certainly be interpreted that way, taking into account Ôe's political views, the boy's solution is never presented as 'false and mis-leading', as Ryan claims (Ryan 1993:455). The boy just follows his ideals to the very end, since he refuses to take any further part in 'the real world'. He dies while being in total peace with himself. And by doing so he is much happier than, for example, Yasuo in *Warera no jidai* who does not have the energy to commit suicide and is forced to keep on living, while struggling with the world around him. Ôe simply says: this is what can happen (or rather: happens) under these (socio-political) circumstances. He leaves the judgement up to the reader, which is of course in line with his existentialist orientation of that period. Ôe offers no solution to the problems facing Japan's post-war youth, not just because that would not be 'existentialist', but also because most likely he did not have one at the time.

Kojinteki na taiken is obviously a different case. Whereas earlier heroes generally ended up exactly where they started or else dead, Bird, who starts out as a typical passive Ôe-hero, towards the end has taken a step forward: he has taken up responsibility, he has grown up and made an 'adult' de-cision: he chooses to let his handicapped baby live and forsakes the escapist solution of going to Africa with his lover. In *Seiteki ningen* this choice would have been considered 'conformist' and 'self-deceiving', but now it is pre-sented as 'the proper one'. Bird proves himself to be a politically correct hero. And having become a dedicated 'family man', he is no longer alone.

There are two points I would like to make here. First of all the transition did not happen overnight, i.e. with the birth of Hikari, as is often suggested. Of course, his son's birth and the mental handicap on top of it played an important part, but there were indications of Ôe's tending toward 're-sponsible, adult' choices in earlier stories and, on the other hand, there are several stories written after Hikari's birth where the hero still opts for non-conformist solutions. Mitsusaburô in *Man'en gannen no futtobôru*, for example, at the end goes to Africa, leaving his pregnant wife and handicapped baby behind, but remarkably enough this decision is not presented as escapist here, but justified by the fact that the baby will be well taken care of and by the fact that Mitsusaburô's wife insists on him going to try and start a new life. Here too, we can see that no matter what opposing choices Ôe's heroes take (suicide, sexual perversion, family man, traveller), they are never re-proached for it in the end, although some of them should be in terms of 'political correctness'.

The second point is that Ôe's conversion to political correctness was not very much appreciated by his audience. The end of *Kojinteki na taiken* has been criticised almost unanimously by both critics and readers.[6] With most critics this is because the ending is improbable in its 'happiness' (the baby's brain tumour suddenly appears to be benign), but with general readers it is the political correctness itself that displeases them. Even later works of Ôe which received good critical reviews never recaptured the interest of his earlier readers and fans. In the second part of this paper I will illustrate this point.

As for the first point: while *Kojinteki na taiken* may have been Ôe's first full-length novel after Hikari's birth, it was preceeded by a few short stories, among which *Sora no kaibutsu Aguii*, featuring a father who allowed his handicapped baby to die (politically incorrect!) and is now haunted by its ghost, which eventually leads to his suicide. Nevertheless, the fact that *Kojinteki na taiken* ends with the words 'hope' and 'forbearance', and *Sora no kaibutsu Aguii* with madness and suicide, seems to indicate that Ôe preferred one option over the other. The dead man is not envied by the narrator, as might have been the case before.

What has not been pointed out in earlier Ôe studies, however, is that Bird, the protagonist of *Kojinteki na taiken*, appears in an earlier short story called *Fumanzoku* (*Dissatisfaction*, 1962). This short story ends with Bird feeling liberated from the feeling of dissatisfaction which used to plague him; he feels 'adult'. Another short story, indicatively called *Otonamuki* (*Toward Adulthood*, 1963) and written while Ôe's wife was pregnant, has a hero who is similar to J in *Seiteki ningen*:[7] he refuses to get a decent job, flirts with homosexuality, etc., but, contrary to J, in the end he 'conforms'. So, just as with *Kojinteki na taiken* and *Sora no kaibutsu Aguii*, Ôe presents both options. But here his preference is still less clear. Yet another story written around that period (i.e. just before Hikari's birth), *Suparuta kyôiku* (*Spartan Education*), ends with the protagonist solving a situation and going to the hospital to greet his wife and new-born baby.

There are, therefore, indications that the birth of Hikari was not some sort

6. See reviews by, for example, Terada Tôru (Gunzô 11/1964), Mishima Yukio (Shûkan Dokushojin 14/9/1964), Kamei Katsuichirô (Shinchô 1/1965).

7. Both stories were published in the same month.

of 'enlightenment' (in spite of the naming of the baby), 'some bolt from the sky', which completely turned the author and his literature around. Rather there were signs of Ôe's growing up (or, if one chooses, becoming more 'politically correct') before Hikari's birth, and, on the other hand, doubts that still remained even after the birth.

Politically incorrect and popular

Within the scope of this paper it is of course impossible to discuss all the material that appeared on Ôe in Japan in the aftermath of the Nobel Prize. I will select just a few publications which are illustrative of the point I am trying to make with regard to the popularity of Ôe's work, in particular with young people.

The most interesting book I came across in this respect was one called *Ôe Kenzaburô ga kaba ni mo wakaru hon* (*A book through which even a hippopotamus can understand Ôe Kenzaburô*, hereafter referred to as 'Kaba'). The pun 'kaba' (hippopotamus) — 'baka' (idiot) is most likely not unintentional. The cover shows a cartoon of Ôe's head closely resembling that of the animal in the title. This unusual show of disrespect is further intensified by what is written on the cover. As authors of the 260-page publication are cited, 'Ô ken de asobu seinen no kai' (Society of youngsters who amuse themselves with Ô ken', 'Ô ken', of course, being short for Ôe Kenzaburô). Other eye-catching phrases on the cover are: 'Of course published without permission of the author', and '26 secrets about Ô ken which nobody mentions these days'. On the back cover some of these 26 secrets are revealed: 'Ô ken is vulgar!', 'Ô ken is a wanker!', 'Ô ken just loves discrimination!', 'Ô ken hates women!', 'Ô ken is mad about anal sex!', 'Ô ken is a liar!', 'Ô ken was a drug addict!', 'Ô ken is not a so-called post-war democrat!', 'Ô ken is hoping for an atomic war!', etc.

Obviously all these statements are meant to contradict the image of Ôe as it is usually portrayed in the media these days: that of the politically correct humanist, anti-nuclear activist and responsible, caring family man. But the purpose of the authors is actually not to ridicule or vilify Ôe — quite the contrary. The message they are trying to convey is one for young Japanese of today:

Hey you kids, Ôe is not the boring old fart the media is making him out to be. Read his early works and you'll find stories that'll excite you more than any by Murakami Haruki or Yoshimoto Banana ever will (Kaba:85).

The actual content of the book is quite serious literary criticism, and clearly intended to instigate young people to give Ôe a try. The way they try to lure their audience is significant:

For those who hate reading Ôe because they find his recent novels, with themes like 'salvation' and 'healing', stupid, we'll present a selection of sex and violence which remains interesting even today (Kaba:83).

In other words, Ôe used to be politically incorrect, and political incorrectness equals 'not-boring, exciting, worth reading'.

It is remarkable how much attention in this book is paid to *Sevuntiin* and its sequel *Seiji shônen shisu*. The unpublished sequel even gets special mention on the cover, and there is a ten-page synopsis of the story. In one section of the book (called 'Best 5 as introduction to Ô ken, chosen by the twentysomething for the twentysomething', Kaba:83-99), five young people discuss their favourite Ôe books, which they recommend to other young people. Among those five, three put *Sevuntiin* in their 'Best 5' list. Two even place it in the top spot. At the end of the discussion the five make up a united list, in which eventually *Sevuntiin* ends up in the number three spot, behind the short stories *Hato* (*Pigeons*, 1958) and *Sora no kaibutsu Aguii* (Kaba:96). That the latter is in the list and not the novel *Kojinteki na taiken* is another indication that the politically incorrect option is preferred over the correct one. It is also remarkable that none of the lists includes an Ôe-story written later than 1964. At the end of the discussion the five state why they are no longer reading Ôe's recent work (Kaba:94-99).

One had already had enough with *Man'en gannen no futtobôru*, the others still gave some of the recent Ôe a try, but did not find it interesting and gave up halfway.

What it boils down to is not only that later Ôe themes like 'salvation' and 'surviving great personal tragedy' are not as appealing as the 'sex and violence' of the early works, but also that for young people the post-1964 Ôe opus is simply 'not interesting', since they do not feel it tells them anything about their own lives; there is no longer 'identification', no longer 'empathy'.

Does the fact that they are able to empathise and identify with the heroes of *Sevuntiin* or *Seiteki ningen* mean that they condone the actions of fascist assassins and sexual perverts? Not quite. It is more that they identify with the problems and anguish these people are faced with at the outset. Ôe's young heroes are 'just like them'. It is interesting to notice that this was not only the case at the time the stories first appeared, but still true for young people today, over thirty years later, as publications like Kaba make clear.

All five in the discussion first read something by Ôe as a teenager. One of them actually admits he picked up *Seiteki ningen* because the title made him suspect it was porn (in fact, at first he would not have been disappointed as we have a ping-pong ball inserted into a vagina already on page one of that story). As mentioned above, a great part of the discussion is dedicated to *Sevuntiin* under the caption 'Why is *Seventeen* so great?' (Kaba:87-89). Invariably it has to do with a feeling of identification with the protagonist at the outset of the story (one of them confesses that after reading the story he tried what it was like to masturbate twice and then run 800 metres, just like Seventeen does in Chapter Two). Beside the 'universal puberty problems' of the story, they also find the political aspect still very timely: youngsters being drawn into the world of rightist extremism for a feeling of 'belonging' and 'purpose' is something of all places and times, they say. One of them admits he was not aware there was a sequel to *Sevuntiin*, which proves the efficiency of the censorship.

Another thing which is considered 'great' in this (and other early) storie(s), is the sexual terminology. Even in these days, when readers are somewhat used to explicit sexual language, Ôe's vocabulary still seems to maintain some of the shock-effect it undoubtedly had thirty-five years ago. Some of that sexual vocabulary is significantly indicative. The seventeen-year-old boy is a 'chronic masturbator'. A common word for masturbation would be *ji'i*, which literally means 'self-comfort', but Ôe uses the less common word *jitoku*, which means 'self-dirtying/self-staining', and this is no coincidence, since it says a lot about the boy's self-esteem.

It is not only in this book that Ôe's early works, and especially *Sevuntiin*, get a lot of attention. Other post-Nobel publications on Ôe which consider the opinion of the 'ordinary reader' all place great prominence on them. The magazine *Dacapo* for example published the results of a questionnaire among its readers on Ôe in its issue of 15 March 1995. These readers are usually middle-aged or elderly, with a general interest in literature and current affairs, a different audience from the one 'Kaba' aims at. The first conclusion is that only 31.7% of the readers responded to the questionnaire, 'the lowest percentage ever', and of those who did respond about half admitted they had never read anything by Ôe (*Dacapo* 12). This is of course a serious indication of Ôe's limited popularity, even after the Nobel Prize.

Dacapo also asked for the favourite Ôe works of the readers and here too those were mainly early works. In the overall 'Best 5' list only the number five spot had a work dated later than 1964. More than 90% of those who had read Ôe had started with some of his early work and still found those 'most interesting'. The list with 'most boring works by Ôe' on the contrary contained exclusively more recent work (*Dacapo* 13).

The tendency among the 'laymen' to consider Ôe's first six or seven years as a writer as the most important of his oeuvre stands in contrast with the attention the 'specialists' (the literary critics and academics) devote to his early stories, especially those with the most politically incorrect heroes of them all, like *Sevuntiin*.

The major newspapers did not even put *Sevuntiin* on their (otherwise rather extensive) list of 'Ôe's major works' (nor any of the other stories appearing in the 'united Best 5' list in *Kaba*). The list on page 14 of the *Asahi Shimbun* of 14/10/1994, for example, goes directly from *Warera no jidai* (1959) to *Seiteki ningen* (1963), though Ôe wrote no less than 20 novels, novellas, and short stories in between, including *Sevuntiin*.

'Serious' literary magazines, like *Gunzô* for example, also have a tendency to discuss Ôe's debut stories of 1957-1958, and then more or less skip to *Kojinteki na taiken* in 1964. In a special *Gunzô* issue on Ôe of 1995, *Sevuntiin* does not come up once in all the essays by literary critics and Ôe specialists, and is only discussed briefly (two pages) together with some other works in the nearly 100 pages-long section called *Ôe Kenzaburô Sakuhin Gaido* (*Guide to the Works of Ôe Kenzaburô*).

As pointed out above, in the early stories the heroes at the end of the story are still in the same mess (the passive ones), or else they end up dead or in jail (the active ones). Obviously neither type has the right solution. It would be naive to think that Ôe's readers are not able to draw that conclusion themselves. That is why the author, for example, does not need to say explicitly 'do not join a rightist organisation to solve your problems'. The young reader feels reassured: it is not abnormal that he is going through a tough time with no concrete hope for improvement, many others are in the same situation. From *Kojinteki na taiken* on, Ôe does offer a solution, but it is, as the title of the novel suggests, a very 'personal' one, and not one which his young readers were likely to be able to adopt for their own situation. Hence, they lost interest.

References

Dacapo henshûbu. 1995. Kenshô Ôe Kenzaburô. *Dacapo* 231.12-33.
Napier, Susan. 1991. *Escape from the Wasteland*. Cambridge, Mass: Harvard University Press.

Ôe, Kenzaburô:
   1961.   *Seiji shônen shisu.* Bungakukai 15-2.8-48
   1963.   *Sakebigoe.* Tokyo: Kôdansha
   1963.   *Warera no jidai.* Tokyo: Shinchôsha
   1966.   Kassai. *Ôe Kenzaburô Zensakuhin* 1-I, 51-80. Tokyo: Shinchôsha
   1968.   Seiteki ningen. *Seiteki ningen,* 7-116. Tokyo: Shinchôsha
   1968.   Sevuntiin. *Seiteki ningen,* 117-77. Tokyo: Shinchôsha
   1970.   *Okurete kita seinen.* Tokyo: Shinchôsha
   1971.   *Man'en gannen no futtobôru.* Tokyo: Kôdansha
   1972.   Fumanzoku. *Sora no kaibutsu Aguii,* 7-68. Tokyo: Shin-chôsha
   1972.   Suparuta kyôiku. *Sora no kaibutsu Aguii,* 69-99. Tokyo: Shin-chôsha
   1972.   Sora no kaibutsu Aguii. *Sora no kaibutsu Aguii,* 161-209. Tokyo: Shin-chôsha
   1974.   Kimyô na shigoto. *Miru mae ni tobe,* 7-25. Tokyo: Shin-chôsha
   1974.   Miru mae ni tobe. *Miru mae ni tobe,* 117-81. Tokyo: Shin-chôsha
   1976.   *Pinchi rannâ chôsho.* Tokyo: Shin-chôsha
   1981.   *Kojinteki na taiken.* Tokyo: Shin-chôsha
   1983.   *Atarashii hito yo mezameyo.* Tokyo: Kôdansha
Ô ken de asobu seinen no kai, ed. 1995. *Ôe Kenzaburô ga kaba ni mo wakaru hon.* To-kyo: Yôsensha.
Ryan, James. 1993. The Split Personality of Ôe Kenzaburô. *Japan Quarterly,* 444-57.
Watanabe, Katsuo, ed. 1995. *Gunzô Tokubetsu henshû, Ôe Kenzaburô.* Tokyo: Kô-dansha.

A Genealogy of *Sokkyô Shijin* in the Works of Mori Ôgai — From 'Translation' to 'Creative Writing'

Yôichi Nagashima

Mori Ôgai, with all his achievements both as a writer and a career bureaucrat, was an incarnation of the age in which Japan's modernization took place. Ôgai, a giant among the intellectuals of the Meiji and Taishô periods, was all his life concerned with the question of the relationship between Westernization and Japanese cultural tradition. Unlike Natsume Sôseki, another giant author of the age, Ôgai contributed to the modernizing process of Japan through his numerous translations of Western literature. For him translation was a struggle — a constant conflict between his traditional cultural background, his own prejudices and preoccupations, and the Western way of thinking. It was a highly intellectual act. He tried to pierce into the depth of Western culture using language as a pipeline. Through this pipeline he infused new energy into Japanese culture in order to activate and 'modernize' it. He gave Western ideas Japanese words or expressions in order to create a new literature in Japan. But certain modifications were necessary, which inevitably left some visible gaps between the original works and his translations.

Analyzing one of his best and most celebrated translations, *Sokkyô Shijin*, a translation of Hans Christian Andersen's *The Improvisator*, I have shown in my book *Mori Ôgai no hon'yaku bungaku* (Nagashima, 1993), how his peculiar way of re-telling — his creative (mis)understanding — of the original work was accomplished. It was in fact an act of acculturation or Japanization. In other words, the successful Japanization of the original was accomplished by the enormous fame and popularity of *Sokkyô Shijin*, which is considered to be one of the classics of modern Japanese literature.

After having completed *Sokkyô Shijin* (1892-1901, published 1902), Ôgai continued his efforts to 'transplant' Western literary ideas/devices such as the 'first person novel', 'Bildungsroman', and 'quasi-autobiography' into his own creative writings. The scholars of Ôgai's literary activities, however, have paid little attention to his translations. Scarcely anyone has pointed out the organic connection between his translations and his creative writings. Ôgai the translator and Ôgai the novelist were complementary to each other. By viewing his creative works in direct relation to his translations, one can reveal unexpected aspects of his literary world. This kind of study is no doubt very painstaking, but it is nevertheless useful and even crucial, not necessarily for analyzing the influence of the original works on his own writings, but mainly in clarifying the process of how Ôgai adapted and developed borrowed ideas in his own novels and short stories. The process of Japanization was recognizable in his translations, but it was only fulfilled in his own writings. Western literature was an inexhaustible source of ideas for Ôgai; his translations were the means and an intermediary of conveying the examined ideas.

Ôgai spent nearly ten years translating *Sokkyô Shijin*. It is unthinkable that his mental immersion in the work did not leave visible traces in his own writings. This paper is an effort to follow up the hitherto neglected traces of *Sokkyô Shijin* in Ôgai's works from 1910 to 1911, with special emphasis on the novel *Seinen* (*Youth*). This is why I call my paper a 'genealogy'.

Upon completing his first fictional work *Maihime* (*The Dancing Girl*) in 1890, Ôgai began to translate *The Improvisator*, serializing it in the literary magazine *Shigarami-zôshi* from 1892 through to 1901. The whole translation was then published in book form in 1902. After the Russo-Japanese War, Ôgai was promoted to Surgeon-General in 1907. In the following years he eagerly resumed his literary activities by translating quite a number of Western novels and plays into Japanese. At the same time he reembarked upon his creative writing, beginning with a short story *Hannichi* (*Half a Day*) in March 1909. From this time throughout the period of the serialization of the novel *Gan* (*The Wild Goose*) in the literary magazine *Subaru* in 1911-12, similar tendencies could be observed in all Ôgai's works, both in the translations and fiction. In 1909 for example, Ôgai published the following titles among others:

Masui (*Hypnosis*), a short story, June
Saiki (*Creditors*), a play by August Strindberg, June
Vita Sexualis, a novel, July
John Gabriel Borkman, a play by Henrik Ibsen, July-September
Dangozaka, a short story in dialogue, September

In all of them Ôgai's interest was focussed on human relationships driven and governed by 'sexuality' and 'vanity'. As if he would clarify and synthesize this theme, Ôgai wrote the novel *Seinen* (*Youth*), which was serialized again in *Subaru* from March 1910 through to August 1911. Meanwhile he published the marvellous short stories *Fushinchû* (*Under Reconstruction*, June 1910) and *Fujidomoe* (May 1911), and finally in September 1911 he began to serialize the novel *Gan*.

Viewing his literary productions in this period, one cannot avoid noticing a common thread running through all of them; namely a thread composed of the various aspects of a (young) man who, shackled with 'vanity' and (almost) blinded with 'sexuality', still dreams of success or of becoming a writer. 'Sexuality' and 'vanity' described in his own works are woven up with such elements as 'autobiography' and 'Bildungsroman'; all of these elements, by the way, had been the main components of his first fictional work *Maihime*.

Maihime was an incomplete 'Bildungsroman' written under the influence of Hans Christian Andersen's *The Improvisator*. *Sokkyô Shijin* was, as mentioned already, a creative mis-translation of the work, masterfully accomplished but consciously or unconsciously distorted by the author of *Maihime*. These four elements — 'sexuality', 'vanity', 'autobiography', and 'Bildungsroman' — were taken up again by Ôgai after the Russo-Japanese War and forged as the core of his writings from 1909 through to 1912.

In this period Ôgai seemed to want to redeem those expressions and literary devices which were either inadequate, manipulated or eliminated in his translation of *The Improvisator*, due to the differences in the cultural background and the language. Ôgai was in fact preoccupied with an attempt to surpass his previous works by creating a genuine Japanese version of the Bildungsroman. In this context, his three novels *Vita Sexualis*, *Seinen*, and *Gan* were not merely a trilogy but also a series of continuous stories ('adventures') whose chronology and contents preceded the incomplete Bildungsroman *Maihime*: the childhood, the juvenescence and the student-years of the shy and indifferent hero were depicted in *Vita Sexualis*; the vainglorious hero's depraved life in Tokyo in *Seinen*; and the irresolute hero's acquaintance with a woman and his departure to Germany in *Gan*. *Maihime* is a story about a young Japanese student who chooses his career before love during a stay in Berlin. One can catch glimpses of *Sokkyô Shijin* all the way through the trilogy.

The reason why Ôgai wrote works concerning 'sexuality' should not be sought solely in the flourishing naturalistic writings of the time. By the same token it is too convenient to assert that Ôgai wrote his novel *Seinen* simply because he was encouraged by the successful serialization of *Sanshirô* (1908), a novel by his rival Natsume Sôseki. These exogenous motivations cannot fully explain Ôgai's almost obsessive interest in 'sexuality' and 'vanity' at the time of his writing the trilogy. He was more likely spurred endogenously to face his own 'sexuality' and 'vanity' in order to settle an interim account of his life; his Bildungsroman was to become a room for experiment where he could freely examine his inner world, thus enabling him to fictionalize the course of his unsatisfied life, a life of resignation.

One can assume that 'sexuality' was the theme Ôgai really wanted to write about, and the device of the Bildungsroman was used as a framework within which to scrutinize it. Nevertheless, Ôgai's own vainglory and his critical mind veiled the theme in such a manner that his description of 'sexuality' turned out to be somewhat mitigated. For example his short story *Masui* (*Hypnosis*), a story in which a husband finds out that his wife has been hypnotized by a doctor during a consultation, never developed as boldly as *Hakujitsumu* (*Daydream*, 1926), a short play by Tanizaki Jun'ichirô. In the same way the medium of the Bildungsroman was modified or rather abandoned halfway, as can be witnessed in Ôgai's closing remark at the end of *Seinen* which reads as follows:

It seems best to consider the novel *Seinen* to be finished hereby. I have written only a tiny part of what I intended; the number of days in the novel has amounted only to 60-70. In the beginning of the story I have depicted the scene where it began to freeze, and now it is finally winter, but it has scarcely snowed yet in the novel. While I have been writing no more than that, two years have already passed. Anyway, I hereby finish my story.[1]

These words show clearly that the novel was finished unwillingly with no possibility of being continued. Ôgai knew that it was impossible to end a Bildungsroman in a satisfactory way when the hero not only had not suc-ceeded in life (yet) neither was he dead nor had he got married. It was even more difficult for the author to finish a Bildungsroman when the story con-tained certain autobiographical elements. Probably the novel should not have been written as a Bildungsroman when the author was discontent and leading a life of resignation. But, on the contrary, the author could manage to make his account fictitious just by demonstrating that he was able to close the story at any moment in time. In this way he could attain a sort of le-

---

1. This remark is missing in the recent English translation of *Seinen* entitled *Youth* by Shoichi Ono and Sanford Goldstein, 1994.

gitimacy in his story; not the truth, but vividness, plausibility, and even reliability, which only fictional writings could give. Ôgai was aware of this. He knew well that the essence of the novel, this imported art from Europe, consisted of this very point. The novel has its own laws which are not those of daily life: Anything that suits is *true*; you need not necessarily tell *the truth*.

Telling the story of himself, however, Ôgai did not choose the impulsive openheartedness typical for naturalists. Nor did he choose the device of 'confession', which could be grim and pathetic. Instead he transformed the reality of his life, or at times enlarged it, by means of his rich imagination cultivated by his life experience and extensive reading. Thus he published his first fictional work, *Maihime*, which embodied only one truth that 'the hero chose career before love'. In the same way Ôgai continued to fictionalize one truth after another of his alter egos in his trilogy: 'the hero who was interested in the opposite sex' in *Vita Sexualis*; 'the hero who intended to write fiction' in *Seinen*; and 'the hero who was timid and a coward' in *Gan*. The remaining parts of the trilogy were the product of Ôgai's imagination. By fictionalizing these truths repeatedly in different contexts, Ôgai gradually succeeded in mythologizing his own life.

The origin of his mythologizing attempt should be traced back, as mentioned above, to Hans Christian Andersen's *The Improvisator*. In this novel the reserved hero Antonio meets various types of women while encountering breathtaking adventures. In the course of time he gradually cures himself of his shyness and vainglory, finally finds his beloved, and also succeeds as an improvisator. But it is only a fairy tale. In real life, however, Hans Christian Andersen, although he was fond of women, experienced one lost love after another; he remained single all his life, and even to his last day he was shackled by his vanity. For example, when he was photographed — and he liked to be photographed — he curled his hair and always showed his profile from the right. His vainglory was a part of his personality. Nevertheless, he was a lonely man; he endured loneliness and unhappiness in real life by creating myths and tales about himself — giving the illusion of a happy and successful man.

No doubt Ôgai found the same type of a poet as himself in the figure of Antonio, an alter ego of Hans Christian Andersen, but Ôgai, indomitable as he was, did not want to remain a vainglorious and reserved poet forever; he planned to get rid of his weakness — 'vainglory' — and immersed himself in making myths about himself by writing novels and stories. That was exactly what Ôgai had learned from *The Improvisator*, firstly by reading it and later by translating it as *Sokkyô Shijin*.

Seinen or '(Literary) Youth'

Having a close relationship to *The Improvisator*, Ôgai's novel *Seinen* should rather be entitled *Bungaku Seinen, Literary Youth*. He began to serialize it in the literary magazine *Subaru*, instead of the unfinished Bildungsroman *Vita Sexualis*, in March 1910. Needless to say *Seinen* was also a typical Bildungsroman. The hero Koizumi Jun'ichi was for obvious reasons a vainglorious literary youth. He underwent the process of self-discovery through encounters with the opposite sex and his own sexuality. After facing his vainglory and gradually overcoming it, he finally found himself capable of writing fiction.

The frame of Ôgai's Bildungsroman was a true copy of the structure of *The Improvisator*. The subdual of the hero's 'sexuality' gave him an opportunity of self-discovery, which led him further to his writing activities. Though it was a kind of self-discovery, in the case of *Seinen* it was not self-discovery attained by an individual. Neither its process nor its background was explained convincingly; the only things that were described in the novel were the various stages of the ritual, in which the hero adjusted himself to the social system. However, as long as it was the Japanese way of self-discovery — that is by finding one's own place in or one's belonging to society — *Seinen* should be considered as a legitimate Japanese Bildungsroman about the protagonist Koizumi Jun'ichi.

As for the persons in the novel, Ôgai, by arranging three women corresponding to the three women surrounding Antonio in *The Improvisator*, made his story more colourful than any other of the works he had written. Accordingly, Jun'ichi's journey through 'sexuality' became more palpable and realistic. As is well-known, real people were introduced into the novel under pseudonyms (among others Fuseki for Sôseki and Ôson for Ôgai), which contributed to the impression of the reliability of the told history.

Hans Christian Andersen travelled to Naples and Rome, while Ôgai himself travelled to Berlin, the capital of Europe at that time. In both cases they travelled to culturally more civilized cities than those from which they came. By the same token Jun'ichi left his hometown in the provinces and came to Tokyo, the capital of a modernizing Japan. Sanshirô, the hero of Sôseki's novel, had a similar background, but unlike him Jun'ichi visited both Berlin and Rome in a textual context via Ôgai the author and Ôgai the translator. The multilayered structure and the at times impenetrable description of the novel seems to stem from this very fact.

The somewhat unnatural plot of the novel is similar to that of *The Improvisator* — a fairy-like story filled with adventures. Ôgai's intention with

Seinen was to create a Japanese version of the Bildungsroman on the basis of *The Improvisator* but without Christian elements; not a romantic dream-like story in a flowery style, but an eventful and exciting history described in a realistic style. At the time of writing *Seinen*, Ôgai was no longer a romanticist but a mature and resigned realist. It didn't mean, however, that he had lost his passion to dream. For him dreams and fiction belonged to another world where he could round off his youth peacefully. It was and remained his world of healing all through his life.

Just as Antonio was surrounded by different types of women, so was Jun'ichi. Those women who came across him and helped him to find his own self were the pure Oyuki, Mrs. Sakai a widow, and Ochara a geisha. They corresponded to the three women in *The Improvisator* — the devout and pure Flaminia, the voluptuous and passionate Mrs. Santa, and the vainglorious and capricious Annunziata, who were all molded as individuals with their own personalities, and played their roles in the various stages of Antonio's finding his own self.[2] Unlike these, both Oyuki, Mrs. Sakai, and Ochara appear before Jun'ichi almost simultaneously. As Ôgai himself remarked at the end of the novel, the whole story only stretched over a period of 60-70 days. On that point it is debatable whether *Seinen* shoud be regarded as a Bildungsroman. Nevertheless, the readers of *Seinen* get an impression of Jun'ichi travelling through many places and experiencing a lot. This was only made possible by the above-mentioned multilayered structure of the novel.

The novel was composed as a story of the literary youth Jun'ichi, and not as a narrator's recollection. Ôgai's own reminiscence of his younger days, his experiences in life through reading, translating, and writing, and even his reflections at the time of writing the novel, all these elements were merged organically into Jun'ichi's story. Due to this, the whole history assumed a dream-like aspect giving the impression that time was passing very slowly. The novel *Seinen* is in fact a record of Jun'ichi's dream rather than a genuine history of his self-discovery. In chapter 19 of the novel, Jun'ichi has the following dream:

And there, crouching among the green leaves reflecting a white light, was a woman, her long hair disheveled; disheveled too were her long sleeves and her kimono skirt./ ... Junichi and the woman boldly moved closer to one another ... /Junichi moved so close to her he could almost touch her. The face of this un-

---

2. The fourth woman Lala, later Maria, was a heroine of the fairy-like part of the novel which resembled a Christian miracle; for that very reason she was eliminated from the last scene of Ôgai's translation *Sokkyô Shijin*.

known woman suddenly changed into Ochara's, but he thought it not the least bit odd. And then during an interval when they were exchanging quite familiar expressions and fragments of words, the woman suddenly turned into Mrs. Sakai. While he was tormented with his endeavors to support his body in that precarious position even as he tried to shorten the distance between himself and the other, that face was transformed into Oyuki's before he realized what was taking place. /It was at this moment that Junichi was jolted and returned to a state of half-wakefulness. / … Junichi felt the flames of passion in him. … as he repeatedly kept up his dream, he could so clearly sense its outlines and colors it was as if he had grasped the dream with his very hands. He wished he could write his novel that clearly (477-78).[3]

It is no exaggeration to say that the novel *Seinen* is a product of Ôgai writing down his own dreams.

Ôgai's description of the three women is veiled with 'sexuality': Oyuki with her wide-open eyes reminded Jun'ichi of Manet's Nana:

Sitting next to Junichi, Oyuki kept flipping through the foreign magazine on his desk./ … Their kimono sleeves touched. … he caught the odor of a healthy woman. All of a sudden … she moved her body in an exaggerated way. His hip came in contact with hers, and he felt the blunt, resilient resistance of her body (449).

Mrs. Sakai whom Jun'ichi meets at a theatre when the Japanese version of Henrik Ibsen's *John Gabriel Borkman*, translated by Ôgai himself, is performed in Tokyo, is an 'exceedingly attractive woman … and something excessively coquettish was in her large dark eyes' (413). Jun'ichi is at once captivated by her, and before long he becomes 'a man of experience' (426). But the same day he writes in his diary that 'Mrs. Sakai could never be the kind of woman who could be the object of his (my) love'. He is embarrassed by the fact that he has become 'a man of experience' so easily without falling in love. He even accuses himself by writing: 'Why don't I look for a passionate love? I am ashamed of myself for being so spineless!' (426). Afterwards he is in agony, and 'he (I) had come to regard Mrs. Sakai as his (my) enemy' (456). Nevertheless, seized with a loneliness and driven by sexual desire, he is again drawn to her 'beautiful lump of flesh' (513), but only to feel 'a displeasure he could not define' (498), which soon developes into jealousy, those 'feelings of … a very nasty loneliness' (504), when he finds her in the

---

3. Quoted from *Youth*, *op.cit*. Likewise, the numbers after the following quotations refer to the pages in the book.

company of another man. The feeling of defeat, however, makes him equip himself with a means of mental self-defence; thus he becomes a cold-hearted 'bystander', indifferent to women and love. As a result the acting Jun'ichi metamorphoses into the witnessing Jun'ichi. The protagonist metamorphoses into the narrator. At this very moment Jun'ichi thinks that if he 'himself tried to write now, he could probably produce something quite good' (513). Having obtained a point of view from which he is now able to objectify his own self and his life, the literary youth metamorphoses into a writer.

The exciting geisha Ochara appears before Jun'ichi as a beautiful temptation. He decides to 'retreat from this pretty adversary' (471), but he 'could feel at the back of his mind that his vanity' has already been awakened (474). It is Ochara who reminds him of his vanity. As a child Jun'ichi had fancied himself as 'an attractive boy', and now he thinks himself 'a good-looking young man'; vanity has always been something he has cultivated in himself. It is a 'kind of coquetry', a mask. (427). Ôgai does not use the Japanese word 'kyoeishin' for 'vanity' in Seinen; instead he explains it as 'mizukara yorokobu jô' (a feeling of being pleased with oneself) or 'mizukara aisuru kokoro' (a feeling of loving oneself) — the expressions he had used in his translation Sokkyô Shijin.[4]

Having lost Mrs. Sakai, Jun'ichi feels hurt, but in reality what he feels is no more than an unpleasantness, because his vanity has been affronted.[5] When Jun'ichi realizes this, he is cured. He is then convinced that 'a novel might be created' (516). Or rather, he has at last got something to write about.

The theme of a young man suffering from vanity is traced back to The Improvisator. In this sense Ôgai's Seinen is literally the legitimate son of The Improvisator. The narrator of Seinen, however, makes Jun'ichi comment on Ôgai's Sokkyô Shijin as follows:

... he had only looked at Ôson's (Ôgai's) translation of Hans Christian Andersen.

4. In the passage in Chapter 18 where Jun'ichi wonders about the significance of the name card Ochara has given him, one sentence in the English translation by Ono and Goldstein reads as follows: 'Or was it not merely the token of a woman he has felt some slight kindling of love for?' (475). This, however, is a mis-translation, probably due to the translators' ignorance of the meaning of the expression 'mizukara aisuru kokoro'. The name card was the token of the woman who had seen through his 'vanity'.

5. This sentence which contains the same expression 'mizukara aisuru kokoro' as above is translated by Ono and Goldstein as follows: 'It was no more than a wound suffered by his self-esteem' (516).

Jun'ichi could not understand why Ôson had taken the trouble to translate that boring story even if only to kill time (403).

These words of self-scorn are an obvious example of Ôgai's uncured and incurable vanity; his self-scorn is nothing but self-conceit.

References

Mori, Ôgai. 1994. Youth, translated by Shoichi Ono and Sanford Goldstein. *Youth and Other Stories*, ed. by J. Thomas Rimer, 371-526. Honolulu: University of Hawaii Press.
Nagashima, Yôichi. 1993. *Mori Ôgai no hon'yaku bungaku*. Tokyo: Shibundô.
Rimer, J. Thomas (ed.). 1994. *Mori Ôgai Youth and Other Stories*. Honolulu: University of Hawaii Press.

The Lyric Voice in Modern Japanese Poetry:
A Few Considerations

James O'Brien

In the abstract which I submitted to the organizers of the 1995 NAJAKS symposium, I referred to three modern Japanese poets — Kitahara Hakushû (1885-1942), Takamura Kôtarô (1882-1956), and Murano Shirô (1901-75). These three poets were meant to be the focus of an inquiry into problems concerning 'the lyric voice and its effects'. I left the term 'lyric voice' undefined, since I wished to experiment with the widest possible range of ideas in preparing my paper.

Since drafting the abstract, I have narrowed my focus considerably. I will not be dealing with the broad historical and comparative terms indicated towards the end of that statement. Nor will I even take up all three of the aforementioned poets. Instead I concentrate on Kitahara Hakushû, the most accomplished of the three according to the consensus of critics and scholars of modern Japanese poetry. I refer to Hakushû not to reach any definite conclusions on the question of the lyric voice and its effects. I merely sketch an aspect of the problem by looking at four Hakushû poems and leave to a later occasion the challenge of relating these three widely different poets to one another on the basis of their use of a lyric voice.

Before dealing with the poems, I should give a summary of Hakushû's life and achievements. He was born in 1885 in Yanagawa, a small town on the Ariake Bay in Kyushu. During the Edo period Yanagawa had prospered as a harbor town accessible to the vessels which plied their trade along the coast for several centuries. However, like similar provincial harbor towns such as Kurashiki, Yanagawa stagnated under the commercial arrangements set up in the Meiji period. Although he was born and raised during mid-Meiji, Hakushû was not himself disadvantaged by Yanagawa's decline. His father owned the local sake brewery, and the family was well off. The brewery did fail in the long run, as a consequence of a fire and an ill-advised decision to rebuild on a grand scale. However, this occurred only after Hakushû had established a secure reputation as a poet.

As the oldest son, Hakushû would normally have inherited the family business when it was still thriving. However, he proved to be a fragile and sensitive child, more given to reading and daydreaming than to practical pursuits. In late adolescence he fled to Tokyo to escape his father and to begin a career as a poet. As a boy he had written tanka — 31 syllable poems in five lines — and his talent was quickly recognized by the literary establishment in the capital. While still in his twenties Hakushû published two immensely successful volumes of poetry evoking the culture of his home town and region. Then came a third volume, this one depicting scenes in his adopted city of Tokyo.

These first three volumes contained *gendaishi* or 'modern verse'. In general the poems departed from the requirements concerning subject matter, diction, and prosody which had held sway over such classical forms as the tanka and the haiku. Hakushû continued to write this new style of poetry; however, as the years went on, he concentrated more and more on composing modern versions of the dominant classical form, the tanka.

By the time of his death in 1942, Hakushû had been recognized as the nation's most popular writer of free verse during the Taisho and early Showa periods. He was also considered one of Japan's foremost tanka poets and had made his mark as a writer and editor central to the children's literature movement of the 1920's. This children's literature movement, incidentally, has been largely ignored by Western scholars of modern Japanese literature, an oversight which one hopes will be corrected in due course.

The four poems which I will examine in this paper come from Hakushû's second volume of verses, published in 1909. The title, *Memories (Omoide)*, indicates the focus of this volume. In these poems Hakushû looks back to his childhood and upbringing from the vantage point of early adulthood, a time which he spent in Tokyo after escaping from the obligations of family and business and finding his metier. Aware of this autobiographical dimension, many readers equate the poet with the voice speaking in the poems. These works, it must be said, appear to invite such a reading by their direct manner of presentation. Seldom if ever does the poet distance himself from his subject matter by such techniques as irony or comedy.

Hakushû does not, however, suggest his presence through adverting explicitly to a self. Adept at classical methods, he avoids using the personal pronouns. While treating of events which he presumably observed or even participated in, Hakushū provides neither a commentary nor a narrative framework for his depiction of formative experience. The following poem, *Blue Dragonfly (Aoi Tombo)*, is dominated by imagistic brilliance and by a single deed whose motives are implied only.

Blue dragonfly, an emerald look
In the green luster of the eye;
Blue dragonfly, the delicate wing
Glinting on a reed in flower.
Blue dragonfly aloft,
A magician's sleight-of-hand;
Blue dragonfly caught,
Crinkled skin of a diva.

Blue dragonfly beauty,
Fearful even to touch;
Blue dragonfly composure
Grates on the jealous eye.

A grinding leather sandal
Crinkles the blue dragonfly.

青いとんぼ

青いとんぼの眼を見れば
緑の、銀の、エメロウド、
青いとんぼの薄き翅
灯心草の穂に光る。

青いとんぼの飛びゆくは
魔法つかひの手練かな。
青いとんぼを捕ふれば
女役者の肌ざはり。

青いとんぼの綺麗さは
手に触るすら恐ろしく、
青いとんぼの落つきは
眼にねたきまで悩々し。

青いとんぼをきりきりと
夏の雪駄で溜みつぶす。

This poem offers a microscopic look at the scene in question. At the same time the poem's range of imagistic reference is considerable, especially in the second stanza with its magician and diva. Who, one muses, could be describing this odd series of images and the drastic action which concludes the work? Whoever it is seems both protagonist of the action and observer of the entire scene — a kind of shifting viewpoint or, more accurately in this case, a blend of viewpoints. Perhaps the poem coheres primarily by dint of its prosodic technique, an aspect not readily transferable into any language so different from the original as English.

As with any poem the poet's own intelligence permeates the whole, fashioning the materials of a typical childhood experience into a theme which coincides in general terms with that elaborately worked out by Mishima Yukio in his celebrated novel *The Temple of the Golden Pavilion* (*Kinkakuji*, 1956). In both cases someone fascinated by an object of beauty eventually reacts violently and decisively to obliterate that very beauty.

'Blue Dragonfly' exemplifies Hakushû's practice of making his speaker implicit in the words of the poem. These words seem to stand on their own, without a specifically defined figure to voice them. The reader interested in certain kinds of questions regarding poetry will take heed of this impersonal manner of presentation.

Blue Dragonfly is so arranged as to call special attention to certain technical features of the poetry. A highly regular metric pattern underlies the work: each line consists of twelve syllables, an initial unit of seven followed by one of five syllables. The particle 'no' often concludes the first unit, except in two instances where the syntax shifts to the accusative marker 'o.' I have gotten various responses from native speakers when I put to them the question of whether they sense an imminent and radical shift in meaning as they hear these accusative markers occupying the position monopolized hitherto by the particle 'no.' Leaving aside such speculations, the verb following the second 'o' does describe the culminating action of the poem, a drastic one which goes counter to the calm manner in which the entire work is expressed.

The next poem, entitled *Enemy* (*Teki*), again illustrates Hakushû's practice of shifting his ground at the poem's end. In this case, however, the shift is in the prosody rather than in the kind of action being portrayed. This type of shift almost escapes one's attention in the translation; indeed, it is relatively subtle in the original as well.

> The enemy is somewhere,
> He's as if hiding near.
> When I pass through the warehouse shadow,
> When I go to the wholesaler
> For a piece of silver foil,
> When I rub a paper tattoo on my hand,
> Rub it into my skin
> While watching the canal at sundown,
> As I wander the streets alone,
> The enemy is somewhere
> Seeking me, seeking me, never a pause.

敵

いづこにか敵のゐて、
敵のゐてかくるるごとし。
酒倉のかげをゆく日も、
街の問屋に
銀紙買ひに行くときも、
うつし絵を手の甲に捺し、
手の甲に捺し、
夕日の水路見るときも、
ただひとりさまよふ街の
いづこにか敵のゐて
つけねらふ、つけねらふ、静こころなく。

This work, with its actor implicit in the action, evokes the typical childhood fear of a bogy. The protagonist of *Enemy* walks the streets of Yanagawa on tenterhooks, as if he might be set upon at any moment. The movement of the verse in this instance appears to be far less regular than in the previous work — the poet's way of suggesting an edginess in the boy-protagonist perhaps?

Hakushû demonstrates his technical virtuosity in *Enemy*, conveying a sense of irregularity and nervous tension through a metric which turns out to be regular, but in a peculiar way. The opening line of 5/5 syllables is repeated in the final line, the second line of 5/7 in the penultimate, these four lines being part of a pattern whereby the second half of the poem reverses the metrical pattern established in the first half. The eleventh and final line alludes through its language to a famous Heian Period tanka concerned with life's evanescence; this line's three syllabic units suggest prolongation, as if the boy will continue to be haunted by fear.

This poem too seems to speak itself, the description evoking the protagonist's state of mind in an unmediated fashion which becomes partially distorted in the translation. While centered on one emotion, *Enemy* departs from the fixation of *Blue Dragonfly*. The poem instead shifts its focus from place to place, from one activity to another, even though each of these references evokes the fear from which the boy cannot escape.

Despite subtle differences in the functioning of the lyric voice in *Blue Dragonfly* and *Enemy*, both works raise a special problem related to the implicit nature of voice. Although one can sense the poet in the poem by such things as the selection and treatment of materials, treatment including in this case even technical matters of prosody and the like, Hakushû does not project an explicit speaker nor does he create a multiplicity of voices that interact one against the other. Instead, the voice is single and unobtrusive, a factor which helps preserve the sense of a seamless whole in these works.

Sophisticated readers of modern Western poetry sometimes find Hakushû and his peers wanting in poetic excitement. I have heard editors of poetry journals in America express admiration for the poet's descriptive finesse, even as they slight his achievement by referring to the 'descriptive lyricism' of the poems. Such people concede that the poems appeallingly evoke a scene or an ongoing event within a scene in correspondingly appropriate aesthetic terms. However, they seem to believe that the presence of a single voice — a disembodied one at that — results in a lack of the dimensionality and interplay that is so integral to the best modern poetry of our own culture.

To counter such reactions, one needs to probe more fully into modern Japanese poems, whether by Hakushû or his peers. As an experiment in that direction, I wish to introduce two more works, both of which reverberate with symbolic suggestiveness. The first of these poems is entitled *Waterway* (*Suiro*).

Off and on the fireflies glint ...
A hushed waterway in Yanagawa
Where a boat, after theater hours,
Lulls a returning family in the glow
Of old paper lanterns, crest-adorned.

Off and on the fireflies glint ...
The cry of insects under a faint moon,
White walls on either side;
Fear as of a flickering wraith
Tightens its grip.

Off and on the fireflies glint ...
Lowering his pole now and again,
The boatmen passes beneath low bridges
Compacted of soil, redolent of grass,
Steering for the district where talk is hushed.

Off and on the fireflies glint ...
She stands on glistening steps
Where water is drawn for a certain house.

Her skin faintly white,
What does she watch so late in the night?

水　路

ほうほうと螢が飛ぶ……
しとやかな柳河の水路を、
定紋つけた古い提灯が、ぼんやりと、
その舟の芝居もどりの家族を眠らす。

ほうほうと螢が飛ぶ……
あるかない月の夜に鳴く虫のこゑ、
向ひあつた白壁の薄あかりに、
何かしら燐のやうなおそれがむせぶ。

ほうほうと螢が飛ぶ……
草のにほひする低い土橋を、
いくつか棹をかがめて通りすぎ、
ひそひそと話してる町の方へ。

ほうほうと螢が飛ぶ……
とある家のひたひたと光る汲水場に
ほんのり立つた女の素肌
何を見てゐるのか、ふけた夜のこころに。

I cannot detect, either in this poem or in the one to follow, a definite metric pattern of the sort evident in the two poems already introduced. However, like many Hakushû works, *Waterway* has a stable setting, indicated most obviously by the line of refrain which begins each of the four stanzas. It is within this setting that suggestive occurrences take place.

A protagonist occupies the center of this poem, his presence less definitely implied than in *Blue Dragonfly* and *Enemy*. Permeated with ambiguity, *Waterway* requires a considerable effort at imaginative projection by the reader. Let us say that a youth is being ferried home in the boat after spending the evening with his family at the theater. The hour is late, his mind sensitive to intimations from the surrounding darkness. The depiction in the final lines of the woman with her white skin could suggest a romantic rendevous of the sort the youth might well have witnessed at the theater earlier in the evening.

Admittedly these musings are mere speculation, particularly in view of Hakushû's suggestion in the evocative prose preface to *Memories* that this mysterious woman in the dark is tubercular. However, the further one reads this poet, the more one realizes that certain works by him require intuitive daring in the reader. Another poem which underlines this need is entitled *Spinning Wheel* (*Itoguruma*).

Wheel, wheel, the yarn spun in profound quiet.
A mournful evening, wheel softly turning.
On the wood floor where a gold and a red squash lie,
The wood floor of the PUBLIC CLINIC,
An old watchwoman sits all alone.

She is blind, deaf. And when May comes round again,
Her wisps of fragrant cotton drift back from memory.
Even the skeleton looks strange, upright in its glass
enclosure,
And gently falls the slanting moonlight on the canal.

Wheel, wheel, the yarn spun in stillness.
A mournful evening, thoughts softly turning.

糸車

糸車、しづかにふかき手のつむぎ、
その糸頃やはらかにめぐる夕べぞわりなけれ。
金と赤との南瓜のふたつ転がる板の間に、
「共同医館」の板の間に、
ひとり坐りし留守番のその嫗こそさみしけれ。

耳もきこえず、眼も見えず、かくて五月となりぬれば、
微かに匂ふ綿くづのそのほこりこそゆかしけれ。
硝子戸棚に白骨のひとり立てるも珍らかに、
水路のほとり月光の斜に射すもしをらしや。

糸車、糸車、しづかに黙す手の紡ぎ、
その物思やはらかにめぐる夕べぞわりなけれ。

Since the scene does not shift from one place to another, the implied oberver
in this poem might seem even less palpable than the presence which we
imagined to be drifting along in the boat in *Waterway*. In that poem the
implied observer and the assumed figure in the boat both imparted a unity
to what might otherwise be mainly a haunting tableau evoked in subdued
language.

I should mention several references in *Spinning Wheel* that might be
troublesome. The observer of the action described in the poem evidently
stands outside a former public clinic, the skeleton enclosed in a case adding

a confirming note to this identification. What the squashes are doing there on the floor I cannot say in specific terms. However, readers of Hakushû will recognize their poet in the two colors he has given these items.

With its focus on the old, blind woman and its mention of a skeleton, the poem gives rise to thoughts of mortality. Indirect in method and elusive in meaning, *Spinning Wheel* prompts other philosophic musings. The wheel, in turning back upon itself, becomes emblematic of the passage of time; and the woman, occupying with her wheel the poem's very center, partakes of the symbolism as her memories too turn back upon themselves. Perhaps the words which open the final line, 'sono monoomoi', refer to the musings of the observer — these musings joining those of the old woman in the revolving pattern that constitutes the poem.

As mentioned before, a Hakushû poem often compels one to sense the drift of its words by intuition. Absent a speaker who might serve in roles ranging from reliable guide to focus of irony, the poem exists for the reader more on its own, as it were. I would argue an advantage for certain modern Japanese poems because of this orientation. There is much to be said for an art which offers the reader experience unmediated by an explicit persona. When the poem vibrates with symbolism, as it does in *Waterwheel* and in *Spinning Wheel*, one must deal with complexity, albeit of a different sort from that afforded by the manipulation of speaker and persona in modern Western poetry.

By dividing the four poems into two sets, I have perhaps done an injustice to *Blue Dragonfly* and *Enemy*. I admire both poems and find in them certain qualities which they share with *Waterway* and *Spinning Wheel*. Let me pose the following question for discussion: Have I missed certain elements of these two poems that would rescue them for me too from that slightly dismissive category, 'descriptive lyricism?'

References

Kitahara Hakushû. 1970. *Kitahara Hakushû Shû*. Tokyo: Kadokawa Shoten.
This selection of Hakushû's poetry contains authoritative texts of the four poems discussed in this paper. It includes the most detailed notes available on specific works from the poet. The four poems can be located in this volume on the following pages:

Spinning Wheel, 324; *Blue Dragonfly*, 327; *Enemy*, 332; *Waterway*, 356

Varieties of National Narrative in Meiji Japan

Roy Starrs

The idea of literary works as 'national narratives' which contribute in some significant way to the building of a nation's sense of itself has very ancient precedents in Japan, as in other countries and cultures. Just as Virgil is said to have written the *Aeneid* so that Rome would have a national narrative to compete with those of Greece, the *Iliad* and the *Odyssey*, so the oldest extant works of Japanese literature, the *Kojiki* and the *Nihongi*, were compiled by order of the imperial court so that Japan would have a national narrative to rival those of a much older and bigger country, China. As the centuries passed by, literature came to assume an even more predominant role as a pillar of Japanese cultural nationalism: since so much of the nation's culture was imported from continental Asia, it was to the native language and literature that nationalists often turned in their search for the defining characteristics of 'Japaneseness'. We may see this brand of cultural nationalism at work especially in the Tokugawa nativist scholars and revivalists of Shintô such as Kamo Mabuchi (1697-1769) and Motoori Norinaga (1730-1817), who held up literary classics such as the *Man'yôshû*, the *Tale of Genji* and the *Shinkokinshû* as pure expressions of Japanese sentiment — or, in Mabuchi's words, as the 'voice of our divine land'.

When Japanese writers began to read and translate Western literature in the late nineteenth century, they were confronted with some new and quite splendid visions of what a national narrative might be. This, of course, was the golden age of the novel in the West, and it was also the golden age of nationalism — a fervent nationalism based on early nineteenth century romantic, semimystical ideals of the 'national soul'. Nineteenth century nationalism joined together with the nineteenth century novel to produce some very impressive examples of what we might call the 'national novel' — the paragon of them all, of course, being Tolstoy's *War and Peace*, which is undoubtedly the greatest national narrative of the nineteenth century, not only a masterful novel in the usual sense of the term but an epic poem celebrating the Russian people's victory over the invading armies of Napoleon.

On a less sublime level but nonetheless a significant influence in late nineteenth century Japan were the British political novels by writers such as Anthony Trollope and Benjamin Disraeli, which were national narratives of another sort — hardly heroic or epic but still implicit celebrations of the British form of parliamentary democracy. These enjoyed a considerable vogue for a time among Japanese intellectuals, and helped to convince them to take fiction seriously. As the influential mid-Meiji apologist of the modern novel, Tsubouchi Shôyô (1859-1935), pointed out at the beginning of his career, Japanese intellectuals were in the habit of looking down on fiction as an inferior form of literature, since much of Tokugawa fiction had consisted of pornography, adventure stories or simple-minded Confucian didactic tales. The fact that Disraeli in particular, a British prime minister, wrote novels and was apparently proud of doing so — since he did not try to hide the fact, as a Tokugawa gentleman would do, by taking a *nom de plume* — this fact alone was impressive, but the novels themselves, which were among the first ever translated from English into Japanese, also impressed the educated Japanese readers of that day, because, between the lines of a conventional Victorian love story, they managed to squeeze in a serious political message.

Spurred by the obvious disparity between Western and Japanese images and practices of fiction, Tsubouchi published his stirring call to arms, *The Essence of the Novel* (*Shôsetsu shinzui*), in 1885, urging his fellow writers to improve the quality of their fiction so that 'we may finally be able to surpass in quality the European novels ...'. This was obviously an appeal to nationalism and the competitive spirit of the Japanese, but the really surprising thing is, when we survey the bulk of serious literature produced during the Meiji period, we find little overt nationalism in it. Despite both the nineteenth century Western and the traditional native models of national narrative, and despite the obvious pressures on Meiji writers to contribute in their own way to the great nation-building project of their age, no Japanese Tolstoys arose to celebrate their nation's heroic struggle against and ultimate victory over the nineteenth century imperialist West, which had threatened to reduce the divine land to the status of a colony. Japan would have to wait a few more generations for the appearance of a major novelist inspired by this kind of gung-ho nationalism — namely, Mishima Yukio. There were, on the other hand, quite a few imitation Disraelis who tried to contribute to the national political debate. The first of these, Sakurada Momoe, declared his belief that 'the novel was the best means patriotic citizens had at their disposal of enlightening the people and reforming society ...' (Keene 1984:76). Unfortunately, though, the Meiji political novel *per se* cannot be said to have reached any great heights as literature —

although, according to one count, about 250 of them were published. Of these, some 220 were written between 1880 and 1890, when the establishment of the national assembly many of these writers had been campaigning for seemed to remove their *raison d'être* as political novelists. As for the literary quality of these 'political novels', few rose above the level of Tokugawa *gesaku* light fiction, using the same kind of material — for instance, the contest of several lovers for the same *geisha* — but trying, in a very heavy-handed way, to turn it into a modern political allegory: in Toda Kindô's *Jôkai haran* (*Storms in the Sea of Passions*), for instance, the *geisha* is named Oken (rights) and her favorite lover has the unlikely name of Wakoku-ya Minji (popular government in Japan), and when the happy couple is finally united in marriage their wedding reception is at a place whose name suggests the word *kokkai* or 'national assembly' (Keene 1984:78). Of course, it is all too easy for us to make fun of these works now, and their authors must be given credit for at least trying, in an age of strict censorship, to use fiction to communicate a serious political message, which was usually in favor of democratic reform. But even among their contemporaries, some of the leading writers were already strongly dissatisfied with the literary quality of the Meiji political novel. In 1887 Tokutomi Sohô published *A Criticism of the Political Novels Recently in Vogue*, a remarkably lucid and prescient diagnosis of the faults typical of these novels: wooden characters who are merely mouth-pieces of the author, poorly structured and improbable plots, lack of variety in their incidents and characters and, generally, intellectual and psychological superficiality.

But already when Sohô published this criticism a more successfully modern and serious literature had begun to appear in Japan. When one surveys this higher quality literature, however, one is surprised to find how much of it is written in opposition to the brave new world of Meiji and, implicitly, to the national government responsible for creating that world. One of the most familiar narrative patterns in the best Meiji literature or literature written later about the Meiji period is the story of a sensitive man, usually of samurai extraction, who finds that his traditional values are no longer relevant in the crass new society of social-climbing commoners, and this leads him to suffer alienation, failure and sometimes even suicide. This is the basic plot-line of the very first Meiji novel of significance, Futabatei's *Ukigumo* (*Drifting Cloud*, 1886-89), and it would be repeated numerous times again, most notably in the novels of Natsume Sôseki (1867-1916), and even as late as the 1930's in Shimazaki Tôson's *Yoakemae* (*Before the Dawn*). Obviously some of the best Meiji writers could not bring themselves to welcome the rapid 'modernization' they witnessed as an unmixed blessing, even if it did mean that Japan would become a stronger and wealthier nation. No doubt this had much to do with the fact that modernization also meant Westernization and thus, apparently, the destruction of much in the traditional culture that literary men in particular were prone to value. But it should be added that the absence of the large-scale, celebratory kind of national narrative may be ascribed not only to the historical fact of the painfulness of Japan's sudden transition from a 'feudal' to a 'modern' society, but also to a more purely literary factor, which may be summed up as 'the lyrical tendency of serious Japanese literature'. The nineteenth century Western novel as developed by writers such as Balzac and Dickens was able to present, through the multiplicity of its characters and the diversity of its scenes, a large-scale, panoramic view of national life in a particular historical period, and thus is easily viewed as a form of 'national narrative' — even when it did not address a specifically 'national' issue, such as Napoleon's invasion of Russia. But Japanese writers seemed to find this kind of novel very difficult to write. The mainstream tradition of their literature had generally followed a lyrical mode: that is, literature as an expression of the writer's personal feelings, with value being placed above all on the depth and sincerity of that feeling (as we can see by the use of such critical terms as *makoto*, *mono no aware*, *jun-bungaku*, and so on). The most famous consequence of this in the Meiji period was the group of writers known as naturalists, who were supposedly inspired by Emile Zola's school of naturalism, which aimed to bring a new level of realism into the novel by depicting human behavior — including sexual behavior — in a more ruthlessly objective, scientific way than had been common in earlier nineteenth century fiction. Whereas the French naturalists, however, applied this new level of realism to an analysis of society as a whole, their Japanese counterparts applied it mainly to an analysis of themselves, writing 'I-novels' which contained, for instance, scandalous revelations about their own sex lives.

Even Futabatei Shimei, although he was a long-time student and translator of Russian literature, and thus well acquainted with Tolstoy's masterpiece, never attempted to write anything like a Japanese *War and Peace*. Are we to say, then, that the Meiji period — to our great surprise, given that it was perhaps the most frenetic age of nation-building known to history — produced no 'national narratives' of any significant literary quality? If one were to regard the large-scale nineteenth century Western model as the only acceptable model of the national narrative, then one would have to adopt this point of view. But, of course, developments in the theory and practice of fiction, especially of the short story, since the nineteenth century have taught us the various ways in which fiction may take on metaphorical or symbolic overtones, and thus encompass very large areas of meaning within even the smallest areas of text. Using this approach, even a short story can present a meaningful image of an entire nation or period.

Just as Meiji poets took easily to the goals and methods of the French symbolists — because of the long tradition of symbolism in Japanese poetry — so also the best Meiji fiction writers took easily to the new approaches of symbolic fiction, and thus were able to write their own style of what we might describe as national narrative on an intimate scale. Mori Ôgai's short story, *Fushinchû* (*Under Reconstruction*, 1910), is an excellent case in point. At first glance it appears to present a slight if charming vignette from the love life of an upper-class Meiji gentleman, a government official: in a small hotel under reconstruction, he has a brief reencounter with a former lover, a German woman now touring the world as a professional singer. On this immediate level it is a beautifully written, understated story of faded love: the couple find that they cannot rekindle the old flame — sadly, time has taken its toll on their former passion. But the story also works brilliantly on another level: as Ôgai's image of the uneasy mixture of Eastern and Western culture in late Meiji Japan. As the government official himself tells the German lady, not just the hotel, with its awkward mélange of Western and Japanese décor, but the whole country is 'under reconstruction', and the very awkwardness of their meeting, the result not just of lapsed time but of culture clash, echoes the awkwardness of Japan's encounter with the West.

The symbolic approach to fiction, though, was not so much a matter of particular techniques — such as Ôgai's use of synecdoche here, a hotel representing the nation as a whole — as it was a whole new attitude towards fiction as symbolic. Any element of the story can function as a symbol — even the characters themselves. Perhaps the first significant example of this kind of symbolic use of character was the 'superfluous man' of mid 19th century Russian literature, an early symbol of the modern social disease of alienation, appearing in writers such as Lermontov, Gogol, Goncharov and Turgenev. It was precisely from this rather nihilistic tradition of Russian literature, rather than from Tolstoy, that Futabatei Shimei learned what proved to be of most use to him in writing the novel already mentioned, *Drifting Cloud*. As Futabatei himself said, when he began to study Russian literature, he had two motives: a nationalistic one, to know an important potential enemy, and an aesthetic one, to enjoy reading great literature, but soon, he wrote, 'my nationalistic fervor was quieted and my passion for literature alone burned on' (Futabatei 1967:20). It seems that much the same was true for many Meiji writers. Nevertheless, this did not mean that Futabatei became a pure aesthete without any concern for the state of the nation. On the contrary, *Drifting Cloud* may be read as a bitter criticism of the social values encouraged by the Meiji oligarchs. Futabatei's anti-hero, Bunzô, who loses both his job and his fiancée, is on his way to becoming a superfluous man because he is too honest, in the old samurai way, to prosper or even to survive in the ruthlessly competitive society of early Meiji, a *nouveau riche* society of self-made men. As I have said, Futabatei's alienated anti-hero, his superfluous man, became an archetypal character in modern Japanese literature, reappearing again and again in different forms in the work of many of the major writers of 20th century Japan, including Sôseki, Akutagawa, Shiga, Tanizaki and Kawabata. Obviously, then, we might say that Futabatei created a powerful national symbol in this character, and that his novel, *Drifting Cloud*, came to be accepted, by Japanese intellectuals at least, as a compelling national narrative, albeit of a negative or critical rather than a positive or celebratory kind.

Once we accept this more comprehensive idea of a national narrative — that is, as any work of fiction which attempts to present an image of the nation as a whole, whether literal or symbolic, positive or negative — then it becomes clear that the two major writers who appeared in the late Meiji period, Mori Ôgai and Natsume Sôseki, were national narrators *par excellence* and — a point I would particularly like to emphasize — they were national narrators in a way that the writers who came after them were not. Ôgai, for instance, was so constantly preoccupied with the state of the nation that even in a story which seems entirely personal, *Hannichi* (*Half a Day*, 1909), which is about the tensions between his own wife and mother, we still feel larger issues looming in the background. Thus a very perceptive critic, Mishima Yukio, was moved to remark after reading this story: 'I believe it is true to say that Ôgai saw in his own household the failure of Japan's modern age' (Keene 1984:359).

At any rate, to illustrate the way in which both Ôgai and Sôseki were sensitive readers of the pulse of the nation, one could do no better than examine their responses to the disturbing events of late Meiji. The political situation of the late Meiji period was rather volatile: on the one side, a rising tide of liberal democratic and socialist opposition to the status quo, on the other side an increasingly authoritarian and oppressive government of elder statesmen. The climax came in 1911 with the execution of the distinguished socialist leader, Kôtoku Shûsui, along with others, because of their supposed plot to assassinate the emperor.

Ôgai himself had felt the oppressive weight of intolerant authority just the year before when his novel *Vita Sexualis*, a satire on the naturalists' ob-

session with sex, was banned by the censors and Ôgai was personally re-
primanded by the Vice-Minister of War. As a high official himself in the Imperial Army Medical Corps, he of course could not afford to openly criticize
what he considered to be the irrational behavior of higher officials. But his
stories of this period clearly reflect his dissatisfaction — using the symbolic
fictional approach he had by now mastered. *Chinmoku no tô* (*The Tower of Silence*, 1910), for instance, borrows an image from India — the tall towers on
Malabar Hill in which the Parsis dispose of their dead — to symbolize the
way the Meiji government silences people who read, translate or write
'dangerous books', which are defined as 'books about naturalism and so-
cialism'. Ôgai ends the story with a bold rhetorical flourish, condemning all
forms of censorship:

Both art and the pursuit of learning must be seen to be dangerous if you look with
the conventional eye of the Parsi clan. Why is this? In every country and every age,
crowds of reactionaries lurk behind those who walk new paths awaiting an un-
guarded moment. And when the opportunity arises they inflict persecution. Only
the pretext changes, depending upon the country and the times. 'Dangerous Western books' is no more than such a pretext (Ôgai 1994:221).

Just two years after this story was written Ôgai's work underwent a dramatic
transformation, and in an unexpectedly conservative direction — surprisingly
for a writer who had seemed so pro-modern and pro-reform in his scientific
rationalism. The immediate cause was the death of the Emperor Meiji and
the subsequent *junshi* or ritual suicide of his vassal, General Nogi. Like many
of his contemporaries, Ôgai was deeply moved by both events: on the one
hand, the emperor's death bringing to an end a long and remarkable reign;
on the other hand, the general's suicide harking back to the samurai values
of an earlier age. These two events naturally produced a mood of nostalgia
in many people, but in Ôgai they seemed to have produced a lasting change
of heart. It was as if they shocked him into realizing what he really valued:
now that the world of traditional, heroic values seemed to be passing away,
he would devote himself as a writer to preserving its memory. The irony, of
course, is that Ôgai himself up to this point, as both a writer and a doctor,
had done his best to precipitate the very process of modernization which was
destroying the culture he most valued. But he was not alone in his ironic
ambivalence: in this too he was emblematic of the whole elite class to which
he belonged, the Meiji nation-builders.

Before 1912 there seemed to have been two Ôgais: the army officer, a descendant of samurai, and a high-ranking official in the Meiji establishment;

and, on the other hand, the writer, a sceptical rationalist and a lover of Western literature and philosophy, somewhat rebellious in spirit and anti-establishment in many of his attitudes. It was as if the army officer used writing as a means of escape from the oppressive confines of his official life. After 1912, though, the two persona seemed to come much closer together: the essential conservatism of the samurai-class army officer found expression in the writing of historical stories and biographies. For many Western readers, the earlier Ôgai may seem a more attractive writer. But Japanese critics generally regard his historical works as his major achievement. One thing certainly may be agreed upon: in the fiction Ôgai wrote in the last decade of his life, modern Japanese literature finally gained a national narrative of a positive, celebratory kind.

In the four days immediately following General Nogi's *junshi*, Ôgai wrote a story, *Okitsu Yagoemon no isho* (*The Last Testament of Okitsu Yagoemon*, 1912), which is a moving tribute to this ultimate act of loyalty: the faithful samurai Yagoemon commits *junshi* to follow his master into death and, like General Nogi, to atone for a mistake he has committed in the distant past. But what is presented as even more admirable is that, like Socrates paying off his debts before his death, Yagoemon allows himself the privilege of committing *junshi* only after he has discharged his various worldly obligations — even leaving behind enough money to pay for his own cremation. In short, he is a paragon of the samurai virtues of loyalty, courage and dutifulness, and, in the second version of the story, published a year after the first, Ôgai makes it clear that he was rewarded with a brilliant posterity — in proof of which we are offered a genealogical table of almost Biblical proportions, down to the eleventh generation!

Since Ôgai's day, of course, samurai stories of this kind have become a standard part of Japan's popular national myth, functioning in much the same way as do Hollywood Westerns in the USA. But Ôgai's historical fiction is far above the standard: he performed an important service as a national narrator by raising the samurai story to a new level of intellectual and literary sophistication.

From our present point of view in the late 20th century we may judge a story like *Okitsu Yagoemon* to be anachronistic — or worse, potentially to have contributed by its apparent reverence for *bushidô* to the atavistic attitudes and behavior of the ultranationalists and militarists of the early Shôwa period. And it could be argued that, by retreating to the past and its traditional values, Ôgai was trying to escape further censure from increasingly intolerant authorities — in effect, caving in to their intimidation and sacrificing his writing for the sake of his career. But even if this were true or partly true, it would not vitiate the literary quality of Ôgai's historical literature. And when we read that literature as a whole, the impression we are given is far from that of a mindless, reactionary traditionalism. He did not abandon his modern education, his scientific rationalism or his critical intelligence after 1912. In fact, the very next story he wrote, *Abe Ichizoku* (*The Abe Clan* 1913) is a critical, even satirical treatment of the practice of *junshi*: when a certain daimyô dies, so many men end up killing themselves — even men who hardly knew the daimyô — that we have a farcical as well as tragic *reductio ad absurdum* of the whole custom; on the other hand, choosing not to commit *junshi* in this society could lead to equally tragic consequences, as we are shown by what happens to Abe Michinobu. Even though he is ordered not to kill himself, a conflict arises between his samurai duty to obey orders and his samurai sense of personal honor: troubled by rumors that he has failed to commit *junshi* because of cowardice, he finally feels obliged to kill himself in front of his five sons. But the matter does not end there: persecuted by the new daimyô, Abe's whole family is ultimately destroyed, the young and the old, men, women and children, and the story ends with a bloodbath of more than Shakespearean proportions. But with a very modern sense of absurdity rather than with any cathartic sense of tragic greatness; as Ôgai writes of the final fighting in the Abe mansion: 'Just as street fighting is far uglier than fighting in the field, the situation here was even more ghastly: a swarm of bugs in a dish devouring one another'. (Ôgai 1977: 66)

In fact, when one surveys the bulk of Ôgai's historical stories and biographies, one finds that most of them celebrate more quiet virtues than the heroic ones demonstrated in *junshi*. This is especially true of the *shiden* or historical biographies: one author of a recent study of them has aptly characterized their subjects as 'paragons of the ordinary'. (Marcus 1993) Although samurai of the Tokugawa period, they epitomize not so much the martial virtues as the Confucian/samurai virtues of a time of peace, leading quiet lives of moderate, usually scholarly, achievement. These historical biographies are far from being 'blood-and-guts' samurai adventure tales; indeed, the problem with them for many readers may be the blandness of their central characters and the uneventfulness of the lives portrayed. In *Shibue Chûsai*, for instance, Ôgai commemorates the life of a now-forgotten samurai-physician and scholar of that name, whose career, Ôgai felt, 'strangely resembled my own' (Marcus 1993). He celebrates Chûsai's devotion to obscure areas of scholarship such as the study of samurai genealogies as well as his more conventional samurai virtues such as his loyalty to his clan. Chûsai was a man who lived a good life but did not achieve any lasting fame. In rescuing him from obscurity, Ôgai, uniquely among modern writers, created a new order of national narrative, one that celebrates lives of ordinary goodness and achievement. To give further emphasis to this point, he continues the story long past Chûsai's death, to show how he lived on in his descendants and disciples. Thus we are given a powerful sense of the great flow of national life, continuing on from generation to generation, in an undramatic but nonetheless moving way. In this sense it might be said that many of Ôgai's historical works are fundamentally ahistorical rather than anachronistic, in that they aim to present an essentially timeless image of Japanese life as it has existed over many centuries — and still perhaps continues to exist at some subterranean level. A good expression of this may be found in the story *Jiisan Baasan* (*Old Man, Old Woman*, 1915), a simple but moving account of a woman's loyalty to her husband, a samurai who was sent into exile for a rash act of violence. The faithful wife waits thirty-seven years to be reunited with him, and the couple spend their last few years living together happily and idyllically in a small cottage. Although the story is set in the Tokugawa period, it has the timeless atmosphere and symbolic power of a fairy tale. As Ishikawa Jun once wrote:

The two central characters and their fates stand concretely before us, and the world described in the work seems to be something eternal. It is, so to speak, riding the tide of the lives that Japanese have led without break from ancient times to the present (Keene 1984:375).

In other words, it is a form of national narrative which attempts to present a timeless, archetypal image of national life — as do fairy tales or folk tales.

It is interesting to compare Ôgai's literary response to the end-of-Meiji events — especially General Nogi's *junshi* — with Natsume Sôseki's: Sôseki's is far more time-bound. That is, in his 1914 novel, *Kokoro*, he emphasizes the anachronistic nature of the general's act. Why? Because his purpose in *Kokoro* is not so much to celebrate the Japanese tradition, as Ôgai does in *Okitsu Yagoemon*, as to mourn its passing; his mood is elegiac rather than heroic. Thus he emphasizes the fact that the general's act belongs to a now-dead tradition. In the climactic final pages of the novel, when the man referred to as 'Sensei' explains his reasons for committing suicide, he explicitly identifies himself with General Nogi as a man of the past, and tells the young narrator that he reached this decision just two or three days after hearing of the general's suicide. Then he adds:

Perhaps you will not understand clearly why I am about to die, no more than I can fully understand why General Nogi killed himself. You and I belong to different eras, and so we think differently. There is nothing we can do to bridge the gap between us (Sôseki 1957:246).

In contrast, then, to Ôgai's apparent belief in certain timeless features of the Japanese national character and mentality, Sôseki's protagonist subscribes to a kind of historical determinism: especially at a time of rapid modernization, each age has such different values that there is a mutual incomprehension between the different generations. And Sensei identifies himself so closely with the Meiji era that he feels that he cannot survive beyond it. 'On the night of the Imperial Funeral', he writes quite majestically, 'I sat in my study and listened to the booming of the cannon. To me, it sounded like the last lament for the passing of an age' (Sôseki 1957:246). But, as it turns out, the booming cannon also sounds his own death-knell, for as he himself confesses:

I felt as though the spirit of the Meiji era had begun with the Emperor and had ended with him. I was overcome with the feeling that I and the others, who had been brought up in that era, were now left behind to live as anachronisms. I told my wife so. She laughed and refused to take me seriously. Then she said a curious thing, albeit in jest: 'Well then, *junshi* is the solution to your problem (Sôseki 1957: 245).

In this way Sôseki consciously and explicitly creates a correspondence between his characters and crucial events in their lives on the one hand and, on the other hand, important figures and events in national history. A novel such as *Kokoro* thus becomes a symbolic national narrative — but not of Ôgai's positive, celebratory kind; rather it is a national narrative in an elegiac mode. We may conclude from this as from other of Sôseki's works that he was much more pessimistic than Ôgai about the survival of traditional Japanese values in a rapidly Westernizing and modernizing Japan.

Whether in a positive or negative form, however, both Ôgai and Sôseki were exemplary national narrators in their continual engagement with issues of national relevance and in their continual effort to present an image of the nation as they saw it. One of the key questions in the history of modern Japanese literature must be: why were their immediate successors in the Taishô period so noticeably deficient in this area, despite the first tentative budding of what is known as Taishô democracy — which one would have expected not only to encourage but to demand the active engagement of writers in a public or civic discourse? Yet Taishô writers such as Shiga Naoya, Akutagawa Ryûnosuke and Tanizaki Jun'ichirô are remarkably inward-looking, almost exclusively concerned with their own psychological states, seemingly uninterested in the state of the nation as a whole. Was there something about the spirit of the Meiji period which made writers more public-minded, or was it something in the character of Ôgai and Sôseki themselves? Perhaps this amounts to the same thing, since the two writers were very much products of their age. One could point, for instance, to the fact that, in contrast to the Taishô writers, who were more or less 'free agents', both Ôgai and Sôseki were in some sense 'government men' — Ôgai more than Sôseki, of course, but even Sôseki taught in government schools for much of his life and was awarded a government grant which enabled him to spend several years studying abroad. Since both writers benefitted in this way from government patronage, they undoubtedly felt more obliged to contribute to the nation through their writings than did later writers who existed more independently. But this too was very much part of the Meiji reality: as part of its nation-building strategy, the Meiji government sponsored rapid development in all areas of national life, which is why Ôgai was sent to Germany to study army medicine and Sôseki to England to study British literature — in line with the imperial injunction of 1868, which bade citizens to 'seek knowledge throughout the world in order to provide for the welfare of the state'. Thus in their lives as in their work, Ôgai and Sôseki were typical men of Meiji of the elite class, and inevitably felt deeply involved with the nation-building project of that age.

Whether by historical destiny or personal taste, however, the fact remains that Ôgai and Sôseki are still unrivalled as the national narrators of modern Japanese literature. No doubt this accounts for the phenomenon of their continuing popularity and prestige — not just with the Japanese establishment, which is happy to use their images on the national currency, but with the Japanese reading public at large. From a strictly literary or aesthetic point of view, there are probably modern Japanese writers whose art of fiction is superior to theirs — for instance, Tanizaki or Kawabata. But neither Tanizaki nor Kawabata had anything like the sense of national purpose of the great Meiji writers. Because Ôgai and Sôseki confronted large issues of national identity in such a compelling way and at such a crucial moment in modern Japanese history, they continue to possess a moral authority beyond that of any other Japanese writers of the 20th century.

References

Futabatei Shimei. 1967. *Japan's First Modern Novel: Ukigumo*, translated by Marleigh Grayer Ryan. New York: Columbia University Press.

Keene, Donald. 1984. *Dawn to the West: Japanese Literature in the Modern Era: Fiction.* New York: Holt, Rinehart and Winston.

Marcus, Marvin. 1993. *Paragons of the Ordinary: The Biographical Literature of Mori Ogai.* Honolulu: University of Hawaii Press.

Mori, Ôgai. 1977. *The Incident at Sakai and Other Stories*, ed. by David Dilworth and J. Thomas Rimer. Honolulu: University of Hawaii Press.

Mori, Ôgai. 1994. *Youth and Other Stories*, ed. by J. Thomas Rimer. Honolulu: University of Hawaii Press.

Natsume, Sôseki. 1957. *Kokoro*, translated by Edwin McClellan. Tokyo: Tuttle.

Marriages Made in *Otogizôshi*

Lone Takeuchi

It is in the nature of the genre of *fairytales*, Japanese *otogizôshi*, Danish *eventyr* etc., to deal with fundamental universal human issues and to show the wonderful and invigorating array of possibilities for change, while at the same time delimiting the boundaries of what is possible in the society in which they are produced (Warner 1994:xvi). Because the universal features are so immediately apparent in fairytales, they tend to dominate our readings and indeed the scholarly systematization of tales, overshadowing the tradition-specific variation. What follows is a small-scale demonstration of this point, drawing attention to how one such universal association of thematic elements is featured in the specific tradition of classic *otogizôshi* spanning the four centuries between 1300 and 1700.

The thematic association I have in mind is the combination of success or happiness with marriage. It is easily appreciated that this association is probably common to tale traditions everywhere: one need only to consider the similarities between the Danish folk-tale *Klods-Hans*, perhaps best known as retold by Hans Christian Andersen, and the so-called *gekokujô* tales, such as *Saru-Genji sôshi* or *Kootoko no sôshi*, in the *otogizôshi* tradition. Yet on close reading, different traditions expound different social and moral visions. In relation to the theme of marriage, traditions may vary, among other things, as to which occasion or ritual within marriage in its widest sense is regarded as the pivotal one, beyond which happiness is likely to ensue, and a happy ending therefore appropriately can be introduced. In the European traditions that point is the wedding, and the association of marriage with happiness receives its typical expression in the Happy Ending: 'they were married and lived happily ever after', etc. In *otogizôshi*, by contrast, the pivotal occasion of *enmusubi* is the birth of a child, as I wish to show below.

The *otogizôshi* tradition is not monolithic. It is for instance possible to perceive as a minor strand within it the beginnings of the idealized representation of the *yomeiri* marriage conceived as a sequence from *miai* to *miyamairi*, which is also found later in Edo literature. The second half of the seventeenth century saw a peak of permutations of narrative elements as the performed-oral-written *otogizôshi* tradition was reshaped into a written literary genre in stories by Saikaku and others. One crucial aspect of this transformation consisted of questioning or inverting the assumptions of the *otogizôshi*.[1] In 1686 (Teikyô 3) Saikaku, apparently spurred on by the success of collections of stories on filial piety, and in particular the publication of *Accounts of Filial Children of this Country (Honchô kôshi-den (1684 (Teikyô 1))* written by Fujii Ransai, a disciple of the philosopher Yamazaki Ansai, produced an anti-collection *Twenty Unfilial Children of this Country (Honchô nijû fukô)* in which he turned a great many *otogizôshi* motifs upside down in grotesque, sometimes grim ways (not unlike the modern inversion of fairy tales found in *Little Red Ridinghood* by Roald Dahl). In one of these, a silk merchant and his wife settle the matter of the marriage of their daughter to a cloth merchant by quoting a proverb:

A horse is the best company for a horse, — and so is a silk merchant for a cloth merchant (*Muma wa mumazure, kinuya gofukuya sa mo arubeshi*).[2]

Yet however familiar or commonsensical parents deciding the marriage of their child by this kind of reasoning may seem, such cases are, if not totally absent in *otogizôshi*, at least uncommon. In fact, I have come across only one such example, *Saru no sôshi (The Tale of the Monkey)* from the end of the sixteenth century. In the opening scene of this tale the monkey head-priest of Hie (/Hiyoshi) Shrine decides to marry his daughter to a fellow monkey from Enryakuji, rather than to a *daimyô*, who being human and a lay person, is a *gaijin* ('outsider') in the eyes of the head-priest.

The silk merchant's daughter in Saikaku's story is actually the direct opposite of a young girl in *otogizôshi*. Above all she is frightfully eloquent about what she wants:

A good man, no mother-in-law, someone belonging to the Hokke Sect, living in a house that is in a decorous business (*Otoko yoku, shûtome naku, onaji shû no hoke nite, kirei naru shôbai no ie no gyôji wo*).

Not surprisingly, she invites disaster on her indulgent family — there is after all nothing innovative in Saikaku's moral views. In *Saru no sôshi*, however,

---

1. A comparison with the contemporary transition in France represented by Perrault's *Contes* (cf. Warner 1994) might yield interesting results.
2. Ihara, Saikaku: *Ato no hagetaru yomeiri nagamochi*.

the father of the bride is, in fact, the main character who initiates and con-
trols the action. The matter of the *en* having been settled, there follows a
series of celebrations from *yomeiri* to *miyamairi*, that is, from the first meeting
of the bride and the groom (there is no *miai*) to the presentation of their
first-born in the shrine. As a narrative theme, *yomeiri* around 1600 probably
still possessed the charm of novelty and this would partly justify the emphasis on the celebrations of the *yomeiri* and *miyamairi*. The romantic aspect
of love and the birth of a son receives a mere three lines of about ten pages,
and these events seem to be mentioned only to stress that they are
sanctioned by the Sannô Deity of Hie, the divine authority, which in this tale
merges with parental authority.[3]

With *Saru no sôshi* we may well be at the beginning of a conceptualization
of a new ideal of *enmusubi*, certainly its first representation in a scroll. This
ideal of *yomeiri* marriage is represented as the fruit of unchallenged paternal
judgement prudently aiming at a marriage of equals and seems to have come
into its own only during the Edo Period. Around 1700, there appears to have
been a boom in *yome* (bride) and *yomeiri*, judging from the dozens of titles
beginning with *yome(iri)* listed in the *Kokusho sômokuroku* dating from around
that time. Among the more readily available are the etiquette books, *Onna
chôhôki* (*Valuable [Etiquette] Book for Women*), 1692 (Genroku 5), and *Yomedori
chôhôki* (*Valuable [Etiquette] Book for Taking a Wife*) from 1697 (Genroku 10) by
Endô Genkyû, both of which present advice on the proprieties of the *yomeiri*
marriage from *miai* to *miyamairi*. It is, however, not until the *akahon*, booklets
produced for women and children in the eighteenth century and early nineteenth century (in *Kinsei kodomo no ehon-shû*), that we once again find a humorous representation of marriage of rats, cats, ghosts, etc., reminiscent of
Saru no sôshi. It has been suggested that such booklets were intended as jolly,
lighthearted versions of the *chôhôki*, the didactic purpose being clouded by
humorous details (Morishita 1989). Crucially, certain conditions are always
the same in these stories. Above all, marriage must be one of equals, that is
in this context between the same species: thus, rat marries rat, ghost marries
ghost, etc. Furthermore, the fixed format — eleven to twelve pictures with
simple dialogue just like modern cartoons — dictates equal narrative weight
on a fixed sequence of scenes: father and go-between discuss and decide;

3. *Saru no sôshi* is, however, not a prescriptive Confucian text. On a closer reading the
   yomeiri style marriage here turns out to be a vehicle for the celebration of the authority
   of the syncretistic Sannô deity (Takeuchi 1996).

Figure 1. Confinement scene, tracing from
Bakemono yomeiri (ca. 1750).

miai; exchange of betrothal gifts (*yuinô*); return gifts; bride dressing up;
dowry procession; preparing food for the banquet; arrival of bride; banquet;
birth of a boy (Figure 1), and finally, *miyamairi*.

The representation of *yomeiri* in *Saru no sôshi* appears then to anticipate
a Tokugawa ideal. It contrasts with the majority of *otogizôshi* which expound
a different code of behaviour: parents are seldom, if ever, in control of
events, and parental authority never goes completely unquestioned, etc.
Nevertheless, the view of *enmusubi* as constituting an integrated sequence
happily concluded only by the birth of a child (mostly a boy) is essentially
the same, as I would like to show in the following.[4] I have used as the

---

4. Ôshima 1967:95 briefly makes the point that *enmusubi* in *otogiziôshi* is constituted by a
   sequence of events from *miai* to the birth of the child. In fact, this conceptualization
   may well be basic to the Japanese tradition more generally, cf. that the birth of a child
   was the crucial event in a relationship also in the *tsumadoi-kon* as early as the Heian
   Period, as it might prompt a change to shared living arrangements for the parents (cf.
   McCullough 1967).

epicentre of reference *Otogibunko* (with the alternative title *Otogizôshi*), the collection of twenty-three tales probably produced in the middle of the seventeenth century and reissued during the Kyôhô era (1716-36) when it was marketed as an indispensable collection of tales for brides.[5] The approach taken here is to view individual motifs or patterns in relation to the whole of the tale, and to interpret individual tales in relation to a larger number of tales — in the first instance, the tales of *Otogibunko* — but also to other tales, known to have been written or printed during the seventeenth century — although they may, of course, originate much earlier (cf. Bottigheimer 1986, and Pigeot 1987).

It goes without saying that the association of marriage with success is often found in tales of a young person about to enter adulthood. Although there is some variation, such tales tend to be quite gender-specific on the point of how to achieve success: boys and girls act and speak according to two different codes of behaviour. Arguably, boys do not have more freedom of action; they simply have to meet a different set of expectations. Thus, they must show their independence by distancing themselves from their parents, leaving home in quest of success. This is true not only for the successful *gekokujô* (socially upward mobile) male characters, *Kootoko*, *Issunbôshi*, *Saru Genji*, *Monokusa Tarô*; the case of *saishô* in *Hachikazuki* suggests that it is a more general condition. In fact, the very moment *saishô* decides to leave home to follow Hachikazuki, the girl he loves, the bowl springs off her head

---

5. There is tangible proof of the popularity of these *otogizôshi* throughout the seventeenth century, as they are all listed as being in print in contemporary catalogues of published books (*Zôho shoseki mokuroku sakusha-zuke daii*) between 1670 (Kanbun 10) and 1699 (Genroku 12).

Since most *otogizôshi* have been handed down as individual texts, the origins and occasion of which little or nothing is known, *Otogibunko* is the closest that we have to a collection of contemporary literary taste, offering fairly consistent social and moral visions, even if not to the extent of the Tales by the Grimm Brothers. Of the twenty three tales in *Otogibunko*, five are not known in earlier versions, *Kowatagitsune*, *Nosezaru*, *Nekozôshi*, *Issunbôshi*, and *Saiki*, and ten other stories exist in other versions from the Edo Period (Fujikake 1987:32-33). Although we know next to nothing about the compilation, the uniformity of illustrations and lay-out of *Otogibunko* suggests that it is the result of a well considered plan by an editorial mind. The illustrations in a simple Tosa-style are likely to represent imitations of painted scrolls, and it has been conjectured that the blocks were produced around the middle of the seventeenth century (Kan'ei (1624-40) or Kanbun (1661-73) Eras (Yoshida 1984:28). Seven tales exist in what is presumably seventeenth-century hand-coloured 'tanroku-bon' (in fact, distinctly polychromatic) versions of the same printing: *Bunshô*, *Komachi*, *Izumi shikibu*, *Nanakusa*, *Sazareishi*, *Onzôshi shimawatari*, *Shûtendôshi* (Fujikake 1987:24).

to reveal both her beauty and the hidden treasures. In the *gekokujô* tales, the male character's leaving home is narrated differently from tale to tale, but often either his parents or the community are unable or unwilling to support him. In the circumscribed manner of *otogizôshi* discourse, there is the hint of poverty. Thus, Issunbôshi's parents more or less directly let him understand that he is a burden rather than a help to them, and Monokusa Tarô, the apparent lazy village fool, has to be told in plain words to leave and not be a burden to the other villagers. In contrast to these tales, the tale of *Yokobue* in *Otogibunko* illustrates what happens when the parents' will is allowed to prevail: Takiguchi resigns himself to his parents' wish not to see Yokobue anymore, but thereby causes her death.

A girl may refuse to marry, as Bunshô's daughters in *Bunshô sôshi* do, but she cannot leave home except under special circumstances. In *Otogibunko*, only Hachikazuki, who typically is rejected by her father and stepmother, gets away with that. The *otogizôshi* therefore seem to confirm the traditional association of gender and spatial dimensions, male with *hoka* (*soto*) and female with *uchi*, as found, for instance, in the slightly later popular moralizing works, such as *Hyakushô bunryôki* by Tokiwa Tanboku (1729 (Kyôhô 14)):

Men possess the virtue of Yang and manifest themselves, women possess the virtue of Yin and hide themselves. For that reason men are active to the outside and women are in charge of the inside/home. Thus, for a wife to order her husband or for a husband to take orders from his wife, is contrary to the Yin and Yang Principle and therefore necessarily brings ruin to their family. Of this, there are quite a few examples in the past and the present (Tokiwa:269).

The means to success for the male characters is the traditional poetic expression of sensibility — sexuality (*irogonomi*).[6] The male protagonist always initiates courtship with a poem to which the woman must respond capably. Thus, the function of poetry in courtship is gender-specific, while the faculty for poetry is not.[7] When it comes to responding to a man's courtship a wo-

---

6. This feature of the *otogizôshi* tradition is firmly anchored in the Japanese (medieval) perception of artistic, and especially poetic, talent as a means of effecting metamorphosis, and in particular, as an instrument towards salvation in the Buddhist sense. In *otogizôshi* poetic talent provides the protagonist with a means to achieve his aim just like spells in Western tales. In fact, the performance of poetry often quite literally brings about the metamorphosis of the (lowly) character into a higher or sacred identity, in the same way as the lowly object of poetry is transformed into a symbol of spirituality, e.g. oranges into the moon (i.e. a means of salvation) in *Izumi shikibu*.

7. The modern reader may tend to focus on the fact that the ideal of upward social

man in *otogizôshi* has a choice to ponder, the outcome of which nearly always is the same: the woman decides to meet the man. When persuasion is needed there is more often appeal to religious, Buddhist concepts than to social conventions: to resist is sinful and will incur retribution. In *Nosezaru*, the lady is admonished not to be cold-hearted (*tsurenashi*) or stubborn (*kokorozuyoshi*). In *Saiki*, the woman decides to reply to the man's letter believing that she will otherwise be reborn without a tongue — a very harsh punishment given the significance of speech, and in particular *waka*, in the tales. It should be noted that the *otogizôshi* are committed, so to speak, to gentle persuasion. Bunshô's daughters in *Bunshô sôshi* have their minds set on marrying someone of exceptional beauty, talents and rank, while their father Bunshô is more than willing to settle for someone less ideal. Yet the daughters' wish prevails, and Bunshô has no cause for regret as he becomes the father-in-law of the emperor. Parental force invariably leads to disaster. In a story appearing inside *Saru-Genji*, the mother of a young girl (Tennyo) forces her to marry a suitor (Moritô) in order to avoid his resentment, but thereby drives her to suicide. In this connection another story of Saikaku's (*Musumezakari no chirizakura*) again presents an irresistible counterpoint to the code of behaviour in *otogizôshi*. A man and his wife have five daughters. The four older sisters named after the four seasons are married off by their parents, but one after the other dies during pregnancy before they can give birth. In the universe of the *otogizôshi* this line of events is not surprising given the parents' rather high-handed decisions on the marriages. However, when the parents, who regret having forced their fourth daughter to marry and thereby caused her death, advise the fifth daughter, Otome, to become a nun, she rebels: someone who has had the good fortune to be born a human (*ningen*) deserves to have a man. She runs away and marries a robber. But the retroactive morality of Saikaku is displayed in the ending: Otome leads her robber-husband to her parents' house, but, on the way back from the robbery, both fall to their death from a cliff (Ihara Saikaku:442).

It may be instructive to consider one tale in its entirety. *Issunbôshi* in *Otogibunko* is somewhat different from the modern version of the tale. It also presents a degree of variation on the above *gekokujô* tales in the sense that Issunbôshi, a *môshigo* — that is, a child born to elderly parents at the in-

---

mobility (*gekokujô*) is applied to male characters only and overlook that the women these protagonists court, apart from a *hakoirimusume* or two (e.g. the rabbit in *Nosezaru*), are poised, quite exacting women, apparently living a life of leisure without restricting parental presence (e.g. *Kootoko, Saru Genji* and *Monokusa Tarô*). — There are, however, no tales about how they became that way.

tervention of a deity, in this case of Sumiyoshi Daimyôjin — is essentially a trickster, more of a hero, less of a poet. Thus, he does not court by means of poetry or music, but effectively tricks *himegimi* into marrying him. He leads her father to believe that she has stolen some rice by smearing some around her mouth,[8] and the father orders her to leave home. That Isssunbôshi's behaviour represents a transgression is apparent only implicitly from his next move: he decides to take *himegimi* away from the capital, a movement which in the general spatial symbolism of *otogizôshi* as a rule indicates failure. The two are about to embark for his home in the country, when he redeems himself by slaying the demons.[9] He then promptly returns with *himegimi* to the capital and the tale ends happily:

... he [= Issunbôshi] became a *shôshô*, then a *chûnagon*. As his character and appearance from the outset were superior to other people, his reputation was impressive. The *saishô* [his father-in-law] heard about it and was pleased. Later three sons were born. He [/They] lived happily and flourished. In accordance with the pledge of the Sumiyoshi [Daimyôjin] he shall flourish and prosper all his days. I venture the opinion that it is most unlikely that there ever was a more auspicious story than this one (Ôshima 1974:401-2) (Figure 2).

By contrast, a girl leaves the family home only if forced to do so on the death of her mother and the subsequent presence of a stepmother (e.g. *Hachikazuki, Senju*). But whereas a male protagonist succeeds by a sudden display of poetic or musical ingenuity, such skills are not enough to bring a distressed female heroine out of her predicament. When Hachikazuki on her wanderings is asked by the provincial governor who takes pity on her, whether she has any skills (*nô*), her answer is:

No, I have no particular skills, except that I played *koto, biwa,* Japanese lute, *shô, hichiriki* and read *Kokinshû, Man'yôshû, Ise monogatari,* and the eight books of the

---

8. According to Ôshima (1967:49) the rice would be associated with the *mochi* which traditionally in the *tsumadoi-kon* was eaten on a man's third day visit to a woman, when their relationship was recognized.

9. Space interrelates with narrative patterns in *otogizôshi* to form a semiotic system (cf. Pigeot 1988). The tales under consideration all take place in two major narrative spaces. The capital (epitomized by the Court) as the locus of success and happiness attracts the protagonist (*Saru Genji, Monogusa Tarô, Kootoko*); failure, on the other hand, is connoted by the country (*inaka*) (e.g. *Kowatagitsune*) or religious retreat (*shukke*) (e.g. *Izumi shikibu*) or both. The consistency of the setting in *Otogibunko* in particular has been pointed out by Kuroda et al. 1990:17ff).

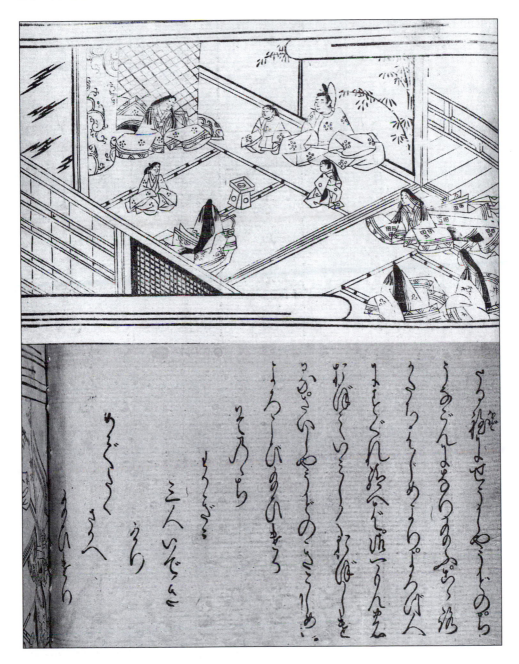

Figure 2. The final picture from the Otogibunko version of Issunbôshi. Notice that the auspicious concluding passage of the tale (cf. quote above) is given emphasis by being written in the drawn-out manner which is also used to highlight poetry (Reproduced by Courtesy of the Trustees of the British Library).

Lotus sutra and other sutras with my mother who brought me up with much loving care.

A somewhat inconsistent answer, one would have thought, but one which the governor immediately accepts: 'Well, with no special skills you can be incharge of the bath (*yudono*)'. (Ôshima 1974:84-85). This position is presumably enough to restore to her the respectability of a household (*uchi*) where she attracts the attention of the youngest son (*saishô*). Once she is courted by him, Hachikazuki can display her poetic skills to good effect. In a sense, therefore, the female voice in the tales is restricted, but perhaps not without a certain pointed irony.

Hachikazuki is traditionally considered a stepmother (*mamahaha*) tale. It has even been called a Japanese Cinderella tale (Mulhern 1979). The instigator of the action is, of course, the stepmother, but it should be noted that Hachikazuki, who declines to identify herself to her family-in-law in order not to bring shame on her father, is not immediately accepted as the governor's daughter-in-law and that the conflict with the mother-in-law, who has ambitions for her son, is acted out as a contest between sisters-in-law (*yomeawase*), which takes up a good deal more narrative space than the stepmother's persecutions. Her position secured, the tale concludes: '… as time went by, she had many sons (*kindachi* "young master") and her/their happiness knew no bounds' (Ôshima 1974:105). Eventually she is reunited with her father, another characteristic *otogizôshi* element. Other *otogizôshi* with female protagonists, e.g. *Senju*, follow a similar sequence of events. The wickedness of Senju's mother-in-law is all the more appalling as Senju and her husband have two sons, a fact which strongly suggests that a happy ending is in stall — which indeed it is, but not until Senju has died and been given a new lease on life with Kiyomizu Kannon's entreaties to Emma-ô. Incidentally, the contrast of these tales to *Ochikubo monogatari*, the classic Japanese stepmother tale, in which the protracted feud with the stepmother is set off by the welcoming parents-in-law, is striking. It has been noted by Ikeda Kikan (quoted in Mulhern 1979) that so-called stepmother tales suddenly increased towards the end of the Muromachi Period. Since a closer reading rather suggests their central theme to be the conflict with the mother-in-law (*shûtome*), their popularity might directly reflect the contemporary spread of the *yomeiri* marriage system where conflicts between daughter-in-law and mother-in-law in the same household would be particularly rife.

While children form part of the Happy Ending of tales such as *Issunbôshi* or *Hachikazuki*, their crucial function in making or breaking an *en* is often conveyed more clearly in a negative way in tales of transgression and punishment, such as *Kowatagitsune* or *Nezumi no sôshi*. Although in the oblique way of *otogizôshi* narration this is never made explicit, it would presumably be obvious to an audience familiar with the sanctioned morality of *otogizôshi* just outlined, that the lady fox in *Kowatagitsune* (*The Tale of the Fox from Kowata*) who falls so passionately in love with a captain (*chûjô*) in the capital, that she leaves the foxes' den without her parents' permission and transforms herself into a human being in order to attract his attention, is misbehaving and does not stand a chance. The captain's parents do welcome her, and she has a son by him, but not even her trusty nurse-maid can help her, when her son (*wakagimi*) on his third birthday is given a dog as present by the captain's nurse. A dog is the obvious animal to detect a transformed fox, and it is in line with the *otogizôshi* fondness for puns that *inu* 'dog' being homophonous with the verb *inu* 'goes away' suggests both the transgression which lies behind the fox's sad fate — namely that she left the foxes' den — and the fate that awaits her as she leaves the captain to return to Kowata mountain, from where she, having become a nun, watches her son grow up. Importantly, the fact that the occasion for the appearance of the dog is the son's birthday places *Kowatagitsune* squarely within the Japanese tradition of stories of the Animal Wife (Origuchi 1924). In this narrative pattern, the child of an animal-human couple causes the mother's true identity to be revealed, often in an indirect manner as in *Kowatagitsune* or *Shinoda no tsuma*, where the fox-mother reveals her tail as she is nursing her child (Origuchi:285). The revelation means the separation of the couple and of the mother from her child: in effect, the fox-mother who has brought about the *en* under false pretext is punished more or less directly by her child by being unable to see the child again.

Otogizôshi have a way of introducing the main character in a few lines, which indirectly forestalls the final outcome of the tale. There are few or no explicit judgements of the characters' actions, and this narrative anticipation may easily be overlooked by a modern reader, less alert to the cultural assumptions against which the tales were told. *Nezumi no sôshi* (*The Tale of a Rat*) is another *otogizôshi* with an animal main character, which judging by the many existing manuscripts must have been very popular.[10] Gon-no-kami ('deputy head') — the title by which the rat is referred to — is evidently of respectable standing. In the opening lines, he is characterized as 'an old rat'

---

10. The possibility of 'mass-production' by *ezôshi* makers is mentioned in *Tenri toshokan zenbon sôsho, Ko-Nara ehon-shû* 1:12.

*Figure 3. Female rat in labour. Tracing from Nezumi no sôshi
emaki (Tenri-bon, late Muromachi Period).*

(*furunezumi*) who, unhappy with his karma of having been born into the Way
of Beasts (*chikushôdô*), wishes to improve the lot of his descendants by
marrying a human being. In plain words, Gon-no-kami is a fool, much too
old to contemplate marriage and with ideas about improving his karma
which, from a Buddhist view-point, can only be termed preposterous. Still
it would not be a tale if he did not succeed in marrying a human being, and
the pictures of the *yuinô* and the *yomeiri* show an abundance of things be-
fitting a Japanese rat. However, the nurse of the bride soon becomes suspicious, and Gon-no-kami is found out. He takes religious orders and meets
an equally disillusioned cat, with whom he retreats to Mount Kôya. Despite
the auspicious wedding ceremonies Gon-no-kami's plans have clearly failed.
If, as it seems, his transgression consisted mainly in his wish to have human
offspring, it is unsurprising that there should be no children. The fact that
rats are highly fertile animals makes the irony of his childlessness stand out.
There is even evidence that this effect was intended by (some of) those who
produced the scrolls: in at least two manuscripts, scenes of a female rat in labour or of female rats washing newborn rats in a confinement scene, each of
which is unrelated to the main story line of the rat-human marriage, occur
towards the end of the *yomeiri* scene (Figures 3-4).[11] That is, they are placed

11. *Tenri toshokan zenbon sôsho, Ko-Nara ehon-shû* 1:55, 90-91, respectively. The hairstyle of
the rats, a faible for the word *tabako* 'tobacco', as well as a rat depicted with a *kiseru*
'pipe' suggest that at least the latter of these scrolls dates from early Edo Period
(*Ibid*:16).

Figure 4. Washing the newborn rats. Tracing from Nezumi no sôshi, beppon (Tenri- bon, early Edo Period).

precisely at the point of the story where a scene relating to childbirth would be expected in an auspicious narrative of a *yomeiri* marriage, such as the later *akahon* already mentioned.

Even when an animal is motivated by a laudable feeling to establish a relationship with a human being, such as wishing to return a favour (*ongaeshi*), the outcome is the same, childlessness and separation. In *Tsuru no sôshi* (*The Tale of the Crane*),[12] the account of the man's saving the crane from the hunter is similar to the well-known folk-tale (*mukashibanashi*) *Tsurunyôbô*. There are, however, two *otogizôshi* variants of what happens after the crane comes to live with the man. In both, the crane brings prosperity to the man. In the briefer version, she subsequently flies away, and the man marries someone else and they have children. In the longer version, the crane, having brought prosperity to the man (*saishô*), and perhaps thereby improved her karma, announces that she intends to die and be reborn as a human, and she exchanges poems with the man. After the crane is reborn the daughter of a courtier, the two are married and have many children.

It has been suggested that the unhappy ending in the *Tsurunyôbô* folk-tale reflects the traditional view that a female should not take the initiative in establishing an *en*, cf. the myth of Izanagi and Izanami, etc. (Kawai 1986: chapter 6). Inside the *otogizôshi* tradition, however, neither transgression nor

12. *Tsuru no sôshi*, too, appears to have been very popular: Yokoyama and Matsumoto (vol 9:493) note the existence of the two printed editions as well as seven manuscripts (*nara ehon*) of this tale dating from the Kanbun era (1661-71) and later.

conditions of punishment seem to be gender-specific. Rather *Kowatagitsune*, *Tsuru no sôshi* and *Nezumi no sôshi* here suggest a more general narrative pattern for describing behaviour which runs against the sanctioned morality, be it a male contemplating marriage in old age or a female giving her passion free rein. In that pattern transgression is coded by difference, namely the incompatibility of an animal-transgressor and a human being, as founded on the Buddhist view that it is unacceptable for someone born into the Way of the Beasts (*chikushô-dô*) to trespass into the Way of Human Beings (*ningen-dô*), bypassing karma. The punishment is separation from the child or childlessness, both of which in *otogizôshi* always signal the break-down of the *en*. In this perspective, it can be clearly seen that the monkey head priest in *Saru no sôshi* knew exactly what he was doing when he preferred a monkey from Enryakuji to a *daimyô* from Kyûshû as his son-in-law.

By consistently valorising children, the vision of *en* in *otogizôshi* seems in agreement with the precepts of Chinese morality expounded in *Shôgaku* (Chinese *Xiao Xue*) and expressed in Japanese by the well-known proverb, *sannen ni shite ko naki wa saru* ('the woman who is childless after three years [of marriage] must leave' (i.e. return home to her parents)). Actual social practices may well have been more pragmatic and at least some contemporary popular moralists appear to have held quite flexible views. For instance, Tokiwa Tanboku (cf. above) rejects childlessness as a reason for divorce and instead recommends that the man might try to have a child by a mistress, or, if the couple cannot agree on this, that they adopt a child of a relation of the husband's instead (*Hyakushô bunryôki*:266).

Be that as it may, *otogizôshi* storytellers may have had several reasons for valorizing the happy *en* with children. Indeed it is probably correct to say that this theme in its variant form of *môshigo*, a child born to an older childless couple at the intervention of a deity, was important to the function of *otogizôshi* as a religious ritual. We know from transmitted written versions, that at the end of the performance the story-teller would exhort the audience to put their trust in the deity invoked in the tale in order that their wishes may come true. This promise of divine favour obviously gained credibility by the success of the main character of the *otogizôshi*. Although people in an audience would wish for various things, an *en* is bound to have been a popular wish, and it is explicitly mentioned in several tales, e.g. *Kootoko*. As an ideal, happy *en* meant children, casting the main character as a *môshigo* (in effect a divine manifestation) was an obvious way of accentuating the miraculous power of that deity. The *môshigo*-theme, which incidentally occurs in more than forty tales, among them *Issunbôshi* (*Sumiyoshi*), *Bunshô* (*Kashima no Daimyôjin*), *Hachikazuki* (*Hase Kannon*), *Senju* (*Kiyomizu Kannon*) (Fujishima

1985:338), therefore represented the story-teller's/deity's unequivocal assurance that the audience's wish for happiness and, in particular, for a happy *en* — i.e. a marriage blessed with children, — could come true. Thus, considerations of social ideals and religious expedience would seem to come together in the motif of *en* in the *otogizôshi* tradition.

References

Araki, James. 1983. *Bunshô sôshi*: The tale of Bunshô, the saltmaker. *Monumenta Nipponica* 38:3.

Bottigheimer, Ruth B. 1986. *Grimm's Bad Girls and Bold Boys: the Social and Moral Vision of Tales*. New Haven: Yale University Press.

Fujikake, Kazuyoshi. 1987. *Muromachi-ki monogatari no kinsei-teki tenkai: otogizôshi kanazôshi ronkô*. Ôsaka: Izumishoin.

Fujishima, Hidetaka. 1985. *Chûsei setsuwa monogatari no kenkyû*. Tôkyô: Ôfûsha.

Gardner, Kenneth. 1993. *Descriptive Catalogue of Japanese Books in The British Library Printed before 1700*. London: British Library.

Ichiko, Teiji. 1985. *Otogizôshi*. Tôkyô: Iwanami shoten.

Ihara, Saikaku. 1991. *Honchô nijû fukô*, annot. by Satake, Akihiro. *Kôshoku nidai otoko etc*, Fuji Akio et al. (annot.). Tôkyô: Iwanami shoten. (= *Shin-Nihon koten bungaku taikei* 76).

Kawai, Hayao. 1986. *Mukashibanashi to nihonjin no kokoro*. Tôkyô: Iwanami Shoten. 1986. (English trans.) *The Japanese Psyche: Major Motifs in the Fairy Tales of Japan*. Dallas: Spring Publishing.

Kinsei kodomo no ehon-shû, Edo-hen, Kamigata-hen. 1985. Tôkyô: Iwanami shoten.

Kuroda, Hideo, Satô Masahide and Furuhashi Nobutaka. 1990. *Otogizôshi*. Tôkyô: Perikan-sha.

McCullough, William. 1967. Japanese Marriage Institutions in the Heian Period. *Harvard Journal of Asiatic Studies* 27, 103-67.

Morishita, Misako. 1989. *Nezumi no yomeiri* — zatsusei no shikake. *Bungaku* 57.7, 23-31.

Mulhern, Chieko Irie. 1979. Cinderella and the Jesuits: an *otogizôshi* Cycle as Christian Literature. *Monumenta Nipponica* 34, 409-47.

Nagatomo, Chiyoji (annot.) 1993 (1692 (Genroku 5)). *Onna chôhôki*. Tôkyô: Shakai shisôsha (= *Gendai kyôyô bunko* 1507).

Origuchi, Shinobu. 1965 (1924). *Shinodazuma no hanashi*. *Origuchi Shinobu zenshû*, vol. 2, 267-309.

Ôshima, Tatehiko. 1967. *Otogizôshi to minkan bungei*. Tôkyô: Iwasaki bijutsusha.

Ôshima, Tatehiko. 1974. *Otogizôshi-shû*. Tôkyô: Shôgakukan.

Pigeot, Jacqueline. 1988. Kyô no hito, inaka no hito: Muromachi jidai monogatari no baai. *Bungaku* 56.2, 8-26.

Ruch, Barbara. 1971. Origins of the Companion Library: Anthology of Medieval Japanese Stories. *Journal of Asian Studies* 30.3.

Steven, Chigusa. 1977. *Hachikazuki*: a Muromachi short story. *Monumenta Nipponica* 32:3.

Takeuchi, Lone. 1996. An *otogizôshi* in Context: *Saru no sôshi* and the Hie-Enryakuji Religious Multiplex in the Late Sixteenth Century. *Japanese Journal of Religious Studies* 23.1-2, 29-60.

Tenri toshokan zenbon sôsho. 1973. *Ko-Nara ehon-shû* 1. Tôkyô: Yagi shoten.

Tokiwa, Tanboku. 1729 (Kyôhô 14). *Hyakushô bunryôki. Kinsei chônin shisô*, ed. and annot. by nakamura Yukihiko. Tôkyô: Iwanami shoten. (= *Nihon Shisô Taikei* 58), 235-302.

Warner, Marina. 1994. *From the beast to the blonde: on fairytales and their tellers*. London: Chatto & Windus.

Yokoyama, Shigeru and Matsumoto Takanobu. 1973. *Muromachi jidai monogatari taisei*. Tôkyô: Kadokawa shoten.

Yoshida, Kogorô. 1984. *Tanrokubon: Rare Books of Seventeenth-Century Japan*. Tokyo: Kodansha International.

Mishima Yukio and Raymond Radiguet: *Tôzoku* and *Le Bal du Comte d'Orgel*

Noriko Thunman

In my article on Mishima's *Tôzoku*, 1948, and Radiguet's *Le Bal*, 1924, (Thunman 1996) I gave my reasons for relating the two works and discussed the shared high degree of authority of their narrators. I did not mention any connections between the two novels on the story level. I would now like to do so briefly, and shall then discuss further the rhetorical features of the narrators. *Le Bal*, in my opinion, served Mishima as an important model of the psychological novel. Mishima wrote psychological novels all his life and we can find the features seen in *Tôzoku* in his whole production. We are perhaps no longer considering a 'model' but rather Mishima as a writer.

1. The stories of *Tôzoku* and *Le Bal*

According to structuralist theory, each narrative has two parts: a story (histoire) and a discourse (discours). The story is the 'what' in a narrative: the content or chain of events (actions, happenings) plus what may be called the existents (characters, items of setting) (Chatman 1993:19).

1.1 Events

Though Mishima wrote that he had Radiguet's *Le Bal* in mind while writing *Tôzoku*, his story is quite different from that of *Le Bal*. In *Le Bal*, François and Mahaut discover their love. The process is slow, a triangle drama of Anne and Mahaut d'Orgel and François de Séryeuse.[1] *Tôzoku* is clearly not an ordinary love story. Of the 164 pages, it is only the opening 13 (until Akihide's sudden return to Tokyo with his mother) that can possibly be called a love story about the two young people.

---

1. See 'Préface' by Bernard Pingaud attached to Radiguet (1983), 39-52.

Chapter One, 'The Origin of the Story' was first published as 'The End of the Love and the Origin of the Story'. Especially this first version of the title shows clearly the intention of the author: the real story begins with Akihide's suffering from not being loved. The whole novel is about Akihide who lost his love, his later decision to solve the problem in his own way and the execution of his decision.

1.2 Characters

The characters in *Tôzoku* are quite different from those in *Le bal*. Akihide is the most important person and has few traits that lead him to the final tragedy. The most essential trait is his covertness. He is, in E.M. Foster's definition, 'flat', because he is predictable and incapable of changing (Chatman 1993:131-2). According to Gerald Prince, characters can be more or less major or minor, dynamic (when they change) or static (when they do not), consistent (when their attributes and actions do not result in contradiction) or inconsistent (Prince 1987:12). Akihide is static and consistent.

Kiyoko is presented as a reflection of Akihide: they are mentally twins. The only difference is that Kiyoko is female, and this gives her a strange, primitive power. 'She is pregnant with power'. Because Kiyoko is a reflection of Akihide, she is also flat, static and consistent, with even fewer traits than Akihide.

Major characters of *Le Bal*, Mahaut d'Orgel and François de Séryeuse, undergo psychological transformations and discover themselves. In that sense, they change in the course of the story and they are dynamic. They are not flat but round, because not predictable. They are sometimes mysteries to themselves. The third major character, Anne d'Orgel, diminishes successively and at the end, in the scene of the Tyrolean hat, he appears shallow. In that sense, he is also 'dynamic'. The only characters who undergo change in *Tôzoku* are Lord and Lady Fujimura. They change under the influence of the triangle drama played by them and Baron Yamauchi, Kiyoko's father. However, they are not main characters.

Thus characters' traits differ greatly, and no one in *Tôzoku* resembles anyone in *Le Bal*. However, two features are common to the characters of the two novels. One is the high-pitched voices of Anne d'Orgel and Baron Yamauchi and his son. This might seem trivial, but it is used in both novels to distinguish the person's aristocratic origins.

The voice of Anne is feminine and falsetto. There are three mentions in Horiguchi's translations:

1. Kare wa ie daidai no, imadewa butai ni dake nokotteiru ano kandakai koe ('Il avait une voix de famille et *ce fausset* conservé au théâtre') (Horiguchi 1983:445).
2. kisei ('*la voix* du comte d'Orgel' — the strange voice in translation).
3. ningen rashiku nai *chôshi no takai koe* ('*d'un rire aux notes* inhumaines, *suraigu*') (Horiguchi 1983:464) (Italics mine).

Anne d'Orgel's high-pitched voice reveals his class more than the features of the face. 'Plus que les traits, la voix décèle la race' (Radiguet 1983:65). The same sort of feminine, high-pitched voice is found in *Tôzoku* to underline the noble origin of Baron Yamauchi:

It (Yamauchi's voice) was an almost feminine, high-pitched voice, frequently heard in the anteroom of the House of Peers (Mishima 1974:44).[2]

The son of Baron Yamauchi shares the same voice quality:

(…) Munehisa grew garrulous. (He talked) in a high-pitched voice that reminded one of his father's (Mishima 1974:84).

In both *Tôzoku* and *Le Bal*, the quality of voice, a high-pitched voice, distinguishes the origin of the characters.

The other common feature is the importance of heritage for the person's character and comportment. Anne is a descendant of court aristocracy, always in good standing with kings and the court. He is worldly and it is important for him to observe the conventions. This makes him totally indifferent to Mahaut's suffering at the end. Mahaut's family on the other hand belongs to an old feudal aristocracy with scant respect for a king. The fact that Mahaut's family long lived on the island of Martinique has changed the family character, and all this, along with Mahaut's childhood, influenced her own character.

Mishima later used the contrast between court and feudal aristocracy in *Spring Snow* in his own way. Kiyoaki's family (marquis) originates from the lower samurai class and belongs to a new class of aristocracy. Thus they lack the real elegance. Kiyoaki's upbringing was entrusted to the Ayakura family of the old court aristocracy, representing the traditional, court elegance.

Both Anne and Mahaut are an extension of their historical heritage, and thus their personalities and value judgements are doomed. Heritage is

2. All translations in this paper are mine unless indicated otherwise.

important even for the minor characters of *Le Bal* such as Mme de Séryeuse and Prince Mirza.

In *Tôzoku*, Akihide's grandfather, father and uncle share the same family trait of covertness. They are masters of concealing their feelings:

The concealing character that was a Fujimura family trait acted as a safety valve. Managing this trait proficiently, his grandfather and father could save much trouble in maintaining their dignity. (...) They were true descendents of people who ate lukewarm meals, carried down long corridors, after passing the poison taster. However, Akihide did not know that the safety valve could be transformed into the most dangerous apparatus for a person with too sensitive a mind. Amour-propre and pride which had been so adeptly protected and never hurt, became unnoticed, ineffectual (Mishima 1974:38).

The only difference is that the inherited covertness works in a different, more dangerous way for Akihide. We can also sense the aristocratic heritage and its influence on the personalities of Baron and Baroness Yamauchi, too.

1.3 Setting

The resemblance between the two novels is all the more striking when we come to the settings. Radiguet himself left a short note on *Le Bal*, which is quoted in the Preface by Jean Cocteau:

Roman où c'est la psychologie qui est romanesque. Le seul effort d'imagination est appliqué là, non aux événements extérieurs, mais à l'analyse des sentiments. (...)
Côté 'mondain':
Atmosphère utile au déploiement de certains sentiments, mais ce n'est pas une peinture du monde; différence avec Proust. Le décor ne compte pas.

A novel in which it is the psychology that is novel-like. The only effort of imagination is applied here; not to external events, but to the analysis of feelings. (...)
'Wordly' side:
An atmosphere useful for conveying certain feelings, but not a picture of the world; difference from Proust. The décor does not count (Radiguet 1993:864).

Radiguet says that the social background of the novel does not exist in its own right but just to give the appropriate atmosphere to the psychological dramas of the novel. What is essential is to analyze sentiments. Mishima most probably read Radiguet's words in Cocteau's Preface included in the

1938 Hakusui-sha version of *Le Bal* in Horiguchi's translation.[3] Here Radiguet's attitude is quite reminiscent of that of Mishima himself who also said that the social background of *Tôzoku* was chosen to facilitate the psychological experiment he wished to perform:

I avoided the disorder of postwar society and looked for the colourless background of the aristocratic society of the 1930s to allow a certain psychological experiment. This method among others was an imitation of *Le Bal du compte d'Orgel* of Radiguet (Mishima 1974:676).

In *Le Bal*, the social background of the novel is the social life of high society. Numerous rendezvous and psychological intercourses are played out at the circus Médrano, in the salon of d'Orgel, at diverse dinners and lunches and at a mansion Robinson, outside Paris, where Society used to meet to amuse themselves.

The first encounter of Akihide and Yoshiko takes place at a hotel in the S highlands where both, with their mothers, have come to spend the summer. The social background of the novel is either a fashionable hotel in the S highlands[4] or the youth soirées of the aristocratic Gakushûin school, or at the Yamauchi summer house in Karuizawa; sometimes at the protagonists' homes. Though both authors chose a similar aristocratic environment, it is interesting to note differences in their descriptions of social life.

Muramatsu says that Mishima's family lived outside the noble circles of Japan and they were not part of aristocratic social life (Muramatsu 1990:49). Mishima was well-acquainted with the way of life of bourgeois families, where acquaintances and relatives met from time to time for marriages or family Buddhistic memorials, and this is also the way of life of the nobles in *Tôzoku*. Baroness Yamauchi belongs to a literary association and composes poetry (*waka*) as did many other women of noble or bourgeois origins. There are no lunches or dinner parties in *Tôzoku* at the homes of the protagonists. Mishima was presumably familiar with the social life of the young people at Gakushûin, and their parties and social life are depicted vividly in *Tôzoku*. One social occasion in *Tôzoku* is the marriage of the son of Kawamori, a close friend of the Fujimuras' in the House of Peers. The narrator says that if one attends a hundred weddings, ninety-nine are other people's and only one is one's own. Society seems to be made up of this one substantial ceremony,

---

3. The question is discussed in my article 'The Genealogy of *Tozôku*' (forthcomming).
4. In the text it is called 'S kôgen', which Mishima later wrote being Shiga-kôgen. See Mishima's *Atogaki* (1953) attached to *Mishima Yukio Sakuhin-shû* I.

but in reality it is sustained by the ninety-nine cases of formalistic courtesy.
(Mishima 1974:146) Compared to the social life of *Le Bal*, the scene of the
wedding is much more formal, almost an empty formality maintained only
by the consensus of the participants. This very emptiness guarantees,
paradoxically, the upholding of the social convention. Those who attend the
wedding of Kawamori seem to be bored:

Those couples have attended too many weddings. Husbands with a sour face
talked business with each others, and wives together with young ladies were absorbed in conversation about girls' operas, cosmetics and men's tyranny and
childishness. Through the dimness of cigarette smoke in a waiting-room glimmered
gloomily white colours, the white necks of women and the reflection of in-
numerable pairs of glasses. The sight of hundreds of people talking and laughing
at the same time was almost a desperate and pitiable sight (Mishima 1974:146).

The participants, despite their noble or high-bourgeois status, seem curiously
vulgar: men talk business and women, girls' operas and cosmetics or men's
tyranny.
    There is also a birthday celebration of a friend of Lady Fujimura, the
Duchess Motoda, at the Club of Nobles. No scene of the anniversary celebration is further described. We can guess from Lord Fujimura's comments that
it is another kind of empty courtesy;

Going now (to meet his wife), what did he intend to do while waiting for the long-
winded meeting of women to end?' (Mishima 1974:100).

While waiting at the Club, Lord Fujimura lunched with the Baron S who was
'*boredom* incarnate' and used to come to the Club to find someone to talk to.
The Club bar was filled with 'the scent of *boredom*'. The Baron S tried to hear
some political news from the Viscount Fujimura who, in turn, got quickly
bored by drinking whisky. The Viscount Fujimura gradually grew to love the
atmosphere of the Club. He was no longer young; solitary old age had
become more familiar to him than youth. He came to feel at home at the
Club together with old Baron S (Mishima 1974:101).
    Thus the life of the nobles described here, especially of the elderly, is
rather tedious. The social life in *Le Bal*, on the other hand, is more enlivened
by human vanity and desires. Prince Naroumof is unhappy, disillusioned,
but not bored. No one radiates boredom in *Le Bal*.
    For neither Radiguet nor Mishima was the setting of the novel primary.

Settings were chosen to facilitate the sort of psychological analysis the authors wished to perform.

Despite the authors' identical intentions, and even though they both chose aristocratic environments, the social intercourse and the atmospheres depicted in the two novels are quite different. It cannot be due so much to the difference in time; the one is from the 1920s, the other from the 1930s.

Jean Hugo said in *Le Regard de la Mémoire*, 1983, that the distance separating the society depicted by Mme de La Fayette from that depicted by Radiguet was not as great as one might imagine, and that there were still many nobles in the first quarter of the 20th century, who played a considerable part in social, literary and artistic life. (Borgal 1991:107) Radiguet knew some of them: Princess Eugène Murat, who served as the model of the Princesse d'Austerlitz, the Count and the Countess de Beaumont and the Prince Firouz de Perse, the model of Mirza. His friend François de Gouy could offer him much information about the old aristocratic families. Radiguet's mother was a Créole, and he claimed to be related, through her, to Tacher de la Pagerie. (Borgal 1991:108, 111-12)

Mishima could not have the same sort of claim concerning his own origin, but he also situated himself near Japanese noble circles through his grandmother Natsu and his friends at Gakushûin. He could have had as good an insight into the everyday and social life of the Japanese nobles as Radiguet did into the French. According to Bôjô, Mishima's friend from Gakushûin days and of an aristocratic family serving the Emperor personally, Mishima really understood the culture of the Japanese nobles (Bôjô 1971: 91-92; see further Ikeda 1994, 1995). In that case, the difference between descriptions of social life in *Le Bal* and in *Tôzoku* , except the boredom which I feel has to do with the author Mishima himself, reflects the real difference in the ways of life of the Japanese aristocracy and the French.

2. Discourse

Analyzing the text of *Le Bal*, Bernard Pingaud pointed out three features: misunderstanding (malentendu), manoeuvre and reversal (renversement), as those which play an important role for the plot.

2.1 Misunderstanding

Misunderstanding is an important mechanism in *Le Bal*. The most momentous misunderstanding is about the triangular relationship of Anne, Mahaut and François. Mahaut sees in François only a friend of her beloved husband. François says to himself that he wishes nothing but the couple's accord and happiness. Anne discovers a 'new' Mahaut the afternoon before the fire, and starts to love her anew. Mahaut disguises her feelings through loyalty to her conjugal obligations. François hides behind his friendship with Anne. Anne is the most unaware and believes simply that he has found a new friend and new feelings toward his wife. The three misunderstand each other and themselves constantly. The narrator shows the reader, by explaining and commenting, the subtle mechanism of their hearts. Le Bal is a

novel in which it is the psychology that is novel-like. The only effort of imagination is applied here, not to external events, but to the analysis of feelings (Radiguet 1993:864).

To achieve this, the mechanism of misunderstanding plays a central role.

If misunderstanding is one of the most important motors of the intrigues of Le Bal,[5] it is also very important in Tôzoku. Akihide saw, wrongly, a sign of complicity in Yoshiko: Yoshiko laughed silently in a car on the way to the station because she knew what her mother was thinking when she wondered for a moment what her husband was doing just then. Akihide asked why she laughed. She thought him childish to ask such a question, flushed and cast him a glance, which Akihide misunderstood as proof of complicity (Mishima 1974:21). Akihide and Kiyoko initially misunderstand each others' intention (Akihide believing her in love with him and vice versa). Akihide's relationship with his parents and with his uncle in Kyoto is also depicted with mutual misunderstandings. Kiyoko's brother misinterprets his sister's calmness, and so on. Lord and Lady Fujimura continuously misinterpret each other's reactions. They never have understood the intention of Akihide, which is perhaps the most tragic unawareness in the whole story.

As each page of Le Bal shows examples of misunderstandings, so does almost each page of Tôzoku. The misunderstandings can be subtle. When Akihide visits his friends after a long interval, they are at first surprised to see him: 'When Akihide entered the study, the air felt fragile as thin glass, everybody listening intensely' (Mishima 1974:62). After a while they start to talk about some friends whom they have not seen for a long time:

Akihide could easily join in their chatter, because he, too, didn't know the news of those friends. This placed Akihide at the same distance in relation to the objects of the chatter, and gradually the three (Akihide's friends) came to believe that he was one of them (Mishima 1974:63).

This is a deluded perspective, an illusion. A little further on:

The scantiness of subjects to talk about after such a long time was difficult to distinguish from that felt by those who meet every day (Mishima 1974:63).

Another kind of misjudgement of distance. The narrator interprets and explains to clarify the nature of misunderstandings/misjudgements.

The only relationship without the least shadow of misunderstanding is that of Kiyoko and Akihide after they confess their intentions. Their accord goes so far that they end up possessing each others' illusions, too. 'Gradually two illusions' — Yoshiko's and Saeki's — 'came to be their common property' (Mishima 1974:124). They became each other's images in a mirror and were almost identical:

And the mirrors could only communicate with each other through their illusions. The form and its shadow reflected each other completely, and it was impossible to distinguish them. It was possible for the form which is at the same time the shadows to smile warmly at the shadow which is also the form (Mishima 1974:124).

They stop being two separate individuals. Their ecstasy at being one with the other attains its height at the end of Chapter Four, when they are sitting and resting on the grass after a bicycle trip to the K meadow, outside Karuizawa. Their accord is so perfect that an image of a ship appears, to carry them away to dreamed illusions, just as in another work of Mishima.[6] There is almost a divine harmony between these two individuals, and the tone of the narrator is elevated and idealistic. Here exists no shadow of misunderstanding, which belongs to the sphere of humanity.

Another passage about Lady Fujimura reveals her unconsciousness of her own feelings:

(...) nothing but love has a right to demand a sacrifice. Lady Fujimura could pass her days during this summer without noticing her renewing love for Lord Yamauchi, Kiyoko's father and her old lover, thanks to the blind mechanism of love. When she met Lord Yamauchi, she was satisfied to feel calm and merry, and

5. Pingaud says, 'Chose curieuse, le mot «malentendu» n'apparaît qu'une fois dans le roman. Mais il n'est guère de page où Radiguet n'utilise le procédé' (in Radiguet (1983), 23), and 'L'emploi systématique du malentendu entraîne une conséquance intréssante sur la narration (*ibid.*, 25).

6. The ship image appears also in the play *Bara to Kaizoku*. Teiichi and Ariko dream of a voyage and the house is 'a pirate ship' which will sail to their kingdom. MYZ (1975) vol. 22.

more intellectually alert than usual. However, as everyone knows, happiness can only be recognized by intelligence. On the other hand, her every worry and pain when she couldn't see Lord Yamauchi during the summer was transformed into a bedeviling, maternal expectation over Kiyoko's and Akihide's relationship, and into a vexed anger she felt repeatedly at the suspicious expression of the Viscount Fujimura — as if he had aquired, for the first time, the right to express openly his feelings about her relationship to Lord Yamauchi — at the Club of Nobles the same day, early that summer, on his return from the journey to see cormorants fishing. This was why Lady Fujimura couldn't believe that love could possibly be such peaceful feelings devoid of pain. Middle-aged women falling in love, which we witness in novels, shouldn't it burst into violent and turbulent flames? (Mishima 1974:140).

Lady Fujimura misunderstands her own feelings and the narrator explains why. The same sort of misunderstanding is richly present in *Le Bal*, where the protagonists misunderstand themselves and each other. Just as Lady Fujimura failed to recognize her own love for Lord Yamauchi, so does Mahaut long fail to recognize hers. The reason Mahaut misunderstands her own feelings is surprisingly similar to Lady Fujimura's:

Ayant jusqu'ici mené de front le devoir et l'amour, elle avait pu imaginer, dans sa pureté, que les sentiments interdits sont sans douceur. Elle avait donc mal interprété le sien envers François, car il lui était doux.

Because she put duty and love in front until now, she had imagined, in her purity, that forbidden feelings are without sweetness. She then misinterpreted her own feelings for François, because they were sweet to her (Radiguet 1983:171-72).

Because their feelings were devoid of turmoil (an illusion that forbidden love should be painful and turbulent, accompanied by the heat of desire), because Lady Fujimura and Mahaut both felt a calm contentment, they misjudged and failed to give their feelings a real name. Nor can François give the right name to his feelings. The narraror interprets the reaction of François and explains why he fails to recognize his own feelings: 'Love entered into the depth of his heart where even he himself couldn't descend' (Radiguet 1993:726)

2.2 Manoeuvre

Another mechanism utilized in *Le Bal* is 'manoeuvre'. The best example is the 'arm' episode: François involuntarily slides his arm under Mahaut's one night in a car. But he does it once again, this time consciously. Mahaut understands that, this time, it is a conscious action and takes it as an insult to their friendship. She tells her husband what François did. Anne, who was surprised to see François' arm under his wife's, is now, after his wife's confession, assured of her innocence and makes light of it. Mahaut is not content with Anne's facileness and tells herself that she should protect herself without Anne's help. François did not attain his goal, and he is very ashamed of himself. The incident also creates an unexpected distance between Mahaut and Anne.

The same sort of calculating appears in *Tôzoku*. Lady Fujimura's asking Niikura to speak to her husband concerning the marriage of Kiyoko and Akihide is one example. The manoeuvre does not succeed, because the intrigue is revealed by Lord Fujimura who guesses rightly that Lady Fujimura has planned the whole thing to get his consent. Lord Fujimura feels, when he discovers his wife's intrigue, that he, at last, can really hate her who has regained her youth through her love for Baron Yamauchi. This, in turn, makes him younger, giving him a passion to hate. This leads to an unexpected dénouement between Lord and Lady Fujimura the same autumn night in the Fujimuras' salon. Lord Fujumura asks his wife about Niikura's move — if it wasn't she who arranged it. Lady Fujumura denies this and they start to argue. To Lord Fujimura's question as to whether she had a guilty conscience, she answers that she has, because she respects Lord Yamauchi more than him. However, she denies it is love. She denies and the reason is very complex: First, Lady Fujimura was ready to tell the truth about Niikura's move. However, Lord Fujimura's suspicion about her and Lord Yamauchi makes her decide to lie. The narrator says that the reason why she cannot ask him herself, but lets Niikura do it, is in fact her bad conscience about Lord Yamauchi, of which she herself is unaware. She intends to admit love for Lord Yamauchi, even though it is a lie (because she is unaware of her own love), just to hate her husband more. But she cannot, because this would involve Lord Yamauchi in the lying. Thus, she decides to say that she respects him.

All this has only one aim: to hate Lord Fujimura, because she despises him so deeply that he is not worthy of the truth. Lord Fujimura, in turn, suddenly sees his wife as an indifferent spectator, while arguing. She perceives his indifference and recognizes for the first time that he is not worth hating but deserves only lies. Her manoeuvre fails to attain the expected result (the clarification of Lord Fujimura's intentions concerning Akihide's marriage), but results in a disastrous climax between the married couple.

The other manoeuvre, also resulting in disaster, is at the beginning of the story where Lady Fujimura, realizing the seriousness of her son's feelings for Yoshiko, makes him an accomplice and interrupts their summer vacation to return hastily to Tokyo so that they may follow the correct social procedure and ask for Yoshiko's hand. Akihide believes, wrongly, that Yoshiko understands his and his mother's intention. Here, too, the manoeuvre results in further misunderstandings and a catastrophic loss of the love.

In both *Le Bal* and *Tôzuku*, then, manoeuvres are doomed to fail, causing new misunderstandings and unexpected effects, effects that seem more grave, more complex and psychologically burdened in *Tôzuku*.

2.3 Reversal

Radiguet creates novelty in *Le Bal* with the help of what Bernard Pingaud calls an optical change. One way is 'reversal': where one expects an ordinary, well-accepted explanation, the narrator presents a different one (Radiguet 1983:21-22). Some examples are:

1. The absence of a person (the husband), whose presence usually embarasses the lovers, embarassed them (Radiguet 1983:169).
2. If separation can create obstacles, it can eliminate some others. (Radiguet 1983:155).
3. It seems that separation makes it easier to disguise onerself. It is just the opposite (Radiguet 1983:155).

Such generalizations are often expressed by maxims.[7] We can find some reversals and a similar logic in *Tôzoku*, too. Akihide and Kiyoko decide not to exchange love letters when she is with her family in Karuizawa and he in Gôra with his family. This does not weaken their relationship, as one might

---

7. This feature is discussed in Thunman 1996.

expect; quite the reverse. It is the total separation (no correspondence) that makes it impossible for them to lie to each other (Mishima 1974:127). Another example of reversal is:

Anyhow, he (Akihide) found lies in old tales. It is a lie of fiction that a man turns into a completely different person after having decided, for certain reasons, to become a thief or to die. Rather, does he not become more like himself through this decision? (Mishima 1974:61).

The opening part of *Tôzoku* presents another case of reversal:

A covert man wishes to keep his feelings secret within himself; appears at first sight to be able to live without getting hurt, as if he is a third party. However, rare stories and secrets have found their hiding place especially in such a person today, and he will be led into an unexpected and old-fashioned tragedy (Mishima 1974:9).

The first assumption seems reasonable, but suddenly the narrator claims the opposite — 'However'. Another example:

Other young men would have thought out adventurous methods such as waiting at a place where she is likely to come, and once she appeared, without leaving her side, attaining one's wish. For him (Akihide) this was totally unthinkable ('yume no mata yume'). 'How can I do something so unrealistic and novel-like?' — This, because he let his imagination work too much on personal, trivial matters so that what a normal person would have realized in action seemed to him too fanciful (Mishima 1974:27).

The first assumption seems reasonably true. It is an idea we usually have about young people. However, Akihide is not like everyone. His dreaming nature makes him incapable of actions easy for others. Here, it is not a question of a general truth, but the truth about Akihide.

Even though the same kind of reversal is found, the rhetoric of *Tôzoku* is more complex. Reversal in *Le Bal* constitutes the psychological logic of the story, and explanations are given in a quick tempo. The psychologies of the characters are juxtaposed in a rapid tempo in transparent lucidity, and the narrator's language leaves no ambiguity. The narrator of *Tôzoku* is very lucid, too, but his explanations are sometimes not as transparent as those of *Le Bal*'s narrator's. To quote one example:

A man who aims to commit suicide often gives an impression of not thinking seriously about death. This is not true. He succeeds in forming a clear-cut judgement on death to the limits of his understanding. This shallowness differs only very slightly from unseriousness. Though slight, the difference exists: a normal person who wants to live regards death as something more than the understandable, i.e. an α added to the understandable. The α is nothing but a safety-valve, but the person thinks that an abyss exists in the α. Rather, the abyss hides itself in the frivolity and the shallowness of the thought of the one who is to commit suicide (Mishima 1974:99).

Here the narrator tries to explain Akihide's joviality after his decision to commit suicide. He becomes sorrowless, glad and frivolous as if he has forgotten death: 'Because he came to know death for the first time, just as a man who came to know love for the first time, he got frivolous' (Mishima 1974:99). The first utterance, 'A man who aims to commit suicide ...' is the narrator's logic. Does not common sense state the opposite?: 'Those who think of suicide think very seriously of death'. This is not stated, and the narrator introduces his own logic from the start.

The logic of the passage is complicated: first, there is the assumption that a person who is to commit suicide seems to be thinking of death without seriousness. Then, the assumption is partly denied; no, this is not so, but he understands death in a certain, limited way. The second assumption follows: this kind of shallowness differs only slightly from unseriousness. The importance of the slight difference is emphasized in the following sentence. If we use A for the first assumption, the logic so far can be transcribed as follows:

{A} → {not A but B} → {B ≠ unseriousness} → {the importance of B ≠ unseriousness}

Then comes a new assumption: a normal person understands death as something plus α to what is understandable for him. This sentence is in contrast with B (He who intends to commit suicide succeeds in understanding death in a clear-cut way). A would-be suicide thinks that he really understands death, whereas a normal person thinks that death is something more than the understandable. Then follows a new contrast: an ordinary person supposes the existence of an *abyss* in the α, the ununderstandable, but the abyss perhaps exists in the *shallowness* of the thoughts of a suicide. The last contrast seems to be there merely for rhetorical effect, and it is not easy to understand what the narrator really means. Thus the passage consists of reversals, but in a more complex way than in *Le Bal*. A commonly accepted assumption is omitted (A suicide thinks/has thought very seriously of death). We can say that the logic is full of contrast and antithesis not easy to accept. Compared to this, maxims and general truths in *Le Bal* seem more logical and easily acceptable.

Radiguet spoke repeatedly of the importance of 'banality' and 'simplicity'. In *Règle du Jeu* we read: 'Treatises on the art of writing have something excellent to say, and it is approximately: write readably' (Radiguet 1993:454). In *Conseils aux grands poètes*, Radiguet writes:

'Try hard to be banal', we suggest to a great poet. The search for banality will safeguard him against strangeness, which is always detestable. This strangeness, which tires us often in Rimbaud, is never to be found in Ronsard (Radiguet 1993: 409).

Mishima was a good disciple of Radiguet, but not on this point. The passages quoted above about Akihide's attitude toward death cannot be said to be easy to understand ('lisible'). The rhetorical apparatus of the narrator is antithesis and contrast, and it works on several levels, successively modifying the previous assumptions.

2.4 The subtle mechanism of the heart

Both *Tôzoku* and *Le Bal* utilize the mechanisms of reversal, misunderstanding and manoeuvre as the essential motors of the intrigues, despite some differences in the narrators' rhetoric. What Mishima learned from Radiguet was, in my opinion, how to write a traditional psychological novel in which the subtle mechanism of the heart is best rendered with the help of optical changes such as reversal, misunderstanding and manoeuvre. The narrator, using his own assumptions, often counter to common sense, explains the movement of the characters' feelings and thoughts. All his life Mishima wrote psychological novels in which the most important thing is not actions and adventures but the characters' feelings and thoughts. We can also see a similar kind of psychological mechanism playing an important role in his later novel *Spring Snow*, 1969, even though the rhetoric of the narrator is altered and the distance between the narrator and the characters is greater.[8]

Conclusion

We have seen that *Tôzoku* and *Le Bal* share important common features, especially at the discourse level. At the story level, there is no common

---

8. First published in *Shinchô*, from September 1965 to January 1967.

feature regarding the events, but there is a common underlying view of the characters: that their personalities are predetermined by their genealogy. We have also seen a more superficial similarity: voice quality as a class-marker. As for the settings, an underlying similarity has been found in the intention of the authors when choosing their social environments. This does not mean that the social life depicted in the two novels is similar, probably because the real life of the nobles in France and in Japan is different. Besides, Mishima's own temperament has coloured the picture of the way of life of the Japanese nobles, giving it a marked atmosphere of boredom.

At discourse level, the kinship is striking. In both novels, the narrators, with great authority, explain and comment on the subtle mechanism of the hearts of the characters with the help of optical changes, misunderstanding, manoeuvre and reversal. The rhetoric of the narrator of *Tôzoku* has been found, far removed from that of Radiguet's narrator, to be burdened with pseudo-philosophical arguments, which disappear in the later *Spring Snow* (1969), just to reappear in the following novel, *The Temple of Dawn* (1970).

Disciple or not, Mishima seems to have found in Radiguet's work a good model of what he himself wished to realize: a psychological novel played in a social environment which is free from everyday worries and which allows the characters to be concerned only with their hearts.

The narrators in Mishima's works are usually accorded a high degree of authority — like an almighty God — and his novels totally lack the dialogic elements seen in Dostoevsky.[9] In this sense, too, it is easy to understand that Mishima has fallen for the lucidity of the narrator of *Le Bal* who can explain all, better than any of the characters.

Mishima loved to be a despotic director of the story, and his narrators are as despotic as he himself. The first writer of his like whom he found was Raymond Radiguet, and this explains the enthusiastic words he wrote repeatedly about Radiguet and *Le Bal*.

References

Bakhtin, Mikhail. 1984. *Problems of Dostoevsky's Poetics*, edited and transl. by Caryl Emerson. Theory and History of Literature, vol. 8. Manchester: University of Manchester.

9. See Bakhtin (1984).

Bôjô, Toshitami. 1971. *Honô no Genei*. Tokyo: Kadokawa-shoten.

Booth, Wayne C. (1961) 1991. *The Rhetoric of Fiction*. Chicago: The University of Chicago.

Borgal, Clément. 1991. *Raymond Radiguet — La nostalgie*. Paris: PUF.

Chatman, Saymour. (1978) 1993. *Story and Discourse*. Ithaca: Cornell University Press.

Chatman, Saymour. 1990. *Coming to Terms*. Ithaca: Cornell University Press.

Cocteau, Jean. (1926) 1964. *Lettre à Jacques Maritain*. Paris.

Genette, Gèrard. 1983. *Narrative Discourse Revisited*. Translated by Jane E. Lewis. Ithaca: Cornell University Press.

Horiguchi, Daigaku. 1984. *Horiguchi Daigaku Zenshû*, vol. 1. Tokyo: Ozawa-shoten.

Hugo, Jean. 1983. *Le Regard de la Mémoire*. Paris: Actes Sud.

Ikeda, Yuriko. 1994. Bôjô Toshitami. Heian Nobleman who was Exiled to the Twentieth Century, I. *Waseda Journal of Asian Studies* 16. Tokyo: International division, Waseda University.

Ikeda, Yuriko. 1995. Bôjô Toshitami. Heian Nobleman who was Exiled to the Twentieth Century, II. *Waseda Journal of Asian Studies* 17. Tokyo: International division, Waseda University.

Ikujima, Ryôichi. 1953. *Shôsetsu no Bigaku*. Tokyo: Hakusui-sha.

Magny, Claude-Edmonde. 1950. *Histoire du Roman Français depuis 1918*. Paris: Seuil.

Mishima Yukio. 1974. *Tôzoku in Mishima Yukio Zenshû*, vol. 2. Tokyo: Shinchô-sha.

Mishima Yukio. 1989. *Mishima Yukio Hyôron Zenshû*, 4 vol. Tokyo: Shinchô-sha.

Muramatsu, Takeshi. 1990. *Mishima Yukio no Sekai*. Tokyo: Shinchô-sha.

Prince, Gerald. (1987) 1991. *Dictionary of Narratology*. Aldershot: Scholars Press.

Radiguet, Raymond. 1983. *Le Bal du Compte d'Orgel*. Paris: Gallimard.

Radiguet, Raymond. 1993. *Œuvres Complètes*, Edition établie par Chloé Radiguet et Julien Cendres. Paris: Stock.

Shimazaki, Hiroshi & Mishima, Yôko. 1972. *Teihon Mishima Yukio Shoshi*. Tokyo: Bara Jûji-sha Co. Ltd.

Thibaudet, Albert. 1924. La Psychologie Romanesque, in Raymond Radiguet. 1983. *Le Bal du Comte d'Orgel*. 229-37. Paris: Editions Gallimard.

Thunman, Noriko. 1996. Mishima's *Tôzoku* and Radiguet's *Le Bal du Comte d'Orgel*. *Florilegium Japonicum*, ed. by Bjarke Frellesvig and Christian Morimoto Hermansen, 333-42. Copenhagen: Akademisk Forlag.

Culture and Society

The Control of Danish Subsidiaries in Japan: Socio-Cultural Interfaces

Lars Bonderup Bjørn

According to Ouchi & Maguire (1975), there are two modes of control: behavioral and output control. When managing large portfolios of companies, as multinational corporations often do, output control is usually the mode prefered. Output control provides unambiguous performance measures, easy to administrate and monitor. Also, output control makes it possible to compare subsidiary performance across countries, thereby providing the headquarters with clear resource allocation criteria.

However, each market is unique and when it comes to Japan, modes of control also differ somewhat from those of most other countries. Japanese organizations are characterized by a lower degree of output control compared to behavioral control. The controversial issue is whether this pattern is due to cultural necessity or to the result of a more or less random development.

If we accept that cultural necessity creates the unique pattern of control in Japan, the socio-cultural interface between a Danish headquarter and its Japanese subsidiary becomes an interface between the headquarter's drive towards output control and the subsidiary's drive towards behavioral control. In this paper, it is argued that not only is it possible to explain the unique Japanese pattern of control as a cultural necessity on the basis of Gouldner's (1960) norm of reciprocity, but also this norm prevents the efficient use of output control in the socio-cultural interface and it necessitates rather specific modes of behavioral control: expatriate managers sent to Japan should not be part of the usual rotation (a behavioural mode of control) as suggested by Edström & Galbraith (1977), but have to stay in Japan for several years or possibly be part of a more sophisticated mode of control.

The paper is based upon interviews with Danish and Japanese managers from 14 Danish subsidiaries in Japan. The interviews support the general suggestions and add rich descriptions to the overall picture of the socio-cultural interface, which so far has hardly been considered within business research.

In this study, it is assumed that the headquarters' control over subsidiary activities is achieved through two principal control modes as it was suggested by Ouchi & Maguire (1975). One is *behavior control*, the other *output control*. The former mode is a specification of the appropriate behavior expected from the controlled entity. The latter is a specification of the wanted outputs through e.g. budgets, plans, etc. while the appropriate behavior is left to the judgement of the entity controlled.

To be able to specify the behavior leading to the output wanted, behavior control presupposes knowledge of cause-and-effect relationships (Ouchi 1977). Output control presupposes no such knowledge. However, output control is at a disadvantage in accepting behavior by individual entities that may have an overall negative effect. What is approved behavior in one country may not be accepted in another and may even prove unethical by some local conventions. To the contrary, behavior control has the advantage of preventing such disapproved behavior while allowing for centralized control on the basis of local contingencies.

On the other hand, by its very lack of behavior specifications, output control is at an advantage in facilitating adaptation to local contingencies without requiring any knowledge of cause-and-effect relationships. This way of adapting to local conditions is a decentralized mode of control. For this and the following two reasons, output control has been a preferred mode in the headquarters' efforts to control their subsidiaries (Martinez & Jarillo 1989; Egelhoff 1984): First, output control measures facilitate cross-subsidiary comparisons. This improves the basis from which the marginal and scarce resources are distributed throughout the organization. Secondly, by simply comparing numbers, it is easy to administer output control. Behavior control requires a much more significant effort if the appropriate behavior shall be specified throughout the organizational hierarchy (Ouchi 1977).

For some time, it has been common knowledge among business economists that US, Japanese and European parent companies differ with regard to their relative use of the two control modes (Franko 1978; Egelhoff 1984). US companies tend to apply output control significantly more than European and Japanese companies while Japanese companies tend to apply behavior control significantly more than European and US companies. European companies seem to exercise a medium use of both control modes.

It is important to recognize that there is no one right combination of output and behavior control. Rather, a number of critical factors should be taken into consideration in evaluating the control system. If cause-and-effect relationships are well-known, behavior control may prove most efficient for reasons of scale economies. If there is a need for adaptation to local conditions, output control seems appropriate. If there is a need for adjusting to local conditions while cause-end-effect relationships are well-known, a combination of output and behavior control may turn out to be the right choice.

Yoshino (1975; 1976) argued that Japanese companies would experience difficulties in adjusting management practices to local conditions because of the lacking tradition for using output control. History has more or less proved his assertions right. However, if the argument is reversed, there should be some truth to the claim that European and in particular American companies are good at adapting to the local conditions in Japan. This claim seems to have been disproved by history, though one cannot take the misery of foreign companies in Japan as a proof of ill-suited control modes. Other explanations have been given, spanning from political bureaucratic barriers to labour shortages.

The results derived from a qualitative case-study of 14 Danish subsidiaries in Japan reported in this paper suggest that an emphasis on output control in the overall control system causes severe problems in the relationship between the subsidiary and the headquarters. The somewhat surprising conclusion is that adaptation to local conditions in the case of Japan means emphazising behavior control. Not tradition but social norms dictate the use of behavior control in the headquarters' control over their Japanese subsidiaries.

Methodology

Data has been collected through interviews with CEO's and functional managers from 14 Danish subsidiaries in Japan. The interviews lasted 2-7 hours, the typical interview lasting appr. 4 hours. The companies were selected from the member list of the Danish Chamber of Commerce Japan and had to hold legal status as a KK (limited liability company). The parent company of each subsidiary had to be of Danish origin: The headquarters had to be located in Denmark, hold the management rights over the subsidiary, and if knowledge could be obtained on the issue, the parent company should have Danish owners or have its historical basis in Denmark. Further, it was emphasized, first, that the subsidiaries showed a willingness to collaborate and an interest in the purpose of the study. This was considered necessary in order to gain access to valid information and to facilitate the development of trust between the researcher and the respondent. Next, it was emphasized that the subsidiaries varied in the number and positions of Danish employees. In particular, a purely Japanese-employee subsidiary, a subsidiary with a Danish director and a subsidiary with a Japanese director and one or several Danish employees were chosen on purpose. The subsidiaries varied in size, with the largest one constituting 25% of the total concern turnover and the smallest one holding less than 1% of the total turnover.

The research design was cross-sectional though historical relations were taken into account in order to understand the present situation. However, past performance is expectedly multi-caused. Also, for reasons of future competitive needs, business organizations cannot reasonably be judged on the basis of historical events alone. Therefore, it is prefered to stay descriptive and explanatory (Emory & Cooper 1991).

The interviews aimed at exploration rather than at testing prespecified hypotheses. Therefore, a semi-structured interview guide was used. The 7-S framework of Waterman, Peters & Phillips (1991) and Galbraith's *Concepts of Organization Design* (1977) constituted the basis upon which questions were asked. Obviously, as the interviews were progressing, earlier interviews to some degree influenced the questioning in later interviews. However, the particular problems of the company researched were the primary focus of each interview.

Case-studies suffer from a lack of reliability, since the same data cannot be collected from a replicated study. However, here the case-study aims only at describing the problems so that hypotheses can be formulated. These hypotheses, of which only a small part are stated in this paper, are currently being tested in a formal study based on closed questionaires sent to all Danish subsidiaries in Japan and Germany. Still, in order to secure a minimum of validity of the data collected, each respondent was asked to sign a written resume and make corrections to the resume if any misunderstandings had occured. The importance, objectives and possible implications of the study were emphasized to the respondents at the beginning of each interview. Also, the respondents were encouraged to ask any questions of concern with regard to the interview and its use through publications, accessibility, etc.

The norm of reciprocity: Socio-cultural differences

The norm of reciprocity applies to every society throughout the world (Gouldner 1960). Whenever people give something, they expect something in return. Work in return for payment is but one example. However, across cultures social norms differ with regard to *what* and *when* something received must be reciprocated. In Denmark, the norm of reciprocity is fairly loose.[1] For example, there is no expectation that an old lady will pay a person for helping her cross the street. Still, she receives help. However, there is an expectation that the helper will receive the same kind of help when it is needed later on. In a public setting, or what could be termed a relationship between two individuals from different groups, the Japanese norm of reciprocity is rather strict (Benedict 1946, Doi 1981). Receivings have to be returned almost immediately and at rather fixed rates. Wedding ceremonies provide such an example. The guests bring a fixed amount in cash as a present and recieve in return a thing at the value of a fixed share of the cash amount. No exceptions are allowed.

Another important feature about the Japanese norm of reciprocity is that the return has to come from the person that received something in the first place. Again, the Danish norm is more loose, allowing for a wide variety with regard to *who* provides the return.

These differences are important to the way the headquarters-subsidiary relationship is perceived by managers and described in text books. For the headquarters' managers, the headquarters-subsidiary relationship is founded on a well-defined set of *roles* with a set of *tasks* attached. For example, the headquarters create a liaison role to take care of communications and production problems in relation to the Japanese subsidiary, or they send out an expatriate as the executive officer of the subsidiary. However, the Japanese norm requires that social exchange goes on between the *person* receiving something and the *person* giving something. Form is important, contents are not. In other words, the headquartes tend to think of the relationship between the headquarters and the subsidiary as a relationship between two organizations while the Japanese employees see the relationship as a relationship between persons. Also, the headquarters tend to think of the relationship as a relationship of specific tasks. The Japanese employees think of the relationship as a relationship where personal obligations are reciprocated by any task.

---

1. It seems reasonable to argue that the norm of reciprocity is fairly loose also in many other European countries and in the US. However, to avoid intra-group differences the paper is only concerned with the relationship between Denmark (a Danish headquarters) and Japan (a Danish subsidiary in Japan).

The norm of reciprocity: Behavioral consequences

Compared with the looser Danish norm, the strict Japanese norm of reciprocity has remarkable behavioral consequences. Whenever a conflict is solved,
at least one person has to give up a claim (Black & Mendenthal 1993).
Thereby an obligation to give a return has been created. However, because
the Japanese norm allows for no flexibility with regard to by whom and
where the repayment is made, the Japanese seek to avoid conflicts. Otherwise, an obligation may lead to a rather long series of reciprocations in order
to balance the account. On the other hand, since the Danish norm allows for
more flexibility, it is acceptable to two Danish parties that one makes a dis-
claim. Rather, an expectation is created that any future conflict between any
two persons can be solved by at least one of the parties disclaiming some of
the controversial issues.

During the interviews, Danish managers expressed this difference between Japanese and Danish behavior in clear terms. However, somewhat surprisingly, it appears that, after a period of adjustments, some Danish managers are more comfortable with the Japanese behavior than with the Danish behavior. To quote a manager from a succesful Danish company in
Japan:

... at the Danish meeting, the experience is that personal points of view are expressed strongly so that a compromise can be reached on a clear understanding of
each others' positions. During meetings with the Japanese the parties very carefully
expose points of view in the first round. In the second round a little more is ex-
posed, and so on and so forth. When a clear sense of each others attitudes has been
reached, a decision is made. By the way, it is typical at the Danish meetings that
if a person takes too deep a breath, another will start talking. At the Japanese
meetings one experiences long pauses with nobody saying anything, rather
thinking about how to comply with the others' wishes so that a consensus solution
can be reached ... We find the Japanese meetings very comfortable.

Typically, the Japanese behavior described here has been interpreted as a desire for consensus. However, as stated above, this behavior is better seen as
conflict-avoiding behavior. Throughout the remainder of this paper, conflict
avoidance helps explain Japanese behavior and it helps us understand the
interfaces between Danish and Japanese co-workers.

In order to avoid a conflict, it is sometimes necessary to stay passive.
Therefore, one finds passivity quite common among the Japanese employees.
However, to the Danish expatriates, the passivity causes severe frustrations

from time to time. There appears to be a discrepancy between the Danish and the Japanese co-workers' attitude towards how to approach a conflict. The Danish expatriates take the position that conflicts should be actively solved while the Japanese employees take the position that conflicts should be passively shied away from in the hope that they will fade out as time passes. For example, the expatriates' experience was expressed in the following two statements:

... it is a typical problem that one does not receive any information from the Japanese employees if something turns out different from what it was supposed to.

The Japanese employees can be characterized as lacking willingness to tell you when bad news come forth. You will get a honest answer if you ask, but you have to ask.

Also, seemingly the conflict avoidance strategy pursued by the Japanese employees encourages them to shirk responsibility for their own acts. The Danish expatriates have no sympathy for this behavior:

An important point about the Japanese employees is that they do not take responsibility for their own actions. It is an annoying problem that mistakes are hidden ... An employee had made a mistake that was in obvious conflict with our policies. When I asked him why he had made the mistake, he answered that he certainly had suggested the mistake but that a superior had approved it. The Japanese are scared of direct confrontations.

However, this statement may also be interpreted as a case of *amae* (Doi 1981), the Japanese employee making a case of self-indulgence as a manifestation of his close relationship with the company. In that case, the reaction from the Japanese employee is a reaction of surprise, since he so obviously had misjudged his relationship with the company.

The Japanese norm of reciprocity: Another setting

The discussion above concerned the Japanese norm of reciprocity with regard to public settings. However, it appears that the Japanese norm has two faces as indicated by the *amae* interpretation above (Doi 1981). Relationships taking place in public, or to be more precise, between persons of different groups are quite different from relationships taking place in more private settings,

settings where both persons belong to the same group. For the sake of convenience, what makes a person an insider or an outsider of a group will not be discussed here. However, attention will be drawn to the distinction between relationships.

When applying to the private setting, the Japanese norm of reciprocity is loose to a degree comparable to the Danish norm. Some may even claim it to be looser. However, Danes would probably also claim that the norm of reciprocity differs between private and public settings. But anyway, the difference is less significant. What makes the borderline between private and public settings so much more clear in the case of Japan is that a special and rather well-defined language and set of formalities apply to the public setting. In the extreme, this sometimes results in a Japanese employee expressing one point of view in public while stating the exactly opposite point of view in private. Moreover, while in Denmark such behavior is considered bully, in Japan it is found both acceptable and normal.

It is important to understand the nature of the private norm of reciprocity. It removes the rigidity that exists in public settings thereby facilitating organizational effectiveness. To the subsidiary, it is important to create a private atmosphere so that the organization can work smoothly. However, to the Danish expatriate used to manage the company in a way familiar from Denmark (though with a flexible mind), the separate natures of public and private settings causes problems. A manager with 19 years of experience from subsidiaries in South-America and South East Asia stated the following:

It is annoying that the Japanese employees are so taciturn when regular management meetings are held. They prefer to stay silent rather than expressing their opposing view to the CEO. The meetings are characterized by me talking, the rest listening. After the meeting I have to confront the Japanese employees one by one — if necessary — at my office, since it is easier to express my point of view to the Japanese employees more directly without them loosing face. Besides, the Japanese seem more willing to express their opinion when we are alone.

However, not only the subsidiary needs to create a private atmosphere, also the relationship between headquarters and the subsidiary needs this flexibility. But even if such an atmosphere is created, the relationship is still left with some problems stemming from the public norm of reciprocity. For example, one of the subsidiaries investigated had a request from the headquarters that product prices be reduced in order to gain market shares. However, the Japanese employees ignored this request. One reason was that the subsidiary was a self-contained profit center. However, this problem could be overcome by technical corrections. The second reason was that the Japanese employees felt uncomfortable about breaking the price structure in the market. It is considered inappropriate to take such actions provoking conflicts.

Creating a private atmosphere in the headquarters-subsidiary relationship faces severe problems of its own. First, the geographical distance prevents the development of closer relationships. It has long been known that even in physical proximity the physical framework is influential as to whom people socialize with (Scharpf 1977). Secondly, the cultural gap is large (Hofstede 1991). The problems expressed by the expatriates concerning their adaptation to the Japanese subsidiary may be blown up when the interaction is less frequent and an understanding never reached. Actually, several expatriates were quite familiar with bad mention of the Japanese circling around in the headquarters. Interestingly, in spite of their annoyance, the expatriates themselves expressed warm-hearted feelings about the Japanese, and they took the position of either defending the subsidary or that of the negotiator in the middle. Further, within a few companies an effort towards illuminating the negative attitude in the headquarters had turned out quite succesful. Amongst other things, these efforts included the cautious choice of employees for working assignments in relation to the Japanese subsidiary, presentations about Japan in the headquarters whenever expatriates or Japanese employees were on a visit, dinners arranged between Danes and Japanese whenever they visited each others companies, and in a rather extreme case, all Japanese employees were flown to Denmark on a visit.

However, in spite of these efforts and the few succesful cases, most expatriates were rather pessimistic with regard to the effect of these socialization efforts. One of the more succesful companies expressed comparatively strongly that they hoped that both the Danish and the Japanese employees would have a feeling of belonging to the same company.

The norm of reciprocity: Double-edged conclusions

Also the understanding of self is said to differ between the Japanese and the Danes (cf. Doi 1986). In particular, among insiders the interpersonal relationships are considered organic in Japan, i.e. to say that a person behaves opportunistically to a group to which he belongs is literally to say that he is cutting his own leg. Further, this has been interpreted in such a way that to the Japanese freedom basically means the freedom to behave as one pleases without being responsible to others (Doi 1981). To the Dane, freedom is understood in terms of individual rights. Further, one is responsible for the way these rights are used. Therefore, self is independent of the others.

In accordance with these observations, some Danish expatriates expressed their admiration for the Japanese employees. Outstanding for their loyalty, the Japanese employees were thought of as easier to manage. In one company, the group behavior was characterized as psychologically important for the motivation of the employees. Nobody would leave their fellow employees alone in the evening if a job needed to be done. The whole working group would stay after the regular working hours to help getting the job done. By itself, this illustrates a fairly loose norm of reciprocity. Help is given with an allowance for reciprocation at a later and unspecified point in time.

Further, should an extraordinary need arise, the Danish expatriates found the Japanese employees outstanding in their inclination to stay at the job. Also the Danish employees are willing to stay over-time, but they have to be asked, one manager explained. The Japanese employees simply stay on by their own initiative. However, one expatriate was particularly critical to this description. He found that the Japanese employees do indeed stay on work during the evenings if necessary, but the only reason as he saw it was that over-time payment provided them with an incentive to stay. The Danish employees would receive no over-time payment, but rather have to flex their time in order to get even with the company.

Whether the Japanese show their great willingness to stay over-time for cultural, group oriented reasons or for reasons of incentives has been debated among anthropologists and economists for some years. Two extreme positions are found in the works of Nakane (1973) and Koike (1984). Nakane's work suggests the Japanese employees' loyalty to be culturally bound while Koike favours a more rationalistic, incentive based approach. However, the discussion above may in fact prove both of them right, their arguments referring to different social settings. If the Japanese workers stay on at work during the evenings for reasons of over-time payment, this may be because they consider their relationship to the company to be at a distance, i.e. they do not feel like insiders with the company. As outsiders, i.e. where a public setting exists, the natural inclination for the Japanese is to expect immediate reciprocation. This they find in the over-time payment. On the other hand, if the Japanese employees think of themselves as insiders to the company, they expect no immidiate reciprocation. On the contrary, they may in fact be satisfied with the prospect of long-term employment or higher bonuses at the end of the year, irrespective of the incentive scheme provided by over-time payment.

The norm of reciprocity: Balancing one edge, falling off another

While the Danish expatriates find the loyalty of the Japanese co-workers unique, they complain about the lack of initiative and independence. Naturally, this complaint is related to the collectivistic behavior often claimed or assumed among scholars of the Japanese social organization (Nakane 1973; Doi 1981; 1986; Lebra 1992). The degree of collectivism versus individualism in various countries has been measured by the Dutch business sociologist Geert Hofstede (1991) in a study of IBM subsidiaries in 53 countries. Here, Denmark is found to be the ninth most individualistic country (score 76 of 100) while the Japanese is placed as the twenty second (score 46 out of 100). While these results confirm that the Japanese are more collectivistic than the Danish, the study also cast some doubt on the extreme nature of Japanese collectivistic behavior. Thus, Doi (1986) argues that the Japanese are much aware of their self and historically have placed some emphasis on both individual superiority and the individual's opposition to the group.

Further, a closer examination of the relationship between the lack of initiative and independence on the one hand and the specific collectivistic behavior of the Japanese on the other reveals a more muddled picture. First of all, as the entity they constitute, groups may show much initiative. Secondly, individuals may show initiative and yet constantly accept to be overruled by the group for reasons of both individual and group interests. This is so, if the group possesses a strong entrepreneurial spirit encouraging group members to show initiative and suggest ideas on the understanding that group interests must be considered. If such consideration is not given, the individual will be punished or maybe even ostracized. However, since any society has social norms, we may in fact consider the Japanese and Danish society to be ruled by partially congruent social norms, each allowing for initiative but with quite different regards to other people. In this sense, the 'individualistic' Danish behavior and the 'collectivistic' Japanese behavior may be seen as points on a continuum of still stronger social norms rather than as contradictions.

Still, we are left with the statements by the expatriates expressing disappointment with regard to the lack of initiative and independence of the Japanese co-workers. However, if the Japanese employees consider the Danish expatriates as outsiders to their group, the Japanese norm of reciprocity prevents the Danish expatriates from obtaining knowledge of the initiative and independence expressed in-group. To the manager such a relationship is fatal. The manager will have to depend on no other ideas than his own. Further, the manager does not have many possibilities to influence and move the groups of employees, since the process of reciprocation must take on the strictly formalized form, i.e. the management of the subsidiary becomes rule driven. Therefore, both the expatriates and the headquarters have to work on the creation of insider relationships. Otherwise, inefficiency results.

The norm of reciprocity: Are the Japanese irresponsible?

That the Japanese are not totally free from initiative has already been illustrated in one of the above quotations in which a Danish expatriate expressed his annoyance with regard to the lack of responsibility shown by a Japanese employee. In this case, the employee showed to much initiative. The lacking feeling of responsibility is also indicated in Doi's (1981) discussion of freedom in Japan versus the West. However, if the norm of reciprocity is considered once again, we will see that the seeming lack of responsibility reported by the Danish expatriates is caused by differences in the control basis rather than being the case per se:

Because of the strict norm of reciprocity as it applies to public settings, the Japanese seek to avoid conflicts. Therefore, the conclusion suggests itself that the Japanese are highly unlikely to make promises at all. However, another commonly stated feature about the Japanese is that they deny the existence of universal concepts, not only considering each situation as highly unique but also as subject to change with changing circumstances (Doi 1981; Wolferen 1989). Of course, by itself this indicates an irresponsible attitude to the Westerner or Dane. However, to the Japanese, responsibility becomes a matter of promising something that is possible when promised. Should the circumstances change, as they are likely to, the responsibility disappears. Surprisingly, in one of the interviews an expatriate thought of this as a positive feature about the Japanese:

We find the Japanese employees to be very pragmatic and good at achieving something positive from critical or bad situations. The perception of a given situation changes extremely fast in the mind of the Japanese, and they therefore show a remarkable ability to adjust to changing situations.

In general however, such an attitude was quite understandably seen as impossible to manage by the Danish expatriates. Still, one explanation is missing. Whatever is promised by the Japanese cannot just be promised without considering the interests and obligations of others. Rather, in order to avoid conflicts, it is critical that any promise is checked with those people that are likely to be influenced by the promise. In this sense, the Danes appear irresponsible, often making promises without being completely sure that the obligations can be met. Rather, to some degree, it is hoped that luck or at least influenced circumstances will make it possible to meet the obligation. Accordingly, the Danish expatriates argued that the Japanese outlook on the world has both its pros and cons:

The way the Japanese have their meetings is definitely not quicker, but it facilitates a much firmer backing of the decision reached. The problem is that the Japanese do not feel obligated by the decision whenever a new situation arises, and it is therefore difficult for us Danes to be clear about which decisions are still in effect and which are not.

It seems that what we see here are two different social systems for dealing with the unpredictable nature of future matters. However, the practical problems in handling these differences were much greater than the differences themselves. This will be illustrated on the basis of a discussion of the company's planning systems.

The norm of reciprocity: Planning the future

Practically, all companies make plans concerning their future development. There is, of course, some variation with regard to the specification of plan contents and the planning horizon, but in any case at least a budget for the coming year is found. In the Danish headquarters, the plan expresses not only the prospects for a specified period, but it is also the basis on which employees, departments and subsidiaries are evaluated. Plan fulfilment is critical to a positive evaluation.

Obviously, plan fulfilment is only expected as long as the underlying assumptions do not change. If a new situation appears, there is a need for some degree of plan adjustment. However, there are limits to how far the adjustments can be made. For example, many investments are irreversible once they have been made, and the consequences of actually carrying out the investment therefore reach well into the future. And it is even worse, if the management is not even aware of the need for adjustments. Often this knowledge is in the hands of the employees who are close to the problems, but the employees have no incentive to report the need for adjustments since the management's awareness of this only creates trouble in relation to the evaluation of the employees' performance. This is in essence one of the classical Danish management problems: How to motivate the employees to report the need for adjustments?

However, because of the Japanese norm of reciprocity such problems do not exist in the same form. Rather, a plan to the Japanese employee seems outdated as soon as the assumptions of the plan are broken. The Japanese employee acts on the basis of the new situation, but not in an uncoordinated way as one might expect. On the contrary, the social system encourages a new consideration of the existing obligations (Nakane 1973). However, this means that while the actions stay coordinated, the response to changes is not very fast. This was expressed by a Danish expatriate in the following manner:

Systems are a key word in the management of the Japanese subsidiary and in the Japanese society in general, and they seem to work so well that very often the Japanese are not prepared and not ready to handle a breakdown ... The Japanese employees' clinging to the systems makes them hard to manage in a company where there is a need for initiative throughout the organization. It is a problem that the employees at the bottom of the organization lack independence to a large degree and cannot or will not make decisions without confirming them with a superior.

This respondent also complains about the lack of independence. However, in one sense the Japanese show more initiative than the Danish employees, namely in their response to changing circumstances.

While many positive and negative aspects of both Danish and Japanese employees could be listed, we shall here evaluate the interface situation in particular: When Danish headquarters manage their Japanese subsidiaries. In this case, the Danish managers have experience with one problem type — the lacking incentives to report a need for adjustments — whereas the Japanese employees they manage are naturally inclined to report such needs. However, the same employees are not used to working with the planning systems familiar to the headquarters and the Danish expatriates. This lack of orientation towards planning in our sense of the word causes annoyance among the Danish expatriates and in the headquarters. A very balanced statement by an expatriate expresses the problem quite well:

the Japanese employees have proved unable to follow a general planning system, and therefore I have chosen to formulate the goals to myself, and to control the company through daily interaction instead ... In the Japanese subsidiary ... it is hard to find any connection between objectives, strategies and activity plans, there is no connection between long time planning, budgets and operational decisions. From time to time this causes anger in the headquarters, and therefore they send out someone to teach the Japanese how to do things. The Japanese employees quickly show their ability to copy the system, and they do as told, but the following year the problem arises once again: There is no connection between objectives, strategies and budgets. Nor did the headquarters understand why things worked out so badly from time to time, even though budgets and perspectives seemed fine, but probably this was caused by the lacking contextual frame and by the lack of planning in the Japanese subsidiary.

The control of Danish subsidiaries in Japan: Behavior or output control?

The planning system constitutes a basis in an output control systems as described by Ouchi & Maguire (1975). Therefore, even though output control is a popular mode of control in headquarters-subsidiary relationships, the discussion above suggests some caution with regard to the use of it. Also, the previously mentioned mental perception of the headquarters-subsidiary relationship suggests an emphasis on behavior control or more personal control modes. Further, also the need for creating a private setting in order to enforce a flexible norm of reciprocity suggests that the relationship should build on the personal modes of control. Finally, both the interviews and other scholars' observations on the Japanese economy caused an even stronger belief that output control should be abandoned in the relationship between Danish headquarters and their Japanese subsidiaries. These findings have been published elsewhere (Bjørn 1995).

While there are strong arguments in favour of behavior control, the conclusion is rather abstract in nature. Behavioral modes of control span across many more concrete instruments. For example, according to Edström & Galbraith (1977) managers are transfered for three reasons. First, a lack of qualified personel in the subsidiary may cause the subsidiary to ask the headquarters for personel to fill out positions when local personel cannot be found or be easily trained. Secondly, international business organizations may transfer managers in an effort to develop managers for positions of responsibility. However, this necessitates a more proactive personnel department in the headquarters since managers may be transferred between subsidiaries and to and from the headquarters. Thirdly, transfers may be used for organization development, in particular in order to maintain the structure and decision processes. As such transfer is a strategy for developing a more decentralized coordination, and it becomes a process of control based on socialization.

However, these arguments are based on the assumption of roles as the correct way of understanding headquarters-subsidiary relationships. The findings of this study therefore add a fourth argument to the list, namely transfer in order to bridge differences in the social systems of each organization. In this case, a transfer is not seen as the organization filling out a role, but rather the transfer becomes a highly personal matter, the intention being to incorporate the expatriate in the subsidiary with the task of controlling the subsidiary. However, the expatriate does not assume the role of a foreign body but the role of an insider. Obviously, this is self-contradictory, since the control by an insider can be nothing but self-control and therefore apparently no control by the headquarters. However, the Japanese social organization necessitates this kind of control, and therefore the demands on the expatriate are extreme: The expatriate must give in to the Japanese behavioral norms while staying an important control tool to the headquarters.

References

Benedict, Ruth. 1946. *The Crysanthemum and the Sword*. Boston: Houghton Mifflin.

Bjørn, Lars. 1995. *Danske datterselskaber i Japan – ledelse og organisation*. Copenhagen: Munksgaard.

Black, James Stewart & Mark Mendenthall. 1993. Resolving Conflicts with the Japanese: Mission Impossible? *Sloan Management Review* 49-59. Spring.

Doi, Takeo. 1981. *The Anatomy of Dependence*. Revised edition. New York: Kodansha.

Doi, Takeo. 1986. *The Anatomy of Self — The Individual versus Society*. New York: Kodansha.

Edström, A. & J.R. Galbraith. 1977. Transfer of Managers as a Coordination and Control Strategy in Multinational Organizations. *Administrative Science Journal*, vol. 22, 248-63.

Egelhoff, W.G. 1984. Patterns of Control in U.S., U.K., and European Multinational Corporations. *Journal of International Business Studies* 73-83. Fall.

Emory, William C. & Donald R. Cooper. 1991. *Business Research Methods*. Boston: Irwin.

Franko, L.G. 1978. Organizational Structures and Multinational Strategies of Continental European Enterprises. *European Research in International Business*, ed. by M. Ghertman & J. Leontiades, 111-40. Amsterdam: North-Holland.

Galbraith, Jay R. 1974). Organization Design: An Information Processing View. *Interfaces*, vol. 4, no. 3, 28-36 reprint in: *Organizations by Design: Theory and Practice*, ed. by Mariann Jelinek, Joseph A. Litterer & Raymond E. Miles. Homewood, Illinois.

Galbraith, Jay R. 1977. *Organizational Design*. Reading, Massachusetts: Addison-Wesley.

Gouldner, Alvin W. 1960. The Norm of Reciprocity: A Preliminary Statement. *American Sociological Review*, vol. 25, no. 2, 161-78.

Hofstede, Geert. 1991. *Cultures and Organizations — Software of the Mind*. Copenhagen: Schultz.

Koike, Kazuo. 1984. Skill Formation Systems of the Japanese Firm. *The Economic Analysis of the Japanese Firm*, ed by Aoki, Masahiko. Amsterdam: North-Holland.

Lebra, Takie Sugiyama. 1992. The Spatial Layout of Hierarchy: Residental Style of the Modern Japanese Nobility. *Japanese Social Organization*, ed. by Lebra, Takie Sugiyama. Honolulu: University of Hawaii Press.

Martinez, J. & J. Carlos Jarillo. 1989. The Evolution of Research on Coordination Mechanisms in Multinational Corporations. *Journal of International Business Studies*, vol. 20, 489-514.

Nakane, Chie. 1973. *Japanese Society*. Harmondsworth: Penguin Books.

Ouchi, William G. 1977. The Relationship Between Organizational Structure and Organizational Control. *Administrative Science Quarterly*, vol. 22, 95-113.

Ouchi, William G. 1978. The Transmission of Control Through Organizational Hierarchy. *Academy of Management Journal*, vol. 21, 173-92.

Ouchi, William G. 1979a. A Conceptual Framework for the Design of Organizational Control Mechanisms. *Management Science*, vol. 25, 833-48.

Ouchi, William G. & Mary Ann Maguire. 1975. Organizational Control: Two Functions. *Administrative Science Quarterly*, vol. 20, 559-69.

Scharpf, Fritz W. 1977. Does Organization Matter? Task Structure and Interaction in the Ministerial Bureaucracy. *Organization Design: Theoretical Perspectives and Empirical Findings*, ed. by Burack & Negandhi. Kent, Ohio: Kent State University Press.

Waterman, Robert H. Jr., Thomas Peters & Julian R. Phillips. 1991. The 7-S Framework. *The Strategy Process*, ed. by Henry Mintzberg & James Brian Quinn. Englewood Cliffs, New Jersey: Prentice-Hall.

Wolferen, Karel van. 1989. *The Enigma of Japanese Power: People and Politics in a Stateless Nation*. London: Macmillan.

Yoshino, M.Y. 1975. Emerging Japanese Multinational Enterprises. In: *Modern Japanese Organization and Decision-making*, ed. by E.F. Vogel, 146-66. Berkeley: University of California Press.

Yoshino, M.Y. 1976. *Japan's Multinational Enterprises*. Cambridge, Massachusetts: Harvard University Press.

Ninsokuyoseba — Or How Kamagasaki Works

Christian Morimoto Hermansen

Try asking a resident of Ôsaka if he or she knows where Kamagasaki is, and most likely he or she will answer affirmatively but incorrectly: 'Yes, I know where Amagasaki is' — Amagasaki being a relatively well-off town located northwest of Ôsaka in the direction of Kôbe. I wonder how many of my readers have heard the name of Kamagasaki before? How many have visited this or the similar areas in other bigger towns of Japan — San'ya in Tôkyô or Kotobukichô in Yokohama, for instance? The common term in Japanese for these areas is *Yoseba*, literally a place in which people gather.

The history of *yoseba* is only a couple of hundred years old, and I now have the privilege of studying this history as the topic of my Ph.D. dissertation. I hope to be ready to tell that story in due course, but for now, I shall confine myself to the modern *yoseba*.

Though rarely talked about and hardly ever mentioned in the typical introduction to Japan's society and economy, it is not as if the world has never heard of the existence of day-labourers and *yoseba* in Japan. Five years ago Kamagasaki made international headlines when a protest against police corruption and injustice exploded into a riot, with at least two thousand special riot police troops on one side and as many day-labourers on the other and two or three news reporting helicopters hovering above. For five days the battle went on and a local railway station was set on fire, while the police station was barricaded off like a castle in the civil war period. But, such incidences aside, Kamagasaki and its like might just as well not exist as far as Japan and the world is concerned.

If indeed Kamagasaki is best kept in oblivion, then why try to make it an object of academic concern, rather than its neighbouring areas such as Tennôji?

Kamagasaki is a barometer of the Japanese economy. As one economist stated,

If you check the number of 'cash' workers and add the number of people in the soup-kitchen line, then you can see the trends in the Japanese economy (Koyanagi 1993:76).

Apart from the economy, I might add that I think Kamagasaki reveals over-looked dimensions in the picture of conformist Japan. In a physically very narrow space, one meets the jobless, the homeless, the prostitute, the alcohol abusers, gangsters and guest-workers. It is the *furusato* (home) of people on the move.

Kamagasaki is a *yoseba* of less than one square kilometer (see map). It is framed on three sides by railways: to the North Kanjôsen (Osaka's Loop line), to the West Nankaisen — the connection between Namba and Kôya-san — and to the East the Hankai tramway from Ebisuchô to Sakai. The semi-official name is Airinchiku ('Neighbourlovehood'), and the area is a part of Nishinari-ku.

Two public structures stand out: In the center of Kamagasaki is the Nishinari police headquarters, and in the northwestern corner just opposite Shin'imamiya station one finds the employment center *Airinchi rôdôkôkyô shokugyô anteijo* (literally: Airinchi workers public job stability/security place). To the public domain belong also an elementary school and two parks — a few tens of square meters of dirt of which one is triangular and the other rectangular and located behind the police station; there are neither trees nor grass.

Of private enterprises one finds small stores, restaurants, *pachinko* parlours and street vendors (human as well as mechanical ones), but first of all a huge number of private lodgings. They range from super-cheap hotels at 700 yen a room to so-called business hotels at 2000 yen. The common term for them is *doya*. In 1992 there were 200 of them with a total capacity of more than 20,000 persons (Mizuno 1993:231). These *doya* are rather particular about their customers. Usually no women are allowed, while places such as the Sun Plaza are mostly for foreigners. The latter was built, along with several others, only six years ago, when the bubble economy of Japan could absorb almost unlimited numbers of workers. Other *doya* will only accept guests who work for a particular company, and thus they ought to be classified as *hanba* (see below). The recent reconstruction of many of the *doya*, through which process the number of *mansions* (apartments) has increased, has almost completely erased the formerly typical room: roughly one meter by two meter by one meter. Nowadays one can actually stand erect inside the room, and will usually find it equipped with a colour television set. The guests are single men — day-labourers, *hiyatoi rôdôsha*. According to a popu-

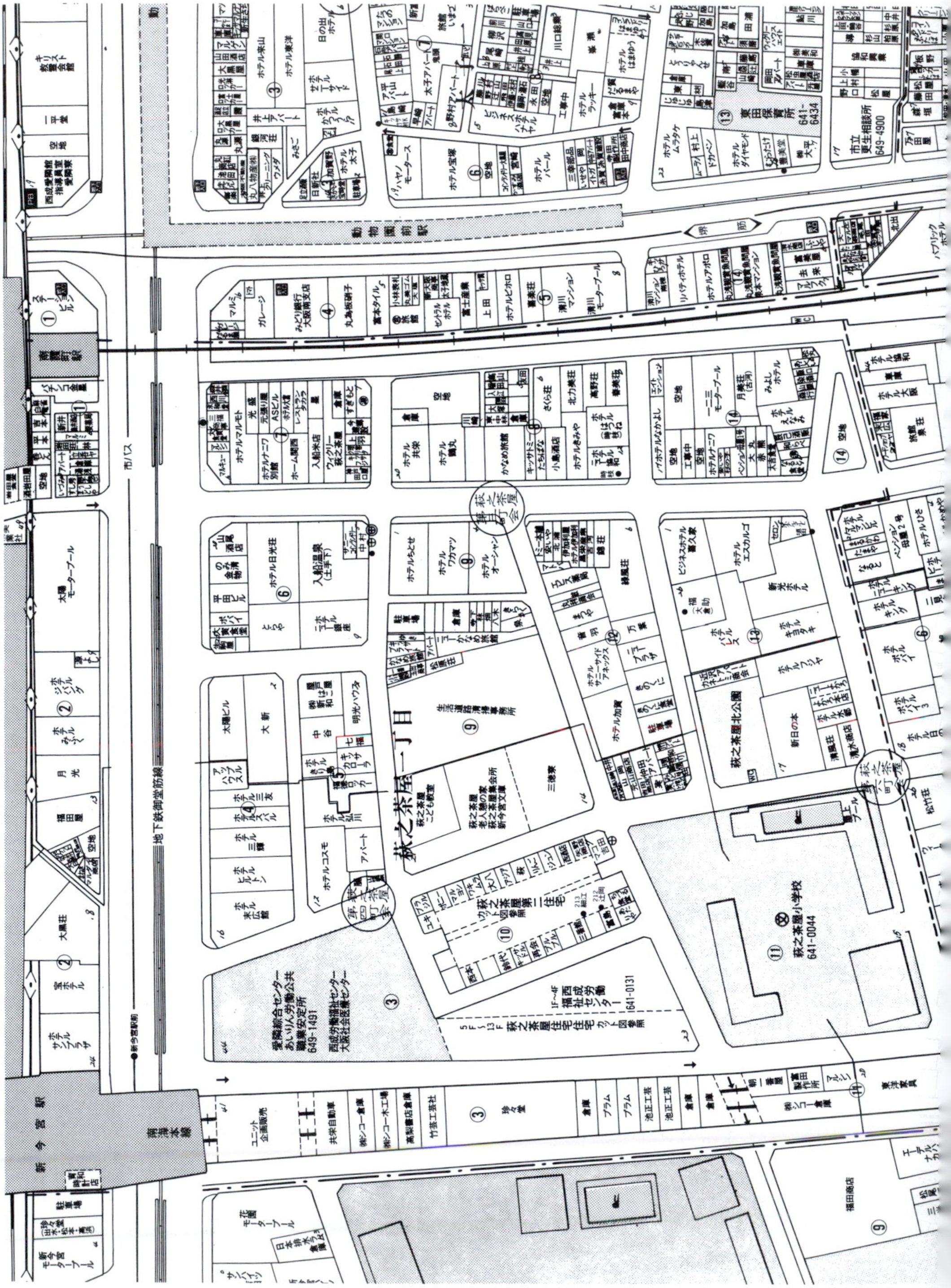
萩之茶屋一丁目
新今宮駅
萩之茶屋小学校
641-0044
地下鉄御堂筋線
市バス
動物園前駅
萩之茶屋北公園

Public map of Nishinari-ku, Haginochaya 1, 2, and 3 chôme = Kamagasaki.

lation survey from 1990, there were 30,745 residents in Kamagasaki, of whom some 15,000 were day-labourers.

If in Japan you have seen a road under repair, a building under construction, or a man with a signboard directing visitors to a specific bar you have also seen a day-labourer. These kinds of job belong to the 3K group — *kitsui, kitanai, kiken* (hard, dirty, dangerous) — to which cleaning of sewage systems and atomic power plants also belong. The person hired to perform them is usually between 20 and 50, male, and to a large degree unskilled for the job. Some of the older men may get jobs which require a lot of routine, and therefore are paid a better salary, but on average the pay per day is 14,000 yen. The hours are from 8 to 5. For the day-labourer there are three kinds of relationships to the job-market: cash, contract or contact.

'Cash' means pay by the day, and when the economy is good, this is the common kind of relationship. To get a job, one goes to the employment center. The day of the employment center begins at 5 a.m., when the shutters are raised, but the job-seeker usually turns up at 4. Contractors, or sub-contractors, looking for workers, will send a car or bus with a job broker who must choose those he wants. It often happens that the broker represents one of the *yakuza*, or gangster bosses. Behind the windshield of the cars a poster announces the day's offer: 'Construction work, 8 persons, 13,000 Yen including lunch, excluding transportation'. No matter what kind of job, one usually gets paid at the end of the employment period and sometimes will have to go to the job broker's office after hours in order to get paid. It is customary to pay the broker a fee for getting the job.

Once the broker has the people he needs, the bus leaves. While waiting for the bus to be filled, those who already have a job will go to the second floor of the employment center, where along the walls some ten small stalls provide breakfast at low prices. Alternatively one may seek out one of the neighbourhood's several coffee shops that offers *môningu sâbisu*, or a bar with *bîru no môningu sâbisu*.

'Contract' is the kind of relationship chosen when the fight for jobs gets fierce. The job seeker makes a contract with the broker and lives at his hanba. *Hanba* are lodges belonging to a job broker company, and can be situated at the place of work, or in the city of Ôsaka, often in the vicinity of Kamagasaki. As long as one stays there, a job, a bed, and three meals a day are guaranteed. It usually costs 2,500 yen a day to live there but life can be very tough, especially if the *hanba* belongs to *yakuza*. Strict rules may have to be obeyed, and infringement is punished severely.

In this contract system the worker must promise to work a specific number of days. The number can be 10, 15 or 30 days. If everything works out all right, there is no problem, but in case of bad weather, holidays, or other events the work may be interrupted, and thus it can take 3 or 4 weeks to get 10 days of actual work done. As every day in the hanba has to be paid for, the worker sometimes ends up coming home to Kamagasaki with a deficit. And should the worker leave before the end of the contracted period, no money is paid; he might even be in for some kind of punishment by the contractor.

'Contact' is for those who have developed good relations with a local boss, so that they can go directly to the work place. The better skilled one is, the better chances one has of getting a job. This direct possibility is thus for a rather limited number of workers.

To sum up, of the three ways, cash, contract and contact, the contract has been the most common since Japan's economic bubble burst.

Around eight or nine in the morning the second part of the day starts for those who did not get a job. Depending on the season, both the natural one and the economic one, hundreds of unemployed line up in front of the windows at the second floor of the employment center behind which clerks are busy checking unemployment insurance books in order to judge whether the client is worthy of payment or not. The idea behind the insurance book is that every day of employment qualifies one for the purchase of a stamp at 200 yen; a month's worth of stamps, bought within two months, entitles the holder to get two weeks of insurance money. This amounts to about 6,000 yen a day.

For many reasons a person may not be able to meet the requirements of the system, be it due to old age, illness or bad weather. Thus left without money he is faced with the following choices: move on to a different *yoseba*; move out of his hotel and sleep outdoors — *aokan* in Japanese; or visit one of the many moneylenders located here and there in Kamagasaki.

The moneylenders are yet another face of the *Yakuza*. One way of borrowing money from them is to bring one's unemployment insurance book and ID card. The lender provides the required number of stamps and seals, the borrower goes to the insurance payment office, and, once he gets the money, he passes on a percentage of it as gratitude money to the moneylender, together with his documents (*Genkimagajin*, no. 6, 1989:104-8). When this situation continues for a longer period, the worker will end up owing a lot of money, and thus may be made use of cheaply by the lender.

In order to help and support the people of Kamagasaki, a network among several organizations has developed there. These organizations address different kinds of people in need. The Kama union organizes wage and work condition negotiations in the springtime, soup kitchens twice a day, and assistance in case of troubles with employers when needed; church groups of various denominations help the children, the aged, the sick, the homeless and the substance abusers; together the union and the church groups go on night patrol during the winter. So if you visit Kamagasaki on a night in January after the *pachinko* balls have fallen silent, you may meet groups of people with a push cart loaded with blankets, cardboard and soup to help people on the street survive.

I think that for almost any topic within the field of Japanology, be it economics, linguistics, social welfare or law, a new perspective on it will be gained by looking into its situation in Kamagasaki or one of the other *yoseba*.

References

Koyanagi, Shinken. 1993. Rôdô to seikatsu. *Kamagasaki Rekishi to Genzai*, edited by Kamagasaki Shiryôsentâ, 68-112. Tokyo: San'ichi shobo.

Mizuno, Ashura. 1993. Yoseba (Kamagasaki) to Otoko to Kazuko. *Kamagasaki Rekishi to Genzai*. Edited by Kamagasaki Shiryôsentâ, 228-57. Tokyo: San'ichi shobo.

Wada, Kensan et al. 1989. *Kamagasaki Sutôrii*. (=*Genki Magajin* 6). Osaka: Burênsentâ.

Ri and Ki in Japanese Thought

Olof G. Lidin

It is not entirely clear when Neo-Confucian thought was introduced into Japan — but certainly not long after Chu Hsi died in 1200. Zen monks visiting China did not only learn about *zazen* 'sitting meditation' but also about *seiza* 'quiet sitting', practised by Confucian scholars. They took a scholarly interest in the last outpour of Confucian thought and they became assiduous students of Confucian metaphysics and natural thought in between their meditation sessions, to the extent that a Zen abbot once complained that there was too much philosophy and too little zazen in the Rinzai (Gozan) temples. However, through the Kamakura and especially the Muromachi periods Neo-Confucian studies were mostly an intellectual sideline and seem never to have become the main occupation of the monks, who were both in name and deed Zen monks. It should be added that also the Kiyowara Confucian scholars from early times took an interest in Neo-Confucian studies.

This would all change in the Tokugawa period when we find the first monks who left Rinzai and established themselves as Confucian scholars. They broke out of Zen Buddhist eclecticism, even often denied Buddhism, and began to preach a Confucian message, leaning toward the native *kami* creed, thereby giving it a distinct Japanese identity. Traditionally Fujiwara Seika (1561-1618) and Hayashi Razan (1583-1657) are mentioned as the forerunners of this new Confucian age and tradition. Whether they left the Buddhist orthodoxy because of conviction or convenience is difficult to say. Fujiwara Seika seems to have been the noble personality who did it out of conviction; Hayashi Razan, on the other hand, might well have done it out of convenience, having plans to rise in the new world that was built by Tokugawa Ieyasu. Fujiwara Seika never accepted a position in official service, but Hayashi Razan happily turned to Tokugawa Ieyasu and entered shogunal service in 1605, establishing a connection with the Tokugawa regime that would last for twelve generations, that is, throughout the Tokugawa era. The Hayashis became the carriers of the Shushigaku *ri* tradition, and whatever new thought appeared to their left or to their right, they were in the centre.

How can their Neo-Confucian *ri* doctrine be simply described? *Ri* can be seen as the totality of the 'wiring' of the universe, as ordained by Heaven. One finds also the expression *tenri*, 'the Inscape of Heaven', in which one can see the close connection between Heaven and its 'wiring' of the world, synonymous with the term *tendô*, 'the Way of Heaven'. *Ri* is, however, not alone — and not sufficient. The 'wiring' is without meaning and useless if it were not for the *ki*, the 'electricity', which makes the whole net come alive.

Ri-ism can be seen as a kind of rational thought, built upon man's ability to reason about things. Man can see *regularities* in things, lines and streaks which individuate. He begins to see order in chaos, and science is born. The unchanging lines and regularities are seen as the *ri* in things, and all these *ri* in things are in turn related to a Heavenly Principle — *ri*, *(tenri)* — the Mother of all individuated *ri* and the ultimate cause of creation and change. *Ri* can accordingly be registered as the same in, for example, each horse and each man not only in his physical appearance but also in his mental and psychic apparatus. In the

original Chu Hsi thought this meant empirical inquiry into individual functions, synthesized by intuitive perception of larger and larger functional systems until one encompasses the one ri permeating all nature, including human nature (Levenson 1954).

These inquiries were expressed with terms, such as *kyûri* (Ch., *ch'iung-li*), 'to penetrate the *ri*' or *kakubutsu kyûri* (Ch., *ke-wu-ch'iung-li*, 'to investigate things and penetrate the *ri*'.

Ri does not and cannot, however, operate alone, it is only the framework or network for the life-giving *ki*, which flows through the lines of *ri*: without *ki* no *ri*, and without *ri* no *ki*. They form the inextricable two sides of the same coin: one does not go without the other. *Ki* is seen in a *ri* perspective and vice versa.

The question is which of the two, *ri* or *ki*, should take precedence over the other. In the orthodox Chu Hsi thought it seems that *ri* has the priority and is valued over *ki*. It is *ri* that represents Heaven — it is tenri in man's nature *(sei)* as well as in all other things — while *ki* represents Earth and comes second, without, for this reason, being secondary. *Ri* comes first because it should, in the human *moral* world, be the essential, unchangeable part which is in control of the *ki* emotional and changeable part of man's psyche. They are in a kind of opposition in the nature of man, which is unfinished and indeterminate, but in nature otherwise it seems that *ki* and *ri* go hand in hand without being in opposition, one functioning due to the other, one being alive because of the other.

In man *ri* appears as his 'basic nature' (*honzen no sei* or *honshitsu no sei*). This is his 'good' nature, which is the same and identical in everybody. Everybody is therefore a potential sage — if it were not for his volatile earthly *ki* nature (*kishitsu no sei*), which obstructs the goodness of his basic *ri* nature. In other words, *honshitsu no sei* is the pure part of man's nature, while the *kishitsu no sei* varies from person to person, as the impure part of man's nature. Desires, emotions, and passions are encoded in his earthly *ki* nature, and man must keep at purifying and polishing, checking and controlling this earthly part of his nature — and perfect his inborn potential.[1]

It is of interest that the *ri* thought served as a conservative force and ideology, supporting the state and the system. The Tokugawa *bakufu* feudal order incorporated and represented *ri* and Heaven in this world, and it became the duty of all people to support the *bakufu seido*, which corresponded to and was in line with the universal *ri* of all things. The feudal socio-political order with the four classes hierarchically ordered in their places was a reflection and embodiment of the cosmic 'natural' order, and so Heaven remained the supreme source of legitimation for the maintenance of shogunal power. Any rebel could be accused of having alienated himself from the *ri* and not being in control of his *ki*.

The term *ki* is a much wider and more difficult term than *ri*. The *ri* can be more or less directly observed and measured, they are after all the streaks and lines and forms of things. The *ki* in all its energy forms is not visible and comes in many categories. We have, for example, 'the great *ki*' (*taiki*), which stands for the whole cosmic atmosphere we live in, the air that surrounds us, and what we breathe in and breathe out. *Kûki*, 'the empty *ki*', is also the air that surrounds us and which we breathe in and out, but is perhaps closer to us than 'the great *ki*', which expresses the air in a wider sense as atmosphere. The two terms naturally overlap in usage. A third term, *fun'iki*, also refers to the atmosphere around us, but then it is the 'air' as it affects us socially. It is the atmosphere of ambience, the '*genius loci*', as a dictionary expresses it. Further, we have *kôkiatsu* and *teikiatsu*, 'high air pressure' and 'low air pressure' and *jôki* (*suijôki*), 'steam', vapour'. Then come the five atmospheric

---

1. Professor Joseph R. Levenson (1954) refers to *ri* as 'ideal form' and *ki* as 'mutable matter'. *Ri* is 'the universal which the intellect apprehends and the senses never reach', while *ki* is part of matter and thus perceptible. *Ki* is here seen as part of but independent of matter. In matter both *ri* and *ki* are indeed perceptible.

ki forces, rain which is under the influence of wood, fine weather which is under the influence of metal, heat which is under the influence of fire, cold which is under the influence of water, and wind which is under the influences of earth. One notices how close the *ki* is to the five elements in Chinese thought. This links to *genki*, the primeval force, 'the protoplasm of Chinese theories of evolution' (Mathews), the stuff of the universe. In early Taoist thought *ki* was born in the emptiness and the *ki* that was light became Heaven and the *ki* that was heavy became Earth. The result was the complementary *ki*, *yin* and *yang*, which in an eternal balance function together and are the origin of all things. *Ki* is then the original and basic stuff of the universe and the force behind all creation. The four seasons of the year can be taken as an example of this interplay when the *ki* force waxes during spring and summer and wanes during autumn and winter. In man it is the same. There is a balance of *ki* that forms man both on the physical and the psychic side. It is the energy that keeps him alive, which can be described as his soul, spirit, heart, mind or life. His *ki* waxes as he grows up and it wanes when he grows old. And all his physical and psychic situations are related to his *ki* force which mysteriously works on two planes and together psychosomatically. In the end, in Taoist thought, all is one and all is *ki*.[2]

The *ri* and *ki* dialectic is anchored in a long Chinese tradition. The *I Ching*, *The Book of Changes*, presents a monistic cosmology, codifying the patterns of universal change — a *ki* universe of change. As change equals *ki*, the first among Chinese classics emphasizes the *ki* side of reality. The question is whether the Chinese have ever left this cosmic view. Chang Tsai (1020-77) in Neo-Confucian thought also described a monistic cosmos, in which the Way (*dao*) and *ri* were immanent in a *ki* totality, and so did many other philosophers both before and after him. There is, however, a Heaven that embodies all the principles of the universe, and the question is whether this Heaven is considered within or outside the *ki* cosmos.

It was in a more rational Confucian world that *ri* came to be emphasized. The virtues, 'goodness', *jen*, (J. *jin*) first among them, became *ri* in man. In the *Ta hsüeh* (J. *Daigaku*), for example, it is said that 'the Way of Great Learning (*ta hsüeh*) lies in making clear the clear virtue; it lies in loving the people, it lies in resting in ultimate goodness'. *Ri* is equal to this clear virtue in man's moral life, it is Heaven and Heaven's Way in man, as in all other

2. *Ki* is also translated with various terms, for example 'breath, states or processes of psycho-physical energy, etc'. (Hoyt Cleveland Tillman), 'mutable matter' (Joseph. R. Levenson), 'ether' (Bodde), 'connotations of material energy, breath of life, atmosphere' etc. (Ian McMorran).

living things, and it is man's duty to cultivate virtue at all times. In Neo-Confucian thought it was then identified with the Grand Ultimate (or Grand Polarity) (*t'ai-chi*, J. *taikyoku*), the one unchanging substance running through all things, yet beyond all things, and giving unity to all things. From the Grand Ultimate emanated the yin and yang , and out of their complementary duality and the operation of the Five Elements all things were born. This was a rational system and a metaphysics that gave a dialectical understanding of reality, both close to and independent of religion. It was the 'practical, real learning' (*jitsugaku*, Ch., *shih-hsüeh*) that occupied Confucian thinkers from Sung times (in contrast to Buddhist learning which was considered 'empty (*kyo*) learning'), until a new *jitsugaku* appeared in the form of modern science in a later age.

If *ri* is the warp of the weave, *ki* is the woof. *Ki* gives life and colour to the pattern, but it has to be disciplined and ordered and not overstep what is heavenly ordained. To use other similes, it is the blood that flows through the *ri* veins, or *ri* are the stable genes while *ki* is the changeable life force. The cooperation of *ri* and *ki* takes place so naturally in animals and plants that we only observe it habitually. Man has, however, the ability to go beyond what is ordained. His blood can overflow and cause high blood pressure and go slow and cause low blood pressure, he can get passionate, and he can get enraged. Man has accordingly to discipline his moral life and not allow his emotions and passions to run wild. Self-cultivation serves to restore the imbalances which occur due to his *ki*- nature. This can lead to rigidity and suppression of the natural life's brocade — and this is what happened in the lives of many over-zealous Neo-Confucian scholars. Yamazaki Ansai (1618-82) and his Kimon School represented the extreme bigot wing of Neo-Confucianists in Japan, while others in the Neo-Confucian tradition turned to the investigation and observation of *ri* in things. For example, Nishikawa Joken (1648-1724) and Kaibara Ekken (1630-1714), and a number of others, turned from moral *ri*-ism to natural *ri*-ism as they began to study astronomy, geography, calendration, botany, and other fields. Both lived on Kyushu and both were influenced by living close to the Dutch on Dejima. Nishikawa was called to Edo by Shogun Yoshimune in 1718 and probably influenced the latter when he relaxed the ban on the import of Western books and allowed scholars to undertake Western studies in, first of all, astronomy in 1720. This wing of Neo-Confucianists, first in China and then in Japan, *could* have led to modern science, and the question is why it did not. One reason could be that thinkers like Kaibara and Nishikawa were by education Confucian thinkers, and when they turned to natural science, they never left, and never needed to leave, their Confucian heritage. A Confucian scholar could, as it were, look either way and yet remain a Confucian. In a Cartesian way Nishikawa rationalized things when he developed the dualism of *meiri* and *keiki*. *Meiri* stood for *ri* studies in the Confucian sense, while *keiki* stood for studies in the European sense. Of interest is that *ki* came to represent the *res extensa* which were studied empirically, while *ri* came to represent *res cogitans*, about which one could speculate philosophically. Thus, he considered his studies to be *ki* studies; likewise Kaibara saw the universe as a *ki* reality and asserted that *ri* was within *ki* and not above it. The whole circle was a dynamic *ki*, and only its inscape was a *ri* ordering, and it was this inner ordering that absorbed them, one turning his interest to astronomy and the other to botany.

In Japan we find that, during Tokugawa, many philosophers turned their interest toward the *ki* and gave priority to the *ki* over the *ri*. One can wonder why? One reason might be that there had been a tendency earlier in Ming China to give preference to the *ki* side of man, while the *ri* side of man was of less interest even if never rejected. There had been one wing of Neo-Confucianist thinkers from Sung times who had stressed the investigation inward in man with the motto that 'the truth of the universe is within oneself' rather than in things outside oneself. Their approach was introspective and meditative and referred to as 'learning of the mind' (*hsin-hsüeh*). Lu Chiu-yüan (also Lu Hsiang-shan 1139-92) had been one such thinker and he related to and connected with Wang Yang-ming (1472-1529) in Ming times, and their thought has often been called the Lu-Wang School. Their intuitionism can be considered a *kakubutsu* limited to man and close to Zen Buddhism. For them the human mind (*hsin*, *J. kokoro*) was the world of truth and the *ri* came to be the *ri* of the human mind, and not a cosmic *ri* to be investigated and found in any organism or phenomenon in the world. Illumination should come from one's inner, not from rationalistic investigation of outer phenomena. The step was perhaps not long from their thought to the thought of Lo Ch'in-shun (1465-1547), who stated that

the *ri* is only the *ri* in *ki* or of *ki*. *Ri* must be observed in the phenomenon of the revolving and turning of *ki*. If one gains a clear understanding of this phenomenon of revolving and turning, one will find that everything conforms to it.

So *ri* ought to be studied and investigated only in a *ki* perspective, and not as something separate and independent. Kaibara Ekken, who was influenced by Lo Ch'in-shun's thought, believed that *ki* contained within it both the *ri* of constancy and of transformation (*ri no jôhen*) and he sought a study of nature that was unfettered by the restrictions of metaphysical ethics, imagining a single 'life principle' (*seiri*) running through all reality. This meant a separation of ethics and nature, which ran against Chu Hsi Neo-Confucian thought. Investigation and study of things came to be a-moral as in modern science. Also Nishikawa Joken saw the *ri* as the visible forms of the *ki* when studied in astronomy and other subjects. He never left his basis in Confucianism. As said above, he dichotomized reality and his study of astronomy and geography was termed the study of the '*ki* of forms' (*keiki*), while orthodox Neo-Confucian studies were termed the study of the '*ri* of the Will of Heaven' (*meiri*). He drew a Cartesian line between heaven and earth and concentrated on earth which was seen as an interplay of *ki* energies and forces.

Among seventeenth century Chinese scholars who later influenced Japanese thinkers was Fang I-chih (1611-71) who sought 'the extended principles of things' and stressed 'the comprehension of seminal forces'. *Kakubutsu* came with him to be widened and directed at that which is external to our minds. Fang I-chih was cognizant of and discussed the works by Jesuit missionaries which were published in Chinese at the end of the Ming Dynasty. He was impressed by the *ri* dimension of these studies, which he found, however, to lack the metaphysics of the *ki* dimension. Whether geocentric or heliocentric, the universe was under a Heaven where *ki* forces operated in yin and yang revolutions. Wang Fu-chih (1619-92), likewise, under the influence of Chang Tsai, expressed that 'within the universe there is nothing but one mass of *ki*', that '*ri* are only visible in the arrangement and pattern of *ki*', and that '*ri* operates within the *ki*'. The *ki* envelops the *ri*, and so phenomena possess life and nature. The phenomena of the world are but 'the temporary forms (*kyakkei*), that is, of *ri* within *ki*'. However, Wang Fu-chih goes so far as to say that 'all is one'. It is a *duum in unum* and only an apparent duality in phenomena, where all *ki* and *ri* are just the two aspects of the same thing. A contemporary of Fang I-Chih and Wang Fu- chih, Ku Yen-wu (1613-82) also held that knowledge had to be rooted in the objective world, external to our minds. Yet another seventeenth century philosopher, Huang Tsung-hsi (1610-95), wrote that 'Between heaven and earth there is only *ki*, there is not *ri*'. All of them were 'realists' who turned away from Chu Hsi and especially Lu-Wang idealism 'in a move to vindicate the earthy, observable particular thing' (Levenson 1954:156), 'turning thought in the direction of things and mind in the direction of matter'. They influenced Japanese Confucian thinkers in the eighteenth century — for example Miura Baien who had read Fang I-chih's works.[3]

It was, then, under the influence of Chinese thought that Japanese emphasized *ki* over *ri*. We find this in Nakae Tôju (1608-48) who accepted Wang Yang-ming and began the Ôyômei tradition in Japan. The *kokoro* (= *ki*), immediate intuition, and 'innate knowledge' (*liang-chih*, J. *ryôchi*) became coincident with the workings of the heart. Thinking was removed from 'scientific' study of *ri* in things, and 'willing' limited to self-control and filial piety. Like Wang Yang-ming he found that each man's *kokoro* can be his own standard within which he realizes his moral mind. Ri was found 'in there' in the mind and not 'out there' in a bamboo. Kumazawa Banzan (1619-91), who was influenced by Nakae Tôju, also gave priority to the *ki* of Heaven and Earth (*tenchi no ki*). He says, 'If man's heart is upright, the *ki* of heaven and earth is also pure in him'. *Kokoro* and *ki* became synonymous and *ri* became subjective and dependent on each person's *kokoro*.

In the following *kogaku* ('ancient school') thought it was again *ki* rather than *ri* that came first. Yamaga Sokô (1622-85) rejected the Neo-Confucian stress on *ri* cultivation and stated that man became like 'dead bones' if he subdued the desires and passions, that is, the *ki* side of his nature. *Ri* was certainly there, but it was the *ki* life that should come first in a *bushi*'s life. So he became the creator of the *shidô*, later *bushidô*, the 'Warrior's Way'. Itô Jinsai (1627-1705) went further when he considered life a spontaneous thing, a life of *ki* and not a life of *ri*, when he stated that 'All between Heaven and Earth is the one original *ki*' (*tenchi no aida wa ichi-genki nomi*) and that the whole universe is a living thing (*katsubutsu*), a one-dimensional *ki* monism. He then came close to original Chinese *ki* thought, as seen above. Ogyû Sorai (1666-1728), likewise, put the life of *ki* first when he considered a life of goodness — *jin* — as that of *ki* and not of *ri*. As he said (*Benmei*), '*Jin naru mono wa toku nari, sei ni arazaru nari, iwanya ri wo ya*', 'Goodness (*jin*) is virtue, it is not human nature (*sei*), so how could it be *ri*?'. According to him, all *ri-ki* thought comprised accretions of a later age, not found in the sacrosanct early Six Classics of the Sages. At the time of Confucius people concentrated on propriety and on how to rule the state. It was the Sung Confucianists who began fruitless speculative thought, leading to forced interpretations about what the Sages had said little or nothing.

---

3. Other seventeenth and eighteenth century 'realist' Confucian scholars were Yen Yüan (1635-1704), Li Kung (1659-1733), and Tai Chen (1724-77), who were also *ki* monists and emphasized that there is no *ri* apart from things.

Sorai only accepted the *kishitsu no sei*, the '*ki* nature', in man and this *kishitsu no sei* was unchangeable. As he said in the *Benmei*: 'Can *kishitsu* possibly be changed?! (*kishitsu wa hen-zubekenya*)'. The *rishitsu no sei* (*honzen no sei*), whether accepted or not, was of less interest. The *ri*, mentioned by Sorai, was *tenri*, the 'Heavenly Inscape', which was limited to the Sages' Way. To understand things in a 'scientific' way was not possible: *ri* should not be studied except in areas where the Sages had already studied it. In spite of the fact that Sorai was both curious and open-minded, he did not deviate from 'sagely' subjects unnecessarily. 'Modern' science, in the form of *ri* study, was not for him, for the simple reason that the Sages had not undertaken such studies. What the Chu Hsi thinkers had achieved, he categorized as 'forced interpretations' (*kenkyô*) of the *kakubutsu* and *kyûri* concepts as they were found in the Classics. In this sense Sorai's approach was much removed from natural science; his 'science' concentrated entirely on sagely areas. No elaboration was needed as regards sagely truths. Scholars should keep to political economy (*keizai*), — and other classical subjects, as the Sages had presented them. Corroboration from antiquity was required for any undertaking to be legitimate.

Ogyû Sorai says in the *Seidan* III:12:

Now the truth (*dôri*) of the Book of Changes (*I Ching*) that 'things grow up from below' is certainly no foolish fancy. In the course of the year, spring and summer are the seasons when the spirit (*ki*) of Heaven descends, the spirit (*ki*) of Earth rises, and the two combine harmoniously so that all things grow. In autumn and winter the spirit (*ki*) of Heaven rises and the spirit (*ki*) of Earth descends; Heaven and Earth separate and cease to be in harmony with the result that all things wither and die. It is also like that in human society.

All natural life forms a circle of *ki* and, and as it is in nature, so it is in society.

There were others in Sorai's time, however, who took a keen interest in the *ri* of things, but they are not mentioned so often as those who dealt with lofty philosophy. Who has, for example, heard of Inô (Inao) Jakusui (1655-1715) who investigated herbs for medicinal reasons and wrote works like *Shobutsu ruisan* and is rightly called the 'ancestor of herbal studies' in Japan? Sorai is mentioned and honoured and every educated Japanese knows his name. Jakusui is not, even though he probably meant more for the daily life of the Japanese than all Sorai's philosophy. Important thought was directed toward the *whole* and not toward the parts; toward the great *why*, and not toward the partial *how*.

The tendency of leading Confucian thinkers was, accordingly, certainly under Chinese influence, to leave *ri-ki* idealistic dualism and turn to *ki-ri* realistic monism. They moved, as it were, from Plato's world of ideas to Aristotle's world of *entelecheia* (entelechy, 'complete actuality'), from idea above to life within things.

Among other thinkers of the first half of the eighteenth century who stressed *ki* over *ri* we find Andô Shôeki (1703?-62) who saw nature (*shizen*) as the 'advance and retreat of the one *ki*' (*ikki no shintai*). It is *ki* advancing (*shinki*) and *ki* retreating (*taiki*) in an eternal perpetuum mobile. Nature and *ki* were for him synonymous. All dualism is rejected and *kami* and Buddha are only cultural creations, as also ethics. Heaven and Earth are a composite term for nature, and the *ki* is the life force which encompasses the whole. Nishikawa Fumio has in his article, *Andô Shôeki ni okeru shizen no gainen*, demonstrated how Andô Shôeki was close to Schelling in European nineteenth century naturalism.

Another thinker in the mid-eighteenth century who stressed the *ki* side of things was Yamagata Daini (1725-67). He was clearly influenced by Itô Jinsai and Ogyû Sorai and like them he saw the operations of Heaven and Earth as an interplay of the *ki* force. There were probably others who saw things in a similar fashion.

Ki-ist thought perhaps reached its finest and final expression in Miura Baien (1723-89) and his *Genkiron*, 'On Primal *ki*' and *Genron*, 'Deep/dark words'. In his *Genron* analysis — he rewrote the work not less than 23 times — *ki* is the supreme One Primal *ki* residing above as well as in things, equal to Heaven and Earth. (One can talk about *tenki* as much as about *tenri* in orthodox Chu Hsi Neo-Confucianism.) The heavenly *ki* is diffused through yin-yang operations to become all things and all bodies. With a terminology that is often not clear, Miura sees balances, or *a* balance, in all nature, all of *ki* origin, coming from Heaven and yin-yang revolutions, which end up in the *jôri* reality of opposites in the temporary forms of the world. All forces are *ki*, active or passive, waxing or waning, in dynamic flux or in static form, in action or in being. All is under a *ki* Heaven — is formed of *ki*.

Miura wrote that 'at the age of thirty I first recognized that heaven and earth are *ki*' and he spent the rest of his life conveying this truth to others. In his enlightenment he saw the oneness of the universe and this oneness can be summarised by the two-letter word *ki*. This primal *ki* is above all opposites. The opposites appear when *ki* comes to operate in all *jôri* configurations.

But as *ki* is individuated, objects are there and they last as long as each *jôri* 'gene' system lasts. Bodies change with time, but the given 'genes' in objects do not, and therefore the jôri laws can be investigated and described. The reason is that the *jôri* only exists within the merged being of yin and yang. Within the life of the *ki*-force, rules and laws exist in objects, which form the essences and regularities which can be the object of observation, and classification. This scientific work, concerned with the *jôri* of things, was for a *ki*-ist philosopher like Miura Baien a business of second importance to be left to 'practical' people, who worked with 'plebeian' matters. Since theirs was not 'lofty' thought, they are not often mentioned, but they were there and they increased in number from mid-Tokugawa.

They can be called the *ri*-ists, the true exponents of the Neo-Confucian tradition — whether in a *ri-ki* perspective or a *ki-ri* perspective — and they were in later Tokugawa more and more influenced by Western *rangaku* thought. It took Arai Hakuseki (1657-1725) no time to discover that Giovanni Battista Sidotti (1668-1715), who smuggled himself into Japan in 1708 and whom he interrogated, had two distinct sides to his thought. On the one side he was the 'irrational' Christian, but on the other side he was the 'rational' thinker, who astounded Hakuseki with his precise knowledge of natural science — a dichotomy that Hakuseki could not understand. Beginning with Hakuseki, however, a new interest was taken in Western science and from 1720 Yoshimune, the eighth Tokugawa *shogun* (r. 1716-45), allowed Western books in Chinese dealing with astronomy, geography, medicine, weaponry, shipbuilding, food, clockwork and perhaps other fields to be read and studied by scholars. This was to develop into *rangaku* studies later in the eighteenth century. Astronomy, medicine, geography and many other fields came then peu-à-peu to be influenced by Western thought until, with a scholar like Yamagata Bantô (1748-1821), it was Western science that came to be in the centre of 'progressive' Japanese thought. Yamagata Bantô can be seen as an important turning point. With him the study of nature became the study of *ri* in things as in Western science. His *Yume no shiro*, (*Daydreams* 1802-20), has rightly been described as 'an intellectual guide for future generations'. But yet, even Yamagata Bantô saw his *ri* studies taking place within a *ki* universe and in a *ki* perspective.

It can be said that the emphasis was on *ki* among leading scholars from the middle of the seventeenth century until the nineteenth century. The *ki* energies and forces were in the center while the *ri* were only encased within them. With Yamagata Bantô and others by the beginning of the nineteenth century the emphasis came instead to be on *ri*, and so we can say it has been until today. Until the middle of the nineteenth century we have *rangaku* studies in a Confucian context: all who studied Western learning were first schooled in Confucianism and all mixed Confucian and Western learning. In the middle of the nineteenth century, however, *rangaku* widened into Western *yôgaku* learning with China rarely mentioned. The acceptance of Western science and the mathematical ordering of the universe spelled a new world-view and paradigm in which *ri* and *ki* were seen in mathematical terms with no apparent need of an ethical Heaven and a heavenly principle beyond things.

But was the way so long from traditional Chinese *ri-ki* thought to modern science? The *kakubutsu-kyûri* aspect of Chu Hsi thought called for the 'investigation of things and the *ri* in things'. This thought was certainly mostly taken in a moral sense, and it was not so clearly defined *what* should be investigated and where the *ri* was to be reached. There was a dichotomy in Chu Hsi thought, inwards and outwards, both in the direction of material life and in the direction of moral life. *Mono* (*butsu*) first of all concerned concrete material objects, while *koto* referred to acts, actions and events. For the Confucian philosopher, not least the Neo-Confucian philosopher, however, *mono* was a wider notion. For him *mono* referred also to human and social relationships, to human beings and their characters, and so to moral life. As a result the line was thin between *mono* and *koto*. Usually moral life came first in Neo-Confucian thought and investigation of things aimed at moral perfection. The moral life of man was further connected with the laws of nature so that the *ri* of man, the *ri* of society, and the *ri* of nature were identical. And all *ri* ended up in the one heavenly *ri*. Therefore, when the Neo-Confucian philosopher spoke about the *ri* of a tree and the *ri* of grass, this was not in the sense of modern science. This *kakubutsu-kyûri* had a moral goal in orthodox Neo-Confucian thought; it was not the search for the laws of nature *per se*. In late Ming China first and in Ch'ing China and in Tokugawa Japan next the investigation of things began to be directed toward the material world and the *ri* (= laws) of things began to be studied independently of ethics, and as a result one finds a pre-modern science both in China and Japan. There was thus a dichotomy in the practice of *kakubutsu*, and perhaps depending on the individual thinker, the investigation turned in an inward moral direction or in an outward scientific direction. Modern European science, which took an interest only in the material world, was therefore not so far away from one side of Chu Hsi thought, and it is also evident that the early scholars who took an interest in European science, like Yamagata Bantô, never felt in conflict with or discarded Chinese thought. As it were, they ended up with 'Copernicus in Confucius'. The *ri* of European science was put in a Confucian setting, and the Confucian natural *ri-ki* order was not questioned. The new European science was also a *kakubutsu-kyûri*, 'a study of the principles of things (*monogoto no ri*)' (Fukuzawa Yukichi), only taken in a limited outward sense, as interest was lost in the moral dimension of *ri* within man. Whereas formerly they focussed on what was 'inner', *ri* studies came to concentrate on what was 'outer', but they were yet considered studies of the principles of heaven (*ten no dôri*). Thus, it is no wonder that when a term was to be found for modern physics it became *butsuri*, a term already in use as a short form of *kakubutsu-kyûri*.[4]

However, with a *caveat*. Whether as *ri-ki* dualists or as *ki-ri* monists, the philosophers, whether Chinese or Japanese, never broke away from *the* tradition. They never stopped harking back to a golden age where man lived in peace and harmony under the direction of wise rulers. Whatever new thought they presented, they always sought corroboration from antiquity. Nothing should deviate from the ancient, *correct* truth — and this was not conducive to a scientific break-through, neither congenial to a new method and a new purpose, as witnessed in Newtonian Europe. They criticised — but never criticised the ancient truth. They brought Heaven down on Earth in *ki*-ist thought, but did not go farther from there. The world governed by Newtonian science and the art of doubt had to wait for the arrival of the West.

Who were right, the *ki*-ists or the *ri*-ists? It can seem that they were both right. It is a fact that in recent modern thought the tendency has again been toward *ki*. First came Darwin who showed that all *ri* in the name of evolution is relative. Then came Einstein and proved that all forms in time and space (*ri*) are relative, while all energy (*ki*) is constant, never lost nor destroyed, neither diminished nor increased. Whatever happens and whatever is done, the mass of energy remains the same, while things appear and disappear and the forms of things adapt according to environment. Thus, there is no entropy in the *ki*; entropy is only found in the ri world, with *ki* coming and going, neither diminished nor increased. No two *ri* constellations are the same; no two finger prints are ever the same; nor are two tree leaves ever the same. The laws, whether they concern land or government, plants or animals, can change and are never eternal, while the energy that gives life to the universe is indestructible and can only be manipulated. In science, Karl Pop-

---

4. Joseph R. Levenson (1954:158-60) perhaps has the best answer why modern science did not develop in China. He thinks that the Chinese empiricists never advanced beyond pre-scientific nominalism, as represented by Peter Abelard (1079-1142) in Europe. They observed things, but they never came to observe things 'with a method and a purpose'. 'They stopped short on the scientist's long way to a universality, now, of laws, which govern the mutual relations of particular things'. As it were, they reached Abelard but not Bacon.

per says, truth is transient. So, it seems that in the light of today's science, the *ki*-ists were closer to the 'truth' than the *ri*-ists. They were the realists while the latter were the idealists. In this light Miura Baien and others were correct when they put *ki* first and *ri* second. And Ogyû Sorai was right when he stated that the *ki* nature could not be changed and that '*ri* is kein fester Bezugspunkt' (*ri naru mono wa teijun naki mono nari*), whereas Chu Hsi was wrong when he stated that *ri* could not change. Chang Tsai and Einstein stand side by side when they declare the indestructibility of matter.

God and the Way above things disappear in Western thought and phenomena of the world become but the temporary forms of change and evolution just like in Chinese *ki* monistic thought. Taoist thought and Western science are in the end remarkably similar. But with a difference: the beyondness of a Heaven and the unity of complexity were never forgotten in Chinese thought, while in modern science the beyondness of a God or a Heaven is rarely mentioned and the enigma of the total natural order is mostly avoided.

Amazing, is it not! The Taoist *ki*-ists three thousand years ago expressed, *mutatis mutandis*, the same thing as Einstein in our day!

As it were, scholars in the west began to measure phenomena of the world both in their *ri* and *ki* dimensions in ways that were not done in the east. The east had its science but it was science in the west that would lead to modern science. By Newton and others a brave new world was created from the seventeenth century onwards, which later reached Japan as *rangaku* and *yôgaku*. (Earlier western technology had reached Japan, beginning with the musket (*teppô*) in the sixteenth century (1543)). This was the world of *scientific rationalism* which by means of mathematics began not only to map but also to control things. Both the *ri* and *ki* have since been split apart and atomized, and the great cosmos has even been traced to a *big bang* at the beginning of time. The modernization of the world has been based on this scientific rationalism which has spread to ever more areas, including the social sciences and experimental psychology. The original thought of *ri* and *ki* has been lost in the cold logic of mathematical structures, without a Heaven, and life (*ki*) and form (*ri*) as ethical Neo-Confucian thought, with a Heaven, have disappeared.

As for the epilogue of Tokugawa *ri-ki* Neo-Confucian thought: with the full-fledged acceptance of the West after 1868, Western science came to rule the Japanese intellectual world, while Confucian thought was left behind. Although not entirely: when new concepts were to be created in scientific nomenclature by Nishi Amane (1826-94) and others, it was again *ri* and *ki* that came to be the *key* terms. *Ri* became part of words like *ri-ka*, 'science', *butsuri-*

gaku, 'natural science', *shinri-gaku*, 'psychology', *chiri-gaku*, 'geography', and so on, words which deal with the form of things. On the other hand, *ki* came to be part of words like *denki*, 'electricity', *kiatsu*, 'atmospheric pressure', *ki-shô*, 'weather conditions', *kishitsu*, 'character', 'disposition', *jiki* , 'magnetism', and hundreds of other words which deal with life and energy in things. In this way one can see a link between Neo-Confucian *ri-ki* science and modern science and a link between the earlier Chinese civilization and the later Western civilisation.

And what became of Confucianism? It returned to the original doctrine of Confucius and became the ethics of modern Japan too, and as ethics it has served Japan and other East Asian countries well (with Heaven rarely mentioned) and continues to do so even today. And for many a Chinese and Japanese the universe is probably also today more a *ki* than a *ri* reality.

References

Levenson, Joseph R.. 1954. The Abortiveness of Empiricism in Early Ch'ing Thought. *Eastern Quarterly* XII/2, 156-65.

The Mythical Construction of Tradition and Contemporary Japanese International Relations

Ideology, Racism and Nationalism Permeating the Relations Between Japan and Other Societies

Mika Merviö

Ideologies, myths and values should always be analysed together with the particular culture which one wants to understand. I see all these to be in a key role in shaping the preunderstanding on which all further understanding is built. Ideologies can be seen as integrated and coherent systems of symbols, values and beliefs, built on socially accepted structures of significance, which always have a connection to culture in general (cf. Geertz 1973:12). In all human behaviour one finds ideologies and values. No research can escape these, and they are also part of research and its results. In short, the relation between culture and ideology, and other forms of human thought and belief, is complex. In most cases one can not just take a couple of useful facts, social values or 'variables' to shape an explanation for the rise, fall or existence of ideology and 'images'[1] within a certain culture. Such seemingly dissonant or undesirable factors as ideology, racism and nationalism deeply permeate the

1. In my research I have used sparingly such terms as 'image' and 'perception', in order to avoid misunderstandings and too close association with behavioural research and research in the field of psychology, which have often given to these concepts specific meanings not in line with my approach. Giving full credit to behaviouralist research on the issue of 'images' and sometimes using it as my material, I find it better to simply avoid terminology which would be prone to cause confusion. When using the concept of 'image' in my research I use it in its broadest sense in English or refer to the malformed preunderstanding behind it — sometimes 'image' is simply used as a translation for the Japanese loan-word 'imêji'. For a good introduction to how identification theory and 'images' and 'national identity' based on those theories have been applied, see Bloom (1990). For applications of psychology-based image theories to Japanese postwar foreign policy, see Iwanaga (1993) and Kurihara (1982). For an example of a survey based report on the development of the Japanese people's 'image of a nation', in this case the Republic of Korea, see Tei (1995).

relations between Japan and other countries, as well as the research on them in most societies.

There is always a danger when using cross-cultural concepts of not ana-lysing how useful and appropriate these concepts are in another cultural con-text. Imperfection of method seems to be inevitable in all social sciences, but as long as we are aware of the imperfections of each approach we are in a position to take advantage of these approaches (cf. Befu 1989:323-43). Awareness of our moderate capacity and limited understanding is related to our ability to accept that we are dominated by our prejudices but at the same time are capable of seeing and understanding things in their light (cf. Ga-damer 1985:321-24). Failure to recognise our limitations and the uncritical use of language and concepts easily lead to simplistic generalisations and in-tellectual imperialism often serving the purposes of nationalism. Indeed, distorted images and distorted research are frequently used for nationalist purposes.

This does not mean that our prejudices and cultural background pre-destine us to serve nationalism. Culture signifies meaningful ways of being in the world, and there are endless numbers of these ways. Meaningful axes of identity, such as race and gender or national identity, are integral parts of all societies and have an inescapable power to influence how individuals craft a self and attach significance to phenomena around them within a par-ticular historical and cultural matrix (cf. Kondo 1990:300-1). Nationalism requires that part of our historical and cultural matrix is ignored. As Ernest Gellner notes, amnesia is essential for nationalism. The modern world has in-herited from previous ages an endless wealth of dialects, of cross-cutting nuances of speech, faith, vocation, and status. For the existence of na-tionalism it is not only important that each citizen learn a standardised, cen-tralised idiom in his primary school, but also that he forget or at least devalue dialect, something which is not taught in school (Gellner 1987:16-17).

The internalisation of the predominant or the 'majority' attitudes and be-liefs serves as a base for defining both the 'majorities' and 'minorities' and their 'characteristics'. Wagatsuma Hiroshi argues that the Korean Japanese and the Ainu[2] often create a 'negative self-image' inseparably associated with

---

2. It should be noted that these two groups are quite different in most respects. For Ainu it is much easier to construct a 'cultural identity' different from the 'mainstream Ja-panese identity' as they have their own language as an important symbol of their own culture, and Ainu also have a long 'independent' history largely apart from the Ja-panese, having been subjugated so late. For them today it is also possible to demand special protection for their culture on the basis of global campaigns to save indigenous

a negative image of their own group as a whole. These people end up believing that there is nothing to be proud of in the culture of their own group and even if they are able to assimilate into the dominant culture they often start to hate the assimilated aspects in themselves. According to Wagatsuma, before the era of ethnic consciousness many American 'blacks' and Japanese Americans 'overdid' it when they tried to attain similar self-identities and life-styles as 'white' Americans (Wagatsuma 1981:304-33).[3] De Vos and Wagatsuma have also studied the Burakumin and found similar types of 'negative self-image' among them. Even a Burakumin 'informant' who was successfully 'passing'[4] and still lived among his own people had an 'image' of his people as somehow unclean. However, De Vos and Wagatsuma also found evidence of defences against 'negative self-images' among the Burakumin. Some studies showed that the Burakumin use their traditional attitudes as a counterbalance to a 'self-disparaging image'. For instance, they believed that they are more filial, more respectful to ancestors, more stringent in the observation of arranged marriages, and more deferential toward persons of higher status when they compared themselves to outsiders (De Vos & Wagatsuma 1972:228-40).

However, all the minority groups are under strong forces of assimilation and change. In spite of the legal struggles and gradual institutional reforms, social discrimination against minorities continues in Japan. The Korean residents are well aware of the historical circumstances which have led to the development of the contemporary Korean community in Japan. The majority of Koreans in Japan naturally want to maintain the Korean language and culture in Japan. However, Korean language proficiency among second, third and fourth generations declines dramatically. As the Japanese Government refuses to accredit the bilingual schools maintained by Korean residents' associations, 86 percent of Korean students attend Japanese schools. As a result it is difficult for new generations of Japan-born Korean residents to

---

cultures. For the Ainu's long political struggle for their social and political rights, see Siddle (1995:73-94), Siddle & Kitahara (1995:147-59), Honda (1993) and an autobiographical work of the Ainu politician Kayano (1990).

3. It should, however, be noted that the members of a 'majority' can also have 'negative images' of 'their own national culture'. In a survey study among Finnish 'intellectuals' most of them found many more negative than positive aspects in Finnish culture (Saukkonen 1993:9-12).

4. With the concept of 'passing' De Vos & Wagatsuma apparently suggest that these people are able to live and socialise with the majority people without being discriminated against for their background or even discovered. This concept seems to come quite close to that of 'assimilation'.

acquire language skills in Korean. Nowadays multicultularism and linguistic variation characterise the life of the Korean community in Japan. Much of the literature written by members of the Japanese Korean community deals with the issues of 'identity' and 'cultural co-existence'. There are no simple answers to issues like these, but the Korean community has shown its ability to overcome discrimination and find flexible solutions, for lack of alternatives, perhaps. Being strongly rooted in Japan (as some 85 percent are Japan-born) and usually in a particular location in Japan, the local culture has become one of the basic elements for the identity of many members of Korean community.

Maher and Kawanishi point out that the members of Japan's largest Korean community in Ôsaka tend to strongly identify with the Ôsaka Japanese dialect known as Ôsaka-ben, while standard Japanese (hyôjungo) is identified with Tôkyô as the language of power, centralisation and the source of discrimination against the Korean community and language (Maher & Kawanishi & Yi 1995:164-66).[5] By their necessity of finding a lasting solution to cultural co-existence in Japan, the Korean community has forced also the majority to face the issues of cultural pluralism and the need for cultural tolerance. Many of the problems of the Koreans in Japan are shared by other foreign residents in Japan — as well as 'indigenous minorities', and their legal battles have removed or resulted in modification of some of the most xenophobic regulations and laws in Japan.

On a more general level the problems that minorities face reveal the hollowness of the categories of 'national cultures' or 'national identities', or even 'ethnic identities'. Creating a 'positive self-image', of course, cannot be limited to living as a full member of a majority group in a nation state which tries to guard the social and cultural rights of the majority of its citizens. We should note that the idea of a 'global culture' is a practical impossibility except in interplanetary terms from the point of view of the outside observer (cf. Smith 1990:171). Similarly the differences between individuals in terms of life-style, thinking and belief-repertoire are too great to allow us to speak of monolithic national cultures. In the modern world there is in most cases enough information and knowledge available for individuals who want to deepen their understanding and widen their view of 'being in the world'; the problem lies in attaching significance and in what we could call a widely spread cultural amnesia. For an individual the first step to escape being a

5. For the issues of the 'identity' and 'cultural co-existence' of the Korean community, see Kimu 1994, Fukuoka 1993, Mâha & Kawanishi 1993:165-81, and Maher & Kawanishi & Yi 1995:165-81).

tool of nationalism is to question the 'images' of 'national identities' (including the universal applicability of both these concepts) and see the fragility and variable nature of human self-identity. Attachment to a group or to a nation can also serve as a defensive mechanism to an individual in the world of threatening scenarios, but this attachment also closes many doors for individual development and for social relations.

However, nationalism in its different forms is still strong, in fact nationalism is constantly seeking new forms.[6] For example, in Finland and the other Nordic countries one frequently encounters research which starts from the assumption that the Finnish or the Nordic welfare systems, managerial practices, work ethics, women's position, education systems and environmental consciousness belong to the most advanced in the world — without really critically and systematically analysing these social phenomena. Within myths there may also exist some truths, but the role of the researcher is to analyse critically how certain myths are formed and used in different ways for various purposes. For instance, the above mentioned Nordic myths and prejudices are not only used for nation building purposes but they also divide the world between Finland (or the Nordic countries) and the Other, without questioning the value or basis of this distinction and without realising the consequences of these distortions. The 'Nordic perspective' in Japanese studies can sometimes just mean that Japan is used as a mirror of our own prejudices: there are already too many books which too easily come up with a list of simplistic claims of similarities or differences between the Nordic societies and Japan.

In the case of Japan and Japanese studies, both abroad and in Japan, national and nationalistic myths deeply affect research on Japan and contribute

6. It may be that 'nations' and 'nationalism' as historical phenomena are past their peak or approaching the point of disintegration and retransformation. Hobsbawm, unfortunately somewhat prematurely, some years ago noted that 'the owl of Minerva which brings wisdom, flies at dusk. It is a good sign that it is now circling round nations and nationalism' (Hobsbawm 1990:183). That optimism apparently echoed the seemingly smooth progress of European intergration. Since then Europe has experienced ethnic cleansings and most possible forms of ethnic fanaticism, and Hobsbawm among others has taken a much more pessimistic tone. I find it hard to believe that ethnic fanaticism, of the type prevalent in the Bosnian war, would find successors worldwide, and for instance in East Asia the Bosnian war and its ethnic symbols and mythologised divisions are usually interpreted as matters beyond human understanding, and not as parts of development which could contaminate the whole world. However, it may be that human savagery and bigotry are not in short supply in any parts of the world, leaving all societies and the entire world system vulnerable to surges of human self-destructive acts of stupidity and irresponsibility.

to the rise of rather distorted 'images'. The researchers of Japan, too, cannot escape being associated with the general understanding of the changing 'status' of Japan. Sepp Linhart proposes the following interesting juxtaposition: 'The higher the status of the Japanese car in the world, the higher the status of the foreign Japan researcher' (Linhart 1993:3). European 'general images' (or distorted preunderstanding) of Japan have a history going back to Marco Polo, and in each European country one can even find some national variations of the mythical and historical sediment which serves as the resource pool for the formation of 'images' on Japan — together with European self-images and understanding of the nature of Japanese 'Otherness'.

In addition to the older tradition of exotic flowerland and samurai images which still taint European views of Japan, the current economic success deeply affects how Japan is seen in Europe. As Linhart notes, the countrymen of the foreign Japan researcher also project their conceptions of Japan onto researchers of the country. One could also argue that this deformed preunderstanding, and the values which it reveals to us, deeply influences the kind of research on Japanese society acceptable in our societies and the kind of relations we can expect to be built between these societies. It is a sad feature of the modern European outlook that for many people it is of vital importance what kind of car they are driving and where these cars come from. Decision-makers full of nationalistic ethos see nothing odd when they get personally involved in the business of car-sales and, while trying to sell cars to Japan or prevent them from being exported from Japan, turn their attention away from the complex and far-reaching question of the overall development of Japanese-European or the Japanese-American relations. It is even worse that some researchers are keeping busy with providing tools and excuses for the trade negotiators of their own government. For instance, much of the American literature on Japan in the field of International Relations these days concerns how the Japanese could be coerced to act in line with the current American policies of trade and defence, without paying much attention to the fact that such tactics fit very badly with the multi-lateralism and globalism of contemporary Japanese international relations.

The mythical construction of tradition — *dentô*

What is often accepted or presented as 'tradition' is a myth. (cf. Gunnell 1979:85)[7] This, however, does not negate the fact that the continuation of

7. By 'myth' in my work I mean a belief which is clearly based on misformed and in-adequate understanding. My intention here is not to contribute to the discussion

society and culture is largely built on the existence of traditions. Tradition can be understood as a transmission of ideas or modes of action through an inherited pattern of thought and practice associated with some fairly well-defined activity and realm of discourse. In this way we refer to a situation where knowledge, beliefs and customs are passed to the next generations, bound together with a body of long-established and generally accepted and authoritative forms of thought and behaviour (Gunnell 1979:88).[8] My research being concerned with distorted preunderstanding,[9] I caution researchers to have a critical attitude towards the existence of any particular 'traditions', especially when 'tradition' is used as a tool by historians of thought or by social scientists to reveal some more or less hidden 'tradition' which only the 'chosen people' are able to identify. Once the 'traditions' are canonised or 'mythologised' they usually start to live their own life, being open to re-interpretations and 'rediscoverings' (cf. Gunnell 1979:85-89, 124-25). It is also clear that researchers as interpreters always stand within 'traditions'. To stand within a tradition does not limit the freedom of knowledge but makes it possible (Gadamer 1985:324). It may also be added that politics as a particular field of human life is also within the scope of hermeneutics coming out of cultural tradition and being part of the understandable world where we live — a world that is. In fact the cultural tradition is a realm of human understanding which is particularly interesting for hermeneutic work (cf. Gadamer 1976:30-31).

Traditions and cultures never exist apart from other traditions and cul-

whether there exist 'myths' which are of such a nature that their factual basis cannot be proved 'right' or 'wrong'.

8. In short, I see culture and tradition both as wide concepts providing the basis on which Japanese 'understanding' and 'thinking' are formed — and in the context of which those can be studied and interpreted by a researcher. As for the concept of 'tradition', it is in research used to refer to both 1) wider cultural and social traditions and 2) to particular narrowly defined traditions. To avoid unnecessary scholastic speculation and dogmatism I have not felt it necessary or possible always to define the exact scope of 'traditions' and have preferred to use the concept of 'tradition' in a way assuming that the general scope of the 'fairly well-defined activity and realm of discourse' can be judged by the reader from the context in which I use the concept.

9. In my work I use preunderstanding in the Gadamerian sense, that meanings cannot be understood in an arbitrary way and that we always place meanings in a relation to the whole of our own meanings or ourselves in relation to it. As for hermeneutical work, it is important to be aware of one's own bias, so that the text in question could present itself in all its newness and thus be able to assert its own truth against one's own fore-meanings (cf. Gadamer 1985:238).

tures. For the culture[10] of humankind and for its future, it is significant that
— to a certain degree — parallel evolution of 'modern societies', the
increased ease of human mobility, and the increase of all types of transnational and transcultural transactions, all together make cultural influences
reach all parts of the world, pushing these to coexist and adjust.[11] A wider
awareness of the cultural interdependence of humankind could already be
counted as progress. The present members of humankind are not witnessing
anything like the 'end of history': the world is full of thriving cultures and
ideological constructions, all in a continuous state of flux. The 'modification'
or disappearance of nation states or some 'political units' may also take place
gradually and peacefully, and would not constitute any loss to humankind.
Cultures cannot be stored in museums to keep their purity untouched.

In Japan the widespread optimism about the results of the 'internationalisation' process (kokusaika) stands in stark contrast to the pessimism
so often voiced by some well-known Finnish researchers, particularly Matti
Sarmela, who are worried about the resistance and vitality of Finnish culture.
According to Sarmela traditional cultures are at the mercy of international
unifying powers of cultural imperialism and Americanisation, which, according to him, have in the last thirty years already destroyed most of the
characteristic local culture of Finland and now the whole culture and Finnish
language are in danger of being wiped out by the currents of Anglo- American mass culture and global market economy (Sarmela 1989:195-99). It must

10. Culture itself I understand as a comprehensive concept (hôkatsutekina gainen), containing
    both bunka, including the material culture (busshitsuteki bunka) and spiritual culture
    (seishinteki bunka), and civilisation bunmei, which cannot be excluded from its as-
    sociations with the idea of national culture and national state and from the political,
    social and legal conceptions born in a particular historical and social context, in-
    terpreted from the context of contemporary time. For the different possibilities of un-
    derstanding and defining culture, see Yamazaki & Ichikawa (1970:537-39).
11. Gellner (1987:18) associates the evolution of the cultural homogeneity of political units
    with the growth-oriented industrial society, when culture is being used as a symbol of
    a political unit. When homogeneity is lacking, it can be attained by modifying either
    political or cultural boundaries. The homogeneity of culture is then used to create a
    sense (part illusory, part justified) of solidarity, mobility, continuity, lack of deep
    barriers within the political units in question. In Gellner's view industrial societies
    engender nationalism but agrarian civilisations and societies are free of that effect. I
    agree with the basic logic of this description of historical process, but I would not use
    'growth-oriented industrial society' and 'homogeneous units' as concepts by which to
    describe all the trends and patterns in world history. The concept of 'nation state' with
    all its myths of homogeneity is also just a linguistic convention on its way to the dusk
    of history.

be noted that Sarmela uses 'traditional culture' in a specific sense, giving more narrowly defined meanings to both 'culture' and 'tradition'. Naturally there are dangers in making too hasty comparisons between Finnish and Japanese internationalisation discourses which are products of quite different social environments.

However, in post-war Japan, too, one can still identify some voices denouncing modernity as a threat to 'culture'. These voices usually resonate with references to the pre-war 'defence' of Japanese culture. Their most well-known representative was the novelist Mishima Yukio, who rejected consumerism and the homogenisation of society spawned by it — and argued that the Japanese *tennô* (for which, as he insisted, the English translation 'emperor' is a misnomer) represented a culture that allowed 'anarchy' within 'aesthetic terrorism'. Mishima simply wanted to separate 'culture' from dehumanising and homogenising 'politics' and in the process rejected the whole modern society, in which he saw no place for a real culture characterised by the 'cultural anarchy' whose symbol is the *tennô* (Najita 1989:15-17). Mishima crowned his career as a known eccentric in Japan with his ritual suicide in 1970 on the balcony of the Self- Defense Forces Ichigaya Base, having been able to generate only little sympathy or understanding, even among those small groups with militaristic ideals he had regarded as the heralds of a brave new future.

It may be noted that in the context of Japanese society, when writing in English, the use of the term 'modern' sometimes needs to be reinterpreted by those who have been used to think in terms of associating 'modern' with Western cultural hegemony and by seeing all 'modern' — 'modern man', 'modern science', 'modern life' or 'modern industrial society' — against the 'traditional', defined on the basis of historical experience (and history writing) of the 'West' (cf. Apunen 1990:3). In Japan the emergence of 'modern society' *(gendai shakai)* is not equated with the process of 'Westernisation', but the *'gendai'* has rather been seen as a conceptual opposite to 'tradition' *(dentô)*, largely defined on the basis of the Japanese cultural past. It should also be noted that in Japanese the term *'kindaika'* refers to that particular process of 'modernisation' which changed the 'traditional society' of the Edo period to the 'modern society' with all its complexities. The 'modernisation' behind the term *'gendaika'* is not so clearly defined in its historical context, and the process of *'gendaika'* is still proceeding in Japan as in many other societies. What these terms reveal is that the 'modernisation' in Japan is usually not seen to be associated with adopting the notions of Western cultural hegemony or superiority. The Japanese 'tradition', considered to be more or less unique, also has its place in the 'modern world', coexisting and even prospering with other 'traditions'.[12]

Exploring the implications of the multifaceted character of the cultural encounter at the core of Japanese international relations has led to the conclusion that Japan is a perfect example of a modern industrialised society facing a need to rethink itself and its intersubjective practices to suit better the changing realities of the world. Japan is a significant part of the world — in many different ways. The multiplicity of Japanese power relations and the ideals of seeking harmony in Japanese social relations have indeed prepared particularly ample ground for such social manoeuvres. The continuation of society and culture is largely built on the existence of continuity in intersubjective social practices, and even in fields like Japanese immigration policies and Official Development Assistance Japanese political traditions and social practices largely determine how the options are defined, and what options are to be avoided.[13] I argue that the mythical construction of tradition and reality, and issues like cultural proximity, ethnocentrism, racism and nationalism — all are immensely important in international relations. In the case of Japanese international relations in the 1990s such issues as internationalisation, globalisation, changing essence of nationalism and ethnocentrism, and the intersubjective practices within all social traditions are all interconnected.

The multiple foundations of academic knowledge

It is a pity that many Western scholars so often take as granted that scientific knowledge and philosophy of science are somehow irrevocably connected to the development of academic scholarship in Europe and the United States.[14]

---

12. My position on the use of the concept 'modern' is that I do not define the term by linking it with some of those narrow Western discourses with their inbuilt notion of Western cultural superiority, and would prefer to associate the concept loosely with diverse social processes in the contemporary world and with the several 'endogenously' defined versions of 'modern' that exist. As I am still writing in English, and the avoidance of the term 'modern' altogether could undoubtedly be interpeted as over-acting, I only warn my readers to be circumspect with the use of this concept.

13. For a deeper analysis of these issues, see Merviö (1995).

14. See, e.g., Gadamer (1990:106-25), where he argues that science (Wissenschaft) is tied together with the sense of Europe, the monolithic nature (Einheit) of Europe and the its role in the discourses of the world (Weltgespräch). After that Gadamer proceeds to analyse in depth the development of some specific concepts from their ancient Greek

Modern science is not a monopoly of Europe and the United States, nor do the European languages, and definitions based on those, have a monopoly to serve as a foundation of the philosophy of modern science.

My understanding of science first of all requires one to be honest to his/her own mind and to work toward widening one's own grasp of the surrounding reality. While the semantic significance will necessarily differ between languages and cultures and even individuals who use language in different ways, this richness also provides the basis for widening one's understanding. As I question the clear-cut conventions on how to define who is sharing common values or identities with others, I also question such concepts as 'Japanese culture' or 'Japanese people' as something existing as clearly definable objects of study or 'concepts' which should be taken as given, not so speak of such strikingly dubious 'concepts' as 'Asia' or 'Asians'.

All that exists can and should be understood only in relation to everything else — otherwise we just close our minds to reality. Thinking too much in terms of 'concepts' widely used in academic or popular discourses of one's closest social and linguistic context can greatly limit the significance of one's study. All concepts in social sciences are problematic: Befu takes as his example how English words like 'behaviour', 'democracy', 'symbols', and the 'individual', with all their implied semantic domains, have been elevated from being mere words to being analytical tools. Even when these terms are very carefully defined, the discourse still remains as a discourse in the English language as long as the defining terms remain in English (Befu 1989: 333).[15] Elevating English from its use in describing ideas in a specific culture in a specific personal way to being a metalanguage to analyse all other cultures and societies of the world is to give some kind of religious meaning to the English language and would represent a kind of intellectual imperialism (cf. Befu 1989:334-35).

This intellectual imperialism does indeed take many forms. It is interesting that even such a critical mind as Professor Ernest Gellner, who has in his works concentrated on issues of nationalism, shows gaping narrow-mindedness in claiming that 'in Japan, democracy can be explained by the

origin to their descendants in contemporary Western philosophy. By his analysis Gadamer presents the history of Western science and the continuity of Western history as something fundamentally unique, and that Western science is a distinguishing characteristic of Europe and a European contribution to the culture of the world. Gadamer goes as far as to argue that we find ourselves totally helpless if we want to place, for instance, the East Asian wisdom in our defined categories of philosophy, science, religion, art and poetry.

American occupation, though perhaps it was reinforced by the subsequent economic miracle' (Gellner 1994:81-82). That kind of categorical statement does not take into consideration that 1) defining 'democracy' or characterising any society as 'democratic' or 'undemocratic' is not unproblematic, 2) that in Japan there was a working parliamentary democracy and rather widespread political participation, including a civil rights movement, long before the American occupation, not to mention that 'constitutionalism and genuine elections' — conditions that Gellner sets for 'democracy' — were largely fulfilled already by Meiji Japan, and 3) that the American military occupation was often working against the democratisation of Japanese society and the American military forces did not provide a particularly convincing model of a democratic institution. It is true that an important part of that basis on which the contemporary Japanese parliamentary system rests was created during the period of American military occupation. However, the social reforms were carried out, sometimes also initiated, by the Japanese government and bureaucracy. Gellner saying that the American army brought democracy to Japan can be interpreted to mean that he believes that the Americans already had mastered democracy and taught it to the Japanese. This kind of view of 'democracy' simply defines it as word of the English language referring first of all to the phenomenon of 'democracy' which exists in the English-speaking countries, most notably Britain and the United States. By this logic Japanese *'minshushugi'* will always remain just an imperfect copy of 'real Western democracy'. Leaving unclear one's criteria of choosing certain terms to refer to worldly phenomena, which are not bound by national borders, makes a researcher appear somewhat similar to the European Commission, which went through a painful process in order to reach a decision about the grounds on which Feta cheese can be called Feta cheese.

However, concepts are tools of thinking and there is no way of escaping abstract conceptual thinking. Nor should we exaggerate the obstacles created

---

15. Applying most concepts of politics already brings with it a critical evaluation of a practice or society; we are descibing it from the vantage point of socially accepted standards of political participation, debate, and accountability. To use just any concepts in our societies can not escape from characterising arrangements and actions from a normative angle of vision (cf. Connolly 1993:22-35). People do not share universal languages, nor is there any shared moral judgement. Connolly points out how the lack of shared moral judgements results in political concepts being essentially 'contested' in their nature (Connolly 1993:10-44). There is a good reason to say that when we add the diversity of semantic domains brought by the multiplicity of languages, we do not have much left of commonly accepted standards on which we could build universally accepted concepts.

by linguistic barriers and 'traditions of thought' to the spread of ideas in contemporary world. However, closing one's eyes to the existence of these obstacles can result in gaping ignorance or arrogance. In many European discourses one still often encounters the notion that Western philosophy is a
White Man's philosophy and that the superiority of the Western tradition of
thought and the civilisation based on it have (permanently) turned Europe
into the centre of the world.[16] In Japan translations (from at least German,
French and English) of current works of European writers of philosophy and
social sciences are readily available.

On the contrary, European readers in most cases find it far more difficult
to obtain any knowledge of fresh Japanese currents of thought. In Japan it
is interesting to notice that, while the translations of the classics of Western
philosophy can be bought in very inexpensive pocket-book editions, these
books quite often find remarkably wide readership; whereas the situation in
Finland, as in many other European countries, is that these classics are yet
to be translated into national languages. As a result, in countries like Finland
the number of people who have anything more than superficial knowledge
of the 'tradition of Western philosophy' is very small. Thus the knowledge
of 'Western philosophy', at least, does not make the Finns more 'Western'
than the Japanese. It may be that intersubjective social practices based on a
'common European heritage' make the Finns also 'honorary Westerners'.[17]
My point here is that in Japan it is often impossible to distinguish 'Western
thinking' from 'Eastern thinking'; we live in an interdependent world which
should have already gone beyond such simplifications and useless categories.
One may also claim that the 'tradition of Western thought' was from the
beginning a highly artificial construction — in particular, that labelling
downplays the significance of the long interaction between Europe and the
Islamic world.[18]

16. Cf. Matsubara (1985:11-20) who in her book analyses the complex relationship between
    European and Japanese traditions of thought — analysing also the misconceptions
    looking at them from both sides.
17. Here I am referring to the silly habit of the South Africans who in the past created the
    category of 'honorary whites' to be able to lure Japanese investors to fuel the South
    African economy. For the absurd situations that the Apartheid rule created for the Ja-
    panese in South Africa, see Yoshida (1989).
18. For an introduction to Islamic philosophy, clearly illustrating the intensity of the
    interaction between European thought and the thought of the Islamic world, Qadir
    (1990).

The myths of race and cultural proximity: writing about politics and international relations in an era of nationalist fervour and racial hatred

When we classify a group as a race we refer at best to generally shared characteristics derived from a pool of genes. Social, political, cultural, and geographical factors, in addition to those of natural selection, all have their affect on this pool. Since genetic compositions of populations vary over time, racial classifications can never be permanent (Outlaw 1990:65-66). Race is a fluid, transforming, historically specific concept parasitic on theoretical and social discourses for the meaning it assumes at any historical moment (Goldberg 1993:74). The linguistic characterisations of racial and ethnic groups tend to change rapidly. Linguistic labels indeed are a decidedly insufficient tool to approach the nature of selected groups of human beings. Even during the last couple of thousand years migration waves have criss-crossed most places on earth and two thousand years is a very short time in the history of human evolution. Consequently, for the modern Frenchman there is no way of knowing if his or her ancestors were Gaulish, Frankish, Burgundian, Norman or from some forgotten tribe (Cf. Gellner 1987:9). Even genetic similarities do not help us to define races, as two populations which are historically unrelated can show genetic similarities even if they have been subject to similar evolutionary forces. Therefore, from the biological and historical point of view, race does not make much sense. However, race continues to play a role as a category used to divide people into groups, usually on the basis of easily recognisable characteristics such as colour of skin. Racial categories are therefore fundamentally *social* in nature. As a tool of social formation race is used for the *rank-ordering* of racial groups (cf. Outlaw, 1990: 65-68 and Skutnabb-Kangas 1988:260-61).

Racial criteria have become part of social reality and even administrative practices in many countries when 'race' has become part of established legal vocabulary. There is a good reason to pay special attention to the situation in the United States in this field, as 1) 'race' based practices have deeply influenced American foreign pollicy and international relations, including U.S.-Japanese relations, and 2) the American 'race' discourse, as a general social discourse as well as an academic one, has a worldwide impact, and obviously is closely followed also in Japan.

In the United States the Naturalisation Act of 1790 passed by Congress employed explicitly racial criteria limiting citizenship to 'free white persons' and, after this act was successfully challenged on behalf of 'blacks' after the Civil War, 'Asian immigrants' became the most significant 'Other' in terms of eligibility for citizenship. In the Ozawa versus United States case (1922), the Supreme Court ruled against a Japan-born applicant for naturalisation (who had lived most of his life in the United States), arguing that

had these particular races (like the Japanese) been suggested, the language of the act would have been so varied as to include them in its privileges.

To circumvent the question of colour, the Court defined 'white' as 'Caucasian'. However, when an immigrant from India, Bhagat Singh Thind, attempted to gain citizenship by arguing that he was Caucasian. the Supreme Court changed its definition again, brushing aside anthropological and historical issues and once again appealing to the popular meaning of the term 'white'. Furthermore, in its 1923 decision against Thind, the Court invoked the criterion of racial assimilability to separate the desirable immigrants from the undesirable ones. Thereby Asian Indians were distinguished from European immigrants, who were deemed 'readily amalgamated with the immigrants already there (Wong, 1993:5).

Even the social success of Asian Americans in the post-war period has not been able to remove all the prejudices against this utterly heterogeneous group of people. Today Asian Americans as whole are more likely to obtain a higher education, are less likely to be unemployed or imprisoned and have fewer children than the average American. In short, they are a model minority if we take American middle-class norms as the ideal.[19] Japanese Americans in particular have often been praised as having the 'right values' as a group to be successful in American society. William Petersen writes that Japanese Americans 'as a group have all the civic virtues — education, diligence, honesty, competence; and if they apply these admirable qualities to public problems the whole community gains thereby'. However, Petersen describes the educational success of Japanese Americans at Berkeley during the 1950s and 1960s in the following way:

Their education had been conducted like a military campaign against a hostile world, with intelligent planning and tenacity,

and 'In a word, these young men and women were squares'. By studying statistics Petersen came to the conclusion that all these Japanese American students were 'squares'. He finds the civic virtues of Japanese Americans useful to American society but as a group and as individuals he regards

19. Cf. Daniels (1990:351-70), where numerous statistics for different Asian American ethnic groups and their increases are also presented. On Chinese Americans, see Tsai (1986).

them as somehow fundamentally different and words like those of 'military campaign' come close to suggesting that there is some kind of Japanese American conspiracy (Petersen 1971:113-16).

However, Asian Americans themselves do not have much in common and usually even less with Asians. For instance, the 'Asian identity'[20] of Japanese Americans is a highly questionable or complex issue. In the 1920s and 1930s immigration from Japan was virtually banned and the Japanese who remained in the United States in most cases had no chance of being naturalised, and were under strong social pressure to show their loyalty to American society and to abandon all the behaviour which would link them with Japan and Japanese culture.[21] This loyalty was, however, questioned by the American authorities in wartime and over 110,000 Japanese Americans were placed in internment camps simply for being of 'Japanese race'. Of these people 70,000 were American-born citizens.[22]

To prove their loyalty to the United States, Japanese Americans volunteered in great numbers to serve in the American armed forces, and the unit consisting of them, the 442nd Army Brigade, became the most decorated American unit in the Second World War, its casualties having grown to three times its original battle strength. In war Japanese Americans in the beginning were sometimes not even trusted with real guns and the 442nd spent its war mostly in Italy, as they were not trusted to help in the war against the Ja-

20. As for the concept of 'identity', I am using it in a loose meaning of 'everyday use' in English and also as a translation for the Japanese word 'aidentiti'. Being aware of the psychological research which has often defined 'identity' in various specific ways, I just want to emphasise that I do not believe that 'identities' can be used as rigid, narrowly defined categories of people which could be assigned for analytical purposes. I rather see 'identities' as vague labels which may be used to characterise how the people define themselves as members of certain groups or as outsiders for certain groups. More general labels, such as 'national identities', are usually based on such a distorted understanding of reality that as analytical tools for research purposes they would certainly prove problematic, but as research objects I find 'national identities' most useful.

21. Japanese Americans who experienced the war years and the time before it tried to be 100 per cent American in their symbolisation and rhetoric. O'Brien & Fujita (1983:226). In Asian American literature, including the literature written by Japanese Americans, the social pressure to Americanise and to be 'more American than the Americans', and the continued insecurity among assimilated Asian Americans, have been common themes in post-war Asian American literature. Wong (1993:77-117)

22. For the history of the internment of Japanese Americans and the wartime hysteria which almost without any reason targeted the Japanese Americans as the enemy within, see e.g. Baker (1990), Smith (1948:261-319), Uchida (1982), Knaefler (1991), Hersey (1988), and Armor & Wright (1988).

panese. When many of these soldiers returned home with their Purple Hearts they still had to meet their parents in the internment camps, the place from which they themselves had left for the war. Those Japanese Americans who served in the Pacific war theatre, often as translators, were frequently regarded with hostility and suspicion, and is some cases were mistakenly shot as enemies (Umezawa Duus, 1987 and Smith 1948:320-28). The wartime stereotypes of the Japanese and the Japanese Americans have remained alive among certain segments of the American population. During the trial of a football player turned actor, Orenthal James Simpson, Senator Alfonse D'Amato created a furore in the American media when he crudely mocked the Japanese American judge Lance Ito on national radio by mimicking a Japanese accent (which Ito does not have) in a manner apparently learned from wartime American propaganda films (See e.g. Reibstein & Miller & Foote & Namuth & Shenitz 1995:26-27).

After the Pacific War Japanese culture remained unpopular in the United States for years. Despite the quota of just 185 immigrants annually until 1965, some 45,000 Japanese immigrated to the United States between 1952 and 1960, most of them being married to American soldiers and former soldiers. When the 1965 Immigration Act finally opened the United States to immigration from most Asian countries, the economic motive to immigrate no longer existed for most Japanese and in fact immigration has since the 1960s been in slow decline absolutely and relatively — unlike the immigration from most other Asian countries to the United States. The social background of most Japanese immigrants and the hostility against Japanese culture has encouraged them to assimilate as soon as possible into American society and to abandon Japanese culture and its symbols. Those whose ancestors arrived at the turn of century in most cases were never even taught to speak Japanese. Nowadays, it is even difficult to make any meaningful predictions about the population of Japanese Americans as data from many of the counties where they are most numerous shows that outmarriage, mostly with 'Caucasians', is above 50 percent of all marriages involving Japanese since the 1970s (Daniels 1990:352-56, and for post-war Asian immigration to the United States in general, see Wong & Hirschman 1983:381-403. For a study analysing the kinship change among Japanese Americans, see Yanagisako, 1985).[23]

23. O'Brien & Fugita (1983:223-40), in their survey of Japanese-Americans tried to test feelings about interacting with 'Caucasians'. Their findings indicated that most second-generation Japanese-Americans (nisei) and third-generation Japanese-Americans (sansei) did not feel much less at ease with 'Caucasians' than with Japanese Americans

The racial criteria developed in American intersubjective practices has quite strongly defined the 'Asians' as the 'Other', which has already made the issue of race a permanent factor in most transactions between Japan and the United States. The rapid assimilation, cultural and even physical, of Japanese Americans into the mainstream of American society reveals how incorrect has been the assumption of Japanese as 'Asians' representing the 'Other'. Social Darwinist theories have undoubtedly left their mark on the American stereotypes and categories of nationalities and ethnic groups. These theories held that acquired mental and emotional states are passed from one generation to the next among different ethnic groups. Italians were impulsive, Germans bellicose and Asians treacherous as the result of these traits being inbred and being part of a hereditary process. WASP Americans were seen to be temperate, moral and democratic, and by definition all the others formed a cultural threat to them. In the United States, nineteenth-century Social Darwinism and its notions of biological superiority and inferiority have by and large been replaced by more subtle ideas of cultural superiority and inferiority (cf. Steinberg 1981:78-80). What also remains are the 'race consciousness' of society and the categories to which people are assigned. The category of 'Asian Americans' is simple enough to be applicable in daily life: anyone who has the 'looks' of an 'Asian' can be treated as an 'Asian' or 'Asian American'.

The case of Japanese Americans, being unique in its history, reveals for its part how misleading it is to create such labels as 'Asian American'. Community cohesion among Japanese Americans is not particularly strong and, for instance, the selective celebration of successful members of the ethnic community, so typical of many groups in American society, often does not work in the case of Japanese Americans, for whom the concept of ethnic identity itself remains vague. Institutionalised racism, such as the continued use of racial barriers to prevent larger numbers of 'Asian Americans' from occupying places in the best American universities, naturally is a cause of frustration to many Japanese Americans for whom it is difficult to comprehend why assignment to such a category as 'Asian American' prevents

(or 'Japanese', as they were asked). Not surprisingly, the *nisei* were somewhat more likely than the *sansei* to report feeling uneasiness among 'Caucasians' and also to report having personally experienced discrimination as an adult. Approximately one-half of all the respondents said that they felt there was discrimination in the employment area, which can be regarded as a very high figure and suggests that there are still many obstacles to the 'assimilation' of Japanese Americans, although most Japanese Americans (in this kind of surveys) are hesitant to admit having feelings of uneasiness with 'Caucasians' as a group.

them from attending the university of their choice. The use of the category of 'Asian American' may appear even more unfair to those 'Asian Americans' representing other ethnic groups than the 'Japanese Americans' or 'Chinese Americans', many of whom are recent immigrants who entered to the United States after the 1965 Immigration Act — or their children — who on average have lower academic averages than the above-mentioned groups and have to compete in the group which has the highest scores of all 'ethnic groups'.

In the United States national census all individuals need to select one ethnic category for themselves and this practice is even sometimes defended as a means to ensure the protection of minorities, since the minorities can thus easily be identified. This practice is out of touch with reality especially in a country where most people have difficulties even identifying all their ancestors in five previous generations. However, even in the ethnicity discourses the 'race' of the author seems to be a highly significant factor. Multiculturalism in American universities has increasingly lead to academic battles on which ways 'balanced' history should be reconstructed for the nation. History and present had traditionally been written by members of the majority WASP population, and when younger scholars with different kinds of 'racial identity' have tried to revise or balance America's past, there have been many voices charging them with 'reverse discrimination' and neglect of the positive values of American culture. Professor Ronald Takaki, who describes himself as a 'scholar of color', is a third-generation Japanese American who relates that even after having earned his Ph.D. in the field of American history he did not know much about the history of his grandparents and the history of Japanese Americans in general. What is amazing is that his 'racial identity' is a significant factor in the United States when his texts are interpreted by people whose family may be even fresher immigrants to the United States but who go on defending the 'traditional' interpretations. In politics the conservatives are trying to 'take back their culture and their country', as some Republican politicians put it, and in many universities conservatives are fighting against all plans to diversify the curricula and in some cases have even reinstituted the older versions of truth (Takaki 1993:109-21).

In fact some, apparently 'white' scholars, like Nathan Glazer of Harvard University, have argued that American 'racial policy' and experience with multiethnic society is particularly liberal and that the 'American ethnic pattern' is based on the idea of 'free individuals' and that 'no group is required to give up its group character and distinctiveness as the price of full entry into the American society'. Nevertheless, Glazer opposes all 'specific treatment' and 'special opportunities' given to any minorities and proposes that all those groups should emulate the example of the white ethnics. Scholars like Glazer simply do not acknowledge the existence of contrary phenomena to the 'American pattern' (Takaki 1994:24-35, analyses in detail Glazer's writings). Apparently Glazer believes that all Americans have maintained the essential characteristics of their cultural past, making America a nation of nations where all people are free and equal. According to this theory, for instance, the Japanese can keep their Japanese identity and social practices while they enter American society. I wonder if the proponents of these theories have ever been to a foreign country or met a person who speaks a foreign language.

The use of racial categories in scientific discourses also tells us something about the society which have produced these. European social science research and research on racism has through its selection of objects of study and in its analytical classifications often become strongly tied to European history or worse, national history (cf. Miles 1993:19-20). In the United States the state itself from its very inception has been concerned with the politics of race. After the already mentioned Naturalization Law of 1790 which declared that only free 'white' immigrants would qualify, it took until the McCarran-Walter Act of 1952, for instance, for those racially categorised as 'Japanese' to become naturalised citizens. Historically, a variety of previously racially undefined groups have required categorisation to situate them within the prevailing racial order. As the whole idea of placing people into clearly definable racial categories is based on ignorance of biology as well as of the history of humankind, the American history of applying racial categories in legislation and administration has for centuries produced absurd definitions and rulings. For instance, the California Supreme Court ruled in *People v. Hall* (1854) that 'Chinese' should be considered 'Indian' and therefore denied the political rights accorded to whites (Omi & Winant 1994:81-82). In 1982–83, Susie Guillory Phipps, who had lived her whole life thinking that she was 'white', suddenly discovered that she was not classified as such, because she had 'black' ancestors. She unsuccessfully sued the Louisiana Bureau of Vital Records to change her racial classification from black to white. Phipps was designated 'black' in her birth certificate in accordance with a 1970 state law which declared anyone with at least 1/32 'Negro blood' to be black. In the end Phipps lost the case and the court upheld the state's right to classify and quantify racial identity. However, at least at the local level this case was successful in raising intriguing questions about the way race is classified in the United States. For instance, Phipps' attorney called as a witness a retired Tulane University professor who cited research indicating that most Louisiana whites have at least 1/20 'Negro' ancestry (Omi & Winant 1994: 53-54). It seems that many of those 'whites' who have supported American racist legislation have not really thought about the consequences of the either-or logic on racial identity — most Louisiana inhabitants would have no chance proving they are not 'black' and changing the legal status of a large group of 'whites' to 'black' would certainly change the nature of 'race relations' in Louisiana.

As the American state institutions and their policies have kept directly intervening in 'race relations' from outside and as in fact the state has been acting as the site of racial conflict, the model of the American state may well be labelled as the 'Racial state' (Omi & Winant 1994:77-91). The American obsession with 'race' is a quite specific case and even in reading texts of American social science, an outside observer is often amazed by the careless way that 'race' and 'ethnic groups' are defined and used — the existence and applicability of these categories being taken unquestioningly.

In American research on ethnicity, identity and race relations it is quite commonplace to proceed directly to the specific question of the American 'whites' and 'blacks' and pretend that on the basis of these findings something could be said in general about 'race' or 'racial identity' and the relations between different ethnic groups. For instance, John Stanfield in his book which aims to be a critical presentation of the methodological distortions and Eurocentrism of American research on issues of race and ethnicity, himself keeps writing only about the 'black & white' cases and refers to similar writings by describing those in such terms as 'most important, sobering analyses of racism ...', 'most influential race relations statements ...', etc. (Stanfield 1993:11). It is telling that Stanfield in his three articles does not refer to any book which has been published in any other language than English. For him 'Eurocentrism' seems to mean only the distortions of the American culture of the 'whites' and he himself shows his indifference to the world outside the United States and even toward the diversity of American society (Stanfield 1993).

In naming or refusing to name things in order of thought, existence is recognised or refused, significance assigned or ignored, beings elevated or rendered invisible. Once defined, order has to be maintained, serviced, extended, operationalised. Naming the racial Other, for all intents and purposes, is the Other. Production of social knowledge about the racialised Other, then, establishes a library or archive of information, a set of guiding ideas and principles of Otherness: a mind, characteristic behaviour of habits, and prediction of likely responses. The set of representations thus constructed and catalogued in turn confines those so defined within the constraints of the representational limits, restricting the possibilities available to those rendered racially other as it delimits their natures. In the end whole societies and cultures are labelled as expressions of the Other (Goldberg 1993:150-51).

In the politics of the United States there have been constant demands for recognition on the part of minority groups who have felt themselves vulnerable to discrimination at the hands of the majority. Recognition also includes the act of naming and defining, and the minorities are usually in a disadvantaged position to do the naming and defining on their own terms. The nonrecognition of the existence of cultural and ethnic differences and the need for a more multicultural society is a severe social problem in the United States, but distorted recognition resulting in misrecognition (and often leading to internalising the misrecognition of others) has inflicted real harm on 'minorities' in the United States (Taylor 1992:25-73). The need to identify every individual's defining characteristics has, in a rather dogmatic way, divided people into more or less arbitrary groups. After all, majorities also always consist of minorities and no-one should be sure of their majority position. Some minority groups indeed share some cultural traits or political opinions but some others share little more than perhaps the colour of skin or some other nonrelevant characteristic.

'Racism' has its various faces. The racism most usually referred to is a form of 'personal prejudice' which is usually consciously used as a guise to defend privilege and to justify the treatment of some chosen people as inherently more valuable than others. Sometimes racism is manifested in more ideological ways using biological and cultural explanations as rationalisations or justifications for the prevailing superior position of a group of people. Racism may also be expressed institutionally in the form of systematic practices that deny and exclude groups of people from access to social resources (cf. Wellman 1993:57-58). The existence of differences in racial characteristics usually serves as the only criteria for how the people are defined and assigned to different groups. Without this arbitrary defining and naming, racism, in the forms presented above, would die out immediately. However, even if the prejudices based on 'racial defining' are overcome, that would still leave many other 'differences' on which to make similar kinds of distinctions, simplifications and polarisations to those on which racism is based. The mechanisms of nationalism and ethnocentrism are largely the same as those of racism: all need to select the ways to distinguish one's 'own people' from others, and once this is achieved the way is open to setting up different criteria on how to treat people in these categories.

Racial or ethnic similarity and linguistic similarities or differences which have been pointed out as expressions of the Other often have profound political significance. Furthermore, racist practices and the preundestanding these have reinforced have proved to be extremely enduring. Popular 'understanding' and 'knowledge' of race or conceptions of shared culture are often simply mythical constructions[24] and a researcher may wonder how it has been possible that even simple misunderstandings and folktales have distorted the minds of so many people for so long a time. Even in European academic literature there has been a tradition of study of the 'Orient' which has largely been based on ignorance, prejudices and generalisations.[25] The non-sense paraphernalia and silly ideas still so often associated with many Asian cultures and societies in Europe is simply frustrating for people who have a living contact with these societies.

Much of European literature on the 'Orient' deals with the Middle East but it is not uncommon that the same conceptions are in careless manner projected onto the whole of Asia. The academic discourse on 'Orientalism' in English is likewise concentrated around the research on the Middle East, and the personal contribution of Edward W. Said cannot be underestimated. Said analyses how Western scholarship has distorted the Eastern cultures on the basis of fragmentary knowledge and imagination, basing his analysis largely on writings about the Middle East. Said shows how science was used to legitimise colonialism or to serve the colonial administration. According to Said, Orientalism and scholarship on the East has never really been freed from colonialism and he argues that Orientalism in the form of American science and culture is still today used to dominate the Eastern people and also that the oriental scholars themselves use American science to feel superior to their own people and in the process become agents of American political and cultural domination. According to Said, the most important science

24. In the sense of myth distorting the reality.
25. For this tradition and its development, see e.g. Said (1981), Said (1991), Said (1993), Schwab (1984), and Thomas (1994:6,8,21-27,31-32,46,53-54,208-9). Jokisalo (1991:15-22) points out, with many examples, that the whole history of Western science and thinking is largely tainted by racism. See also Goldberg (1993:14-89). Even in academic discourses there is often a somewhat belittling tone or tendency to paint the 'Orient' or some Asian society as totally separated from the reality of the 'Western world' and as such a suitable place for a scholar to forget all rules of serious academic work. For instance, Barthes (1982:3), in his book on Japan, explains that for him 'the Orient is a matter of indifference, merely providing a reserve of features whose manipulation — whose invented interplay — allows me to 'entertain' the idea of an unheard-of-symbolic system, one altogether detached from our own'. In short, Barthes studies the Japanese as if they were Martians or fictive people.

institutions and mainstreams are dominated by Westerners and to get jobs the 'native informants' are expected not to rock the boat. This cultural domination has served the American interest of bringing consumerism to the Orient and hooking the Arab and Islamic world into the Western market system. As a consequence there has been a standardisation of taste in the region, symbolised not only by American consumer goods but also by distorted information on the Orient supplied by the American mass media. Said even argues that there is the paradox of an Arab regarding himself as an 'Arab' of the sort put out by Hollywood (Said 1991:324-25).[26]

The biggest problem with Said's presentation of Orientalism is his rather one-sided picture of global cultural standardisation. I do not know how many Arabs get their understanding of being 'Arab' from Hollywood movies but I am ready to believe that Said, perhaps on the basis of his own 'Americanisation', overestimates the importance of American cultural domination even in the Middle East, not to mention most other Asian regions. Ideas similar to Said's work about global cultural standardisation appear in Samir Amin's book 'Eurocentrism', where he strongly criticises global capitalistic universal culture and also explicitly claims that this process has also poisoned China and Japan (Amin, 1989). In their simplistic picture of the proliferation of global capitalistic universal culture Amin and Said come close to the book *The End of History and the Last Man* by Francis Fukuyama (1992), who believes that in the future the American type of liberalism and democracy will prevail all over the world. The main difference is that Fukuyama also believes that this development will lead to a more peaceful and harmonious world. Both Said and Amin have turned around the tradition of Orientalism but still seem to think largely in terms of the categories of 'Eastern' and 'Western', and both also seem to make the most of their references to Western literature.[27] However, for instance in Japan the idea of

26. For a very different, carefully created and balanced, interpretation of the social development of Islamic societies, see Gellner (1985). Gellner (1994:159-69), provides a harsh critique of Said's world view and position as a researcher. Gellner questions Said's conviction of the domination of the world by the West and of the all-pervasiveness of the ills of colonialism.

27. Thomas (1994:25-27), criticises Said (1991/1978) by saying that Said offered an appropriate account of a discourse about one part of the world, from a vantage point of a moment in political history, but it follows also that this will be incomplete and inadequate as far as other strands of colonial representation are concerned. There also seems to be some kind of tendency in the Islamic world among some people to see the 'religious' or 'fundamentalist' option as being opposed to a 'modern' attitude. If 'Muslim identity' is constructed emphasising the religious aspects, even at the expense of

American cultural domination simply appears absurd. American cultural influences are adopted selectively and modified to the local context, as happens with cultural influences from many other directions. In Japan it would be rare to find people who worry about American culture being a threat to Japanese culture. If asked, many would probably question whether Americans themselves are rich in such a thing as culture (*bunka*) — as the stereotype of Americans in Japan would not value highly the cultural sophistication of American culture. Similarly the idea that the market economy is somehow an American cultural monopoly does not make sense in a country which has a substantially higher per capita GNP than the United States.

As Akbar S. Ahmed and Hastings Donnan point out, Said's approach has created serious problems in the academic community of the field, principally because of the manner it has been received. 'Orientalism' itself has become a cliché, and third world literature, especially, is now replete with accusations and labels of Orientalism being hurled at critics and at one author by another at the slightest excuse (Ahmed & Donnan 1994:5). It would be a pity if the critical study of Orientalism turned to uncritical denial of the value of all research in the field, or of research done by someone with the 'wrong' kind of ancestry or background.

However, it remains a fact that Western academic research has made wild generalisations about whole Asian cultures and at the same time popular literature and art, like painting, have reinforced the same conceptions. And the world is not yet free of these conceptions. Many Western societies have simply accepted Europe's Orientalist constructs as substitutes for knowledge. Regardless even of the economic importance Asia is repeatedly said to have

more general cultural aspects, the chosen interpretations of religious truths may be seen to be in contradiction to values (or lack of values) which 'modern' is seen to represent. If then the image of 'Orient' or 'Asia' is constructed largely on the basis of 'Muslim identity' it is no wonder that there is virtually no one in Japan who can share much of this identity or worldview, and the values on which those are built. For the different options of interpreting 'being Muslim' and having a 'Muslim identity', see Waardenburg (1988:27-29). It may also be pointed out that for instance in Britain there has emerged a whole new community of 'Islamic Britain', people who have defined and established their position as an integral part of British society and have their own religious and political practices (cf. Lewis 1994). However, being 'Muslim' in many Western European countries often is interpreted under the influence of old prejudices against the 'Orient'. The negative media coverage, often employing sensationalist images of several existing Islamic societies and their past, has been used to portray 'the Muslims' as some kind of bridgehead in the West for the establishment of an Islamic theocracy or worse. The whole European discourse on 'ethnic relations' between 'Muslims' and others is very much a direct successor of the older 'Orientalism' discourses.

in most non-Asian industrialised countries in the 1990s, the Orientalist constructs of old Europe still taint much of what is written on Asian societies in
these countries. Quite often one gets the impression that many rather want
to continue defining their understanding of 'civilised life' and their own life
in such a way that serious study of Asian societies and cultures is left out of
it.[28] One may find it strange that the Orientalist discourse has penetrated also
some of the Asian academic discourses. In Japan the *Nihonjinron* discourse
can be said to be a natural ally to 'Orientalism': the myth-making mechanism
in both of them is very similar and the discourses can easily 'exchange' wild
generalisations on the uniqueness of Japanese culture and people. Obviously
the Orientalist discourses and constructs have also influenced the Japanese
discourses on Asia, modernisation and internationalisation (cf. Kan 1996:
82-146)

European Orientalism in literature and art has long roots, especially reflecting the long history of close interaction between Europeans and Middle
Eastern people. The core of Western Orientalism had already been created
when the 'Far' East was added to give more room to the imagination; new
forms of exotic oriental inspiration now had endless sources in these fantasy
lands. The diversity and great number of 'Far Eastern' cultures contributed
to the image of Asia and the 'Far East' in particular as an inscrutable and
exotic place — rather than making Europeans question the whole sense of
generalising on Asian countries without first studying them properly. Even
many Western colonialists who were in direct contact with many Asian societies and cultures accepted Europe's Orientalist constructs as substitutes for
knowledge.

For instance, as Australians usually failed to identify with geography,
they accepted most of the European Orientalist notions, and in the Australian
imagination Asia, including the 'Far East', became linked with the 'exotic'
and were seen as places 'far away'. Broinowski points out that even in the
Australian fiction of the 1990s China is described as so remote a place that
by digging straight down and deep enough one could get there, just as
people used to say in Britain. There is also evidence that some Australian
soldiers who fought in Vietnam still thought China was 'the whole of South
East Asia and everybody in that part of the world was Chinese' (Broinowski
1992:14). In spite of diplomatic speeches on the part of some Australian and
New Zealand politicians advocating that Australia and New Zealand should

28. For Western Orientalism in literature and art, see e.g. Kabbani (1986), Winks & Rush
    (eds. 1990), Szyliowicz (1988), Sweetman (1988), and Broinowski (1992).

become more 'multicultural' and look more to Asia, there are not many signs that the great majority of Australians and New Zealanders will change their attitudes toward Asia and make a serious effort to learn about Asian societies and languages. Asian-born people will remain a small and marginal minority in Australia and will be met with strong expectations to 'assimilate'. There is still no sign of appointments to top jobs of Asians (even people who have 'Asian looks') or Asia-literate Australians commensurate with the economic importance Asia is repeatedly said to have (Broinowski 1992:204-5)

The role of travel writing and travel journalism (to which category we still can place much of what is written on Asia even in the more serious European newspapers) should also not be underestimated, as it was largely these writings which produced the rest of the world for the European (and American) readership at particular points of Europe's trajectory. The Eurocentred form of 'planetary' consciousness created its own conventions of representation and those conventions are easily recognised in much European travel writing (cf. Pratt 1992:6-11). The reason why travel writings so seldom challenged the old stereotypes and myths of the Orient, for instance, is that the whole field was defined through which societies, people and events were represented, not on the basis of their own statements but by European 'experts' whose writing presumed the silence of the Orientals themselves (cf. Thomas 1994:23). By denying the Orientals an opportunity to represent themselves the travel books and popular literature kept strengthening the old stereotypes. Later on the tourism industry often kept using the same 'images',[29] and sometimes even living cultural practices are 'corrupted' in order to better cater to the wishes of tourists. In the Japanese case, Japan has never been a target (or victim) of foreign mass tourism and the tourist services are mostly geared to Japanese tourists,[30] and consequently

29. Here used in the sense of distorted idea of reality.
30. For many years the high costs in Japan have made Japan an unaffordable travel destination to great segments of American and European travellers who patronise many other tourist spots around the world. In Japan the tourism industry has largely targeted its efforts at the wealthy Japanese who can afford travel both in Japan and abroad. As of the 1990s, less than four million foreigners entered Japan each year, but the figures for Japanese entering foreign countries are more than ten million (of which about nine million are tourists). The annual figures for Japanese tourists have kept rising steadily whereas numbers of foreigners visiting Japan have not shown a dramatic increase (in 1980 the figures for the foreigners were 1.3 million and for the Japanese 3.9 million). One should note that these figures are for the number of entries and exists, not for the number of people — many of whom travel frequently abroad. *Nihon tôkei nenkan heisei 4 nen* (1992:60-61).

the need for Madame Chrysanthème-type fake operetta geishas or dubious 'modernised' folkdance performances fortunately has remained limited.[31]

In conclusion I would argue that when one uses such simple categories as racial categories or 'Eastern' and 'Western' as starting points of analysis, one already limits the human encounter between different cultures, traditions and societies and distorts reality (cf. Said 1991:45-46). Much of social science literature suffers from the careless use of linguistic characterisations and labels. I am also aware and concerned about how difficult it is to write informative and pertinent text on Japanese society in English or Finnish, when in order to produce a readable text, it is not possible or expedient to keep challenging the appropriateness of all linguistic conventions.

References

Ahmed, Akbar S. and Donnan, Hastings. 1994. *Islam in the age of postmodernity. Islam, Globalization and Postmodernity*, ed. by Akbar S. Ahmed & Hastings Donnan, 1-20, London: Routledge.

Amin, Samir. 1989. *Eurocentrism*. New York: New York Monthly Review Press.

Apunen, Osmo. 1990. *Peace Research, Research Paradigms & A Time of Radical Change. Department of Political Science and International Relations. Unit of Peace Research and Development Studies*. Report 39. Tampere: University of Tampere.

Armor, John & Wright, Peter. 1988. *Manzanar*. New York: Times Books.

Baker, Lillian. 1990. *American and Japanese Relocation in World War II; Fact, Fiction & Fallacy*. Medford: Webb Research Group.

Barthes, Roland. 1982. *Empire of Signs*. New York: Hill and Wang. Original: *L'Empire des Signes*. Genève: Skira, 1970, translated by Richard Howard.

Befu, Harumi. 1989. *The emic-etic distinction and its significance for Japanese studies. Constructs for Understanding Japan*, ed. by Sugimoto Yoshio & Ross E. Mouer, 323-43. London: Kegan Paul.

Bloom, William. 1990. *Personal Identity, National Identity and International Relations*. Cambridge: Cambridge University Press.

Broinowski, Alison. 1992. *The Yellow Lady. Australian Impressions of Asia*. Melbourne: Oxford University Press Australia.

---

31. A certain demand for commercially exploitable 'traditions', however, does exist in Japan. When 'traditions' are marketed, 'genuine' and 'invented' elements are combined in some ratio. Many consumers of these 'reconstructed traditions' are fully aware of the dubious authenticity of these 'traditions'. However, there are limits on how one can use 'traditions' to make profit. If market forces are allowed to decide, there is also a danger that 'exotic' marginal people with their 'traditions', seen as representatives of the Other, are used to market and advertise products and services. The cases of Ainus, American Indians and Sámi people could be used to illustrate this pattern.

Connolly, William. 1993. *The Terms of Political Discourse.* Third Edition. Oxford: Basil Blackwell.

Daniels, Roger. 1990. *Coming to America. A History of Immigration and Ethnicity in American Life.* New York: Harper Collins.

De Vos, George and Wagatsuma Hiroshi. 1972. *Socialization, self-perception, and burakumin status. Japan's Invisible Race. Caste in Culture and Personality,* ed. by George De Vos and Wagatsuma Hiroshi. Revised Edition, 228-40. Berkeley: University of California Press.

Fukuoka, Yasunori. 1993. *Zainichi kankoku - chôsenjin. Wakai sedai no aidentiti. Chûkôshinsho 1164.* Tôkyô: Chûôkôronsha.

Fukuyama, Francis. 1992. *The End of History and the Last Man.* Harmondsworth: Penguin.

Gadamer, Hans-Georg. 1976. *Philosophical Hermeneutics.* Berkeley: University of California Press.

Gadamer, Hans-Georg. 1985. *Truth and Method.* New York: Crossroad.

Gadamer, Hans-Georg. 1990. *Das Erbe Europas.* Second Edition. Frankfurt am Main: Suhrkamp.

Geertz, Clifford. 1973. *The Interpretation of Cultures.* New York: Basic Books.

Gellner, Ernest. 1985. *Islamic dilemmas. Reformers, nationalists and industrialization: the southern shore of the Mediterranean.* Berlin: Mouton.

Gellner, Ernest. 1987. *Culture, Identity, and Politics.* Cambridge: Cambridge University Press.

Gellner, Ernest. 1994. *Encounters with Nationalism.* Oxford: Basil Blackwell.

Goldberg, David Theo. 1993. *Racist Culture. Philosophy and the Politics of Meaning.* Oxford: Blackwell.

Gunnell, John G. 1979. *Political Theory: Tradition and Interpretation.* Cambridge, Massachusetts: Winthrop.

Hersey, John. 1988. Commentary: 'A Mistake of Terrifically Horrible Proportions'. *Manzanar,* John Armor and Peter Wright, 1-66. New York: Times Books.

Hiro, Dilip. 1992. *Black British. White British.* London: Paladin.

Hobsbawm, E.J. 1990. *Nations and Nationalism since 1780. Programme, Myth, Reality.* Cambridge: Cambridge University Press.

Honda, Katsuichi. 1993. *Senjû minzoku ainu no genzai.* Asahi bunko. Tôkyô: Asahi shinbunsha.

Iwanaga, Kazuki. 1993. *Images, Decisions and Consequences in Japan's Foreign Policy.* Lund Political Studies 80. Lund: Lund University Press.

Jokisalo, Jouko. 1991. Rasismi – tulevaisuuden ongelma. *Rauhantutkimus* 4/91, 14-29.

Kabbani, Rana. 1986. *Europe's Myths of Orient.* Bloomington: Indiana University Press.

Kan, Sanjun (Kang Sang-jung). 1996. *Orientarizumu no kanata e.* Tôkyô: Iwanami shoten.

Kayano, Shigeru. 1980. *Ainu no ishibumi*. Asahi bunko. Tôkyô: Asahi shinbunsha.

Kimu, Chanjon (Kim Chan-jung). 1994. *Zainichi to iu kandô. Shinro wa kyôsei*. Tôkyô: Sangokan.

Knaefler, Tomi Kaizawa. 1991. *Our House Divided. Seven Japanese American Families in World War II*. Honolulu: University of Hawaii Press.

Kondo, Dorinne K. 1990. *Crafting Selves: Power, Gender, and Discourses of Identity in a Japanese Workplace*. Chicago: The University of Chicago Press.

Kurihara, Akira. 1982. *Rekishi to aidentiti. Kindai nihon no shinri – rekishi kenkyû*. Tôkyô: Shin'yôsha.

Lewis, Philip. 1994. *Islamic Britain. Religion, Politics and Identity among British Muslims*. London: I.B. Tauris.

Linhart, Sepp. 1993. The Foreign Japan Researcher in a Changing World. *Transient Societies. Japanese and Korean Studies in a Transitional World*, ed. by Jorma Kivistö, Mika Merviö, Takahashi Mutsuko & Mark Waller, 1-17. (Acta Universitatis Tamperensis, Ser. B, Vol. 42.) Tampere: University of Tamppere.

Mâha, Jon C. (Maher, John) & Kawanishi Yumiko. 1994. Nihon ni okeru korian iji jôkyô. *Atarashii nihonkan, sekaikan ni mukatte. Nihon ni okeru gengo to bunka no tayôsei*, ed. by Mâha Jon C. (John C. Maher) and Honna Nobuyuki, 165-81. Tôkyô: Kokusai shoin.

Maher, John C. & Kawanishi Yumiko and Yi Yŏng Yŏ. 1995. Maintaining Culture and Language: Koreans in Osaka/ Ikuno-Ku, Osaka: Centre of Hope and Struggle. *Diversity in Japanese Culture and Language*, ed. by John C. Maher and Gaynor Macdonald, 160-77. London and New York: Kegan Paul International.

Matsubara, Hisako. 1985. *Nihon no chie — yôroppa no chie*. Tôkyô: Sanryû shobô.

Merviö, Mika. 1995. *Cultural Representation of the Japanese in International Relations and Politics. A Study of Discourses and Interpretations between Different Cultural Traditions*. (Acta Universitatis Tamperensis. A-series, Vol. 448.) Tampere: University of Tampere.

Miles, Robert.1993. *Racism after 'Race Relations'*. London: Routledge.

Najita, Tetsuo. 1989. On Culture and Technology in Postmodern Japan. *Postmodernism and Japan*, ed. by Miyoshi Masao & H.D. Harootunian, 3-20. Durham, N.C.: Duke University Press.

Nihon tôkei nenkan heisei 4 nen. 1992. *Nihon tôkei nenkan*. Tôkyô: Sômuchô tôkei kyoku.

O'Brien, David J. and Fugita, Stephen. 1983. Generational Differences in Japanese Americans' Perceptions and Feelings about Social Relationships between Themselves and Caucasian Americans. *Culture, Ethnicity and Identity. Current Issues in Research*, ed. by William C. McCready, 223-40. New York: Academic Press.

Omi, Michael and Winant, Howard. 1994. *Racial Formation in the United States. From the 1960s to the 1990s*. Second revised edition. New York: Routledge.

Outlaw, Lucius. 1990. Toward a critical theory of 'race'. *Anatomy of Racism*, ed. by David Goldberg, 58-82. Minneapolis: University of Minnesota Press.

Petersen, William. 1971. *Japanese Americans*. New York: Random House.

Pratt, Mary Louise. 1992. *Imperial Eyes. Travel Writing and Transculturation*. London: Routledge.

Qadir, C.A. 1990. *Philosophy and Science in the Islamic World*. London: Routledge.

Reibstein, Larry & Miller, Mark & Foote, Donna & Namuth, Tessa and Shenitz, Bruce. 1995. Courting Chaos. *Newsweek*, 17 April, 1995, 26-29.

Said, Edward W. 1981. *Covering Islam: how the media and the experts determine how we see the rest of the world*. London: Routledge.

Said, Edward W. 1991. *Orientalism: Western Conceptions of the Orient*. Harmondsworth: Penguin Books. (First published by Routledge & Kegan Paul Ltd 1978).

Said, Edward W. 1993. *Culture and Imperialism*. London: Chatto & Windus.

Sarmela, Matti. 1989. *Rakennemuutos tulevaisuuteen. Postlokaalinen maailma ja Suomi*. Porvoo: Werner Söderström Osakeyhtiö.

Saukkonen, Pasi. 1993. Nationalismi ja intellektuellit. *Politiikka*, Vol. 35, no. 1/1993, 1-14.

Schwab, Raymond. 1984. *The Oriental Renaissance: Europe's Discovery of India and the East 1660–1880*. New York: Columbia University Press Original: *La Renaissance orientale*, Paris. 1950.

Siddle, Richard. 1995. The Ainu. Construction of an Image. *Diversity in Japanese Culture and Language*, ed. by John C. Maher and Gaynor Macdonald, 73-94. London: Kegan Paul.

Siddle, Richard & Kitahara Kyôko. 1995. Deprivation and Resistance: Ainu Movements in Modern Japan/ My Heritage of Pride and Struggle. *Diversity in Japanese Culture and Language*, ed. by John C. Maher and Gaynor Macdonald, 147-59. London: Kegan Paul.

Skutnabb-Kangas, Tove. 1988. Vähemmistö, kieli ja rasismi. *Linguistica & Philologica-sarja*. Helsinki: Gaudeamus.

Smith, Anthony D. 1990. Towards a global culture? *Global Culture. Nationalism, Globalization and Modernity*, ed. by Mike Featherstone, 171-91. London: Sage.

Smith, Bradford. 1948. *Americans from Japan*. The Peoples of America Series. Philadelphia: J.B. Lippincott.

Stanfield, John H. 1993. Methodological Reflections: An Introduction, Epistemological Considerations, and In the Archives. *Race and Ethnicity in Research Methods*, ed. by John H. Stanfield & Rutledge M. Dennis, 3-15, 16-36, 273-283. Newbury Park, Cal.: Sage.

Steinberg, Stephen. 1981. *The Ethnic Myth. Race, Ethnicity, and Class in America*. New York: Atheneum.

Sweetman, John. 1988. *The Oriental Obsession. Islamic Inspiration in British and American Art and Architecture 1500–1920*. Cambridge: Cambridge University Press.

Szyliowicz, Irene L. 1988. *Pierre Loti and the Oriental Woman*. New York: St. Martin's Press.

Takaki, Ronald. 1993. Multiculturalism: Battleground or Meeting Ground? The Annals of the American Academy of Political and Social Science. *Interminority Affairs in the U.S. Pluralism at the Crossroads*, ed. by Peter Rose, 109-21. Volume 530: November 1993. Thousand Oaks: Sage.

Takaki, Ronald. 1994. Reflections on Racial Patterns in America. From Different Shores. *Perspectives on Race and Ethnicity in America*, ed. by Ronald Takaki, 24-35. Second edition. New York: Oxford University Press.

Taylor, Charles. 1992. The Politics of Recognition. *Multiculturalism and 'The Politics of Recognition'*, ed. by Amy Gutmann, 25-73. Princeton: Princeton University Press.

Tei, Taikin (Chung Daekyun). 1995. *Kankoku no imêji. Sengo nihonjin no ringokukan. Chûkôshinsho 1269.* Tôkyô: Chûôkôronsha.

Thomas, Nicholas. 1994. *Colonialism's Culture. Anthropology, Travel and Government.* Cambridge: Polity Press.

Tsai, Shih-shan Henry. 1986. *The Chinese Experience in America.* Bloomington: Indiana University Press.

Uchida, Yoshiko. 1982. *Desert Exile. The Uprooting of a Japanese-American Family.* Seattle and London: University of Washington Press.

Umezawa Duus, Masayo. 1987. *Unlikely Liberators. The Men of the 100th and 442nd.* Honolulu: University of Hawaii Press. Original: *Buriea no kaihôshatachi.* Bungeishunjûsha. 1983. Translated by Peter Duus.

Waardenburg, Jacques. 1988. The Institutionalization of Islam in the Netherlands, 1961–86. *The New Islamic Presence in Western Europe*, ed. by Tomas Gerholm and Yngve Georg Lithman, 8-31. London: Mansell.

Wagatsuma, Hiroshi. 1981. Problems of self-identity among Korean youth in Japan. *Koreans in Japan. Ethnic Conflict and Accommodation*, ed. by Lee Changsoo and George De Vos, 304-33. Berkeley: University of California Press.

Wellman, David T. 1993. *Portraits of White Racism.* Second Edition. Cambridge: Cambridge University Press.

Winks, Robin W. & Rush, James R. (eds.) 1990. *Asia in Western Fiction.* Honolulu: University of Hawaii Press.

Wong, Morrison G. and Charles Hirschman. 1983. The New Asian Immigrants. *Culture, Etnicity and Identity. Current Issues in Research*, ed. by William C. McCready, 381-403. New York: Academic Press.

Wong, Sau-ling Cynthia. 1993. *Reading Asian American Literature. From Necessity to Extravagance.* Princeton: Princeton University Press.

Yamazaki, Masakazu and Ichikawa Hiroshi. 1970. *Gendai tetsugaku jiten.* Kôdansha gendai shinsho. Tôkyô: Kôdansha.

Yanagisako, Sylvia Junko. 1985. *Transforming the Past. Tradition and Kinship among Japanese Americans.* Stanford: Stanford University Press.

Yoshida, Ruiko. 1989. *Minamia — aparutoheito kyôwakoku.* Tôkyô: Ôtsuki shoten.

Japanese Style Democracy

Sang-Chul Park

Introduction

As Japan began to open to the West because of American pressure in 1854, after 250 years of seclusion policy under the 'Tokugawa Shogunate', it had approximately a population of 34 million. Since then it experienced a reformation, industrialization, etc. Through the 'Meiji Restoration' in 1868 it built a parliamentary system. The Meiji Constitution prescribed a sort of constitutional monarchy and assured an absolute imperial prerogative. As prescribed by the Meiji Constitution, three elected representatives were regarded only as advisers to the 'Tennô' (Emperor), and no Prime Minister in rank of member of parliament existed until 1918 (Pohl 1985:26, Hall 1992:253-324). This situation was changed however with the growing influence of the urban industrial businessman class.

In 1925 popular suffrage for men was initiated. After that, Western democratic rules were transformed by the influence of the Japanese social structure, although the Americans brought their own democracy to Japan in 1945.

The modern political system, a parliamentary representative democracy, builds up a dual chamber system, which consists of Lower House and Upper House. The Upper House has a fixed election period and every three years one half of 252 members are elected anew. The Lower House has 511 members and every four years a new election is held. In reality, however, the election of the Lower House has been held almost every two years on account of political conflicts between the ruling and opposition parties on the one hand and between different factions within the ruling party on the other (Eo 1986:174).

It is remarkable that a vote from rural areas had more value than a vote from urban areas until the end of 1995, because the borders of election districts were laid down in 1947. At that time the division of population was planned. Since then it has been barely changed. The reason is that the conservative politicians, such as Tanaka, Ôhira, Takeshita, Uno, Miyazawa, etc. were elected in the rural areas and they would not change the borders of election districts (Pohl 1980:13).

Political reform has been a hot issue following the 1988-89 *stocks-for-political-favour* recruit scandal which pressed then Prime Minister, Takeshita Noboru, to resign in 1989. Subsequent scandals, including the 1992 Tokyo Sagawa Kyubin money and mob scandal, made the government headed by Hosokawa Morihiro introduce the political reform bills which laid the ground work for the electoral reform bills that were passed by the Diet in late January 1995. Under the new electoral system, 300 of the 500 Lower House legislators will be elected by 300 single seat constituencies and the remaining 200 lawmakers will be filled out through proportional representation. The aim is that voters choose a party rather than an individual. The old multi-seat constituency system has been regarded as one of the causes of political corruption since candidates from the same party have often competed against each other, spending massive funds and distracting policy oriented debates. Under the new election law, political parties which have at least five Diet members, or have obtained 2 percent of the total vote in the previous national election, can receive public funds for election campaigns (Abe et al. 1994:153; *Journal of Japanese Trade & Industry*, No. 1 1995:4-5). In reality, however, the LDP obtains better linkages with industries than other parties. The idea of choosing a party rather than an individual seems to be paradoxical in view of Japanese culture being based on hierarchy and group oriented human relationships.

This article argues about Japanese political perceptions of democracy based on culture, religion, philosophy and history, the main factors in the building of Japanese style democracy, which functions differently from Western style democracy.

Basic functions of Japanese politics

The Liberal Democratic Party (LDP) ruled Japan for over 40 years, and in spite of heavy conflicts within the party and many corruption scandals no one previously would ever have doubted its remaining in power. However, the LDP lost its majority in Parliament in 1993. Former LDP members Hosokawa, Hata, and Mihara built their own independent parties, such as the Japan New Party, New Born Party, and New Party Harbinger, and formed a coalition with the Social Party of Japan (SPJ). After the independent coalition was broken up, the LDP regained power by renewing their coalition with the SPJ (*The Economist*, June 26 - July 2, 1993:63). Opposition parties include the

Buddhist Party, Komeito, the Communist Party of Japan (CPJ), the Democratic Social Party (DSP), the New Liberal Club (NLC), and the Social Democratic League (SDL).

One reason for the dominance of one-party politics is that the party is
itself factionalized, and faction leaders compete for power internally and
represent diverse platforms and constituencies. In fact, the dominant party
system stems from Confucian values based on consensus and stability.
Harmony and cooperation practiced by the single-party system is preferred
to competition between the ruling and opposition parties as favoured in the
West (Neher 1994:954-55).

A focal point of LDP membership lies in the strong hold they have on
their voters in the rural areas. Close contact with their election districts,
'image control', is one of the most important factors leading to re-election.
For example, Tanaka Kakuei influenced the Tohoku-Shinkansen-Line project
deeply. He used his political power in the project to bring the Shinkansen
into his election district, Niigata. This phenomenon can be explained by
personalism and localism. In Japan, voters and candidates have an intimate
relationship based on kinship, belonging to the same region, same schools,
etc. (Flanagan 1968:391-95, Abe et al. 1994:164). Japanese politicians provide
their voters with various benefits through their privately sponsored
organizations. These include job opportunities for voters' children, scholar-
ships for university education, and hosting marriage ceremonies for these
voters. By doing all these things, voters and politicians build up a mutual
credibility and thus a basis for personal relationship (Thayer 1969:94-95,
Hendry 1995:197-98). Through human relatedness, personalism can be
developed as a leader-oriented political system where the emphasis is placed
on leaders rather than on laws. Hence, individual leaders play a significant
role in determining their political interests (Neher 1994:951).

This being so, Japanese politics creates a strong localism related to a
typical close village structure and personalism between voters and candidates. It is also remarkable that the majority of voters are usually more
interested in local politics than in national politics (Richardson 1974:57).

Typical Japanese behaviour involves permanent subliminal competition
between different interest groups, independent factions within existing
parties and individual personalities in terms of social behaviour and manners. An individual personality within a group plays a more dominant role
in Japan than in the West. Great respect for established power structures
introduces a conservative pragmatic attitude in politics. Therefore ideology
plays only a subordinated role (Hendry 1995:197).

Because it lacks clear political ideology, the leader-oriented political system is easily overwhelmed. Generally speaking, the social structure is verticalized resulting in a factionalized party system and factionalism within every group. This factionalism exists from government to business organizations. The main reason for factionalism is that the society is based on conformity and competition. These two factors are complementary rather than exclusive and at the same time create spin-off effects. Under these circumstances, politicians are obliged to follow their faction leaders' values and goals on the one hand and compete with one another on the horizontal level on the other (Ishida 1971:64).

The solidity of a faction depends on a junior leader's loyalty to his leader and his faction's leadership. Unless the junior leaders support their leader, no leader could control his faction efficiently. Thus, the leader of a faction respects opinions of the intermediate leaders and their interests. In this sense, the leader is regarded as a sensitive organization man rather than a dictator (Fukui 1970:46).

The functions of factionalism consist of positive and negative sides. Ironically, factionalism has contributed to democratization in the party. Various financial sources were available for different factions. This prevented the LDP from becoming dictatorial. In fact, factionalism checks the potential dictatorship of the Prime Minister (Eo 1986:250-51). Nominations for important party and government posts are based on the power balance and the interests of factions rather than on personal capability. This is obviously regarded as a disadvantage of factionalism (Fukui 1970:66, Abe et al., 1994:31). Additionally, political corruption linked with various financial sources and a weak prime minister are further negative effects of factionalism.

The basic attitude is based on the relationship between members in different sections within a party. It does not rely on contracts, such as in Western countries, but on sympathy and loyalty. These values are more significant for the Japanese idea than contracts and laws. For this reason, individuality is subordinated.

Group-oriented politics caused strong competition between different interest groups and inside parties. An outwardly united political structure based on strong internal competition is a typical attribute of the political culture (Choi 1983:132-33). A further problem is the close relationship between politicians and industrialists. This ensured on the one hand economic stability and growth through cooperation between politics and economics, but also caused many corruption scandals on the other. The close interlocking between politicians and industrialists stems from the government-led economic policy. Governmental economic intervention has been effective and based on Confucian principles. Confucianism stresses authoritarian rule and hierarchy in power but also emphasizes harmony, stability, and consensus on the other hand. On this basis, a strong government could determine needed directions for the nation and at the same time strengthen the nation's leadership from self interested societal and private forces (Neher 1994:953-56).

The structure of Japanese society

Japanese society is based on Confucianism, Buddhism, and Shintoism. Japan accepted foreign cultures and religions and created its own culture and religion. It is a typical Japanese attribute.

Among these, Confucianism has influenced the society strongly. It contains a strong marked loyalty to the state and high respect for one's senior. These principles contribute to maintaining life-time employment and the seniority principles in the society without any severe problems. The social structure reflects a homogeneous cultural identity on the one hand and a strong competition between the individual groups on the other.

Inside political parties there are many factions competing with one another. However, they never compete vertically. Competion in Japan exists only horizontally. This is the reason why Japanese politics has been relatively stable since the Second World War, although there has been some political turmoil.

Cultural identity

The differences in cultural systems between Japan and the West seem to be enormous. The Western cultural system can be regarded as one that places a great emphasis on individual values. In contrast to this, the Japanese system is based on group values. Japanese people do not decide alone, but rather, will respect the decision of a group. To the Westerner, Japanese behaviour seems to be immature, while the behaviour of the Westerner is regarded as egoistic by the Japanese. Groups such as a family or a company are considered more important than individuals in Japan (Hendry 1995:42-55). These different values result from Asian philosophies which are based on Buddhism and Confucianism. According to Buddhism, no one is allowed to accept symbols as representation of beings to attain the 'No Substantial Being'. Instead, the principle of convenience is in the foreground. This means that a symbol does not represent the 'Being', but emphasizes its existence.

This function in Confucianism is based on the ethic of community. The five classical relationships in Confucianism are father and son, ruler and subject, man and woman, elder and younger brothers, and between friends. It emphasizes their duty and responsibility in the human relatedness and stresses consensus, stability, and harmony in the society rather than in-dividual freedom and interests. Watsuji Tetsuro, a Japanese scientist, wrote about a theoretical basis for Japanese culture in which he focused on the idea of philosophy in human history. He was opposed to any evolutionism of culture as asserted by Western scientists.

Given his opinion, differences in culture do not come from its internal differentiation, but result from natural self distinction in different climates. He considers climate to be an international structure which determines the context in which people live, thereby creating so-called 'Inbetween Being'. Furthermore, he tried to escape the aphorism of *consciousness* philosophy of the Western culture because he regarded it as a wrong way of Western thinking (Heise 1989:84-85). The following quotation illustrates the cultural differences between Japan and Western countries and the way of thinking about group consciousness in Japan. Watsuji Tetsurô thinks the occidental tradition has understood the human being in a one-sided way as *individual*, and neglected the human being in society as a *community* creature. On the contrary, he argued that in the East Asian cultures, especially in the tradition of Confucianism and Buddhism, the human being has always been regarded as having a double nature, i.e. individual and commmunity oriented. He has interpreted the Japanese word 'human being' as 'inbetween' — a word composed by the joining of 'human being' and 'inbetween'. He learned from the Chinese characters and the Buddhist sutra that originally the human being has been understood 'in the world'. Later on, people started to use this conception as individual. Therefore, Watsuji Tetsuro found an impulse of critique on the consciousness philosophy in the conception history and pretended to adopt it for his ethics: With the expression for human being (Ningen) we characterize it as 'in the world' and individual as well. Hence, the human being is not *just* an individual, but neither is he *just* a commu-nity creature. Consequently, in view of this dialectic the double character of human beings becomes visible (Heise 1989:86).

Given Watsuji's theory, a subject in Japan is not defined by an individual identity, but rather by place identity. There is no other physical environment where the subject is allowed to fit in except in his own, because a locality is linked very closely to the individual subject. With this philosophical and cultural background Japan has developed a strong group consciousness.

Furthermore, the strong group consciousness can also be explained by factors, such as geographical narrowness, frequent natural disaster, ancestor culture and the tradition of rice cultivation. For example, the geographical

narrowness, frequent natural disaster and the tradition of rice cultivation require the virtues of consideration for others, compromise, tolerance and close
cooperation in a community. The ancestor culture leads to an intimate
relationship between families, communities, and state (Kobayashi 1987:11-13).

As social groups the companies have two special peculiarities: First, employees are familiar with one another, compared to employees in Western
companies. Second, companies tend to influence the personal life of employees. Employees are influenced by their companies as much as by their
family members. Their thoughts and behaviour are to a great extent influenced by the leader of their company. This tendency has not changed
since the Meiji government (Nakane 1989:181).

Additionally, a native place in the group society is of paramount importance. Politician, industrialist, and scientist will contribute to the development of their native places (*Look Japan*, March 1989:22).

The Japanese social structure

In different degrees every society consists of elements of conformity and
competition. It is a unique characteristic of Japanese society that these two
elements are linked so closely within its social and cultural background. I
will start with two different conceptions of the social structure: First of all,
it is based on basic principles in a society. Secondly, it deals with different
elements as to how to function in a society (Ishida 1989:140).

Basic principles

Japanese group building has in principle two different basic forms: One is
dependent on the common 'Ketsuen', that is justification of a single
individual. The other is 'Jien' which depends on the native place. To
understand the two forms properly, it is necessary to explain their
fundamental relationship. 'Ketsuen' is a relationship of blood relatives or
members of a caste. 'Jien' is a relationship between inhabitants of a native
place. Every individual belongs to a social group which is composed of
'Ketsuen' and 'Jien'.

Chie Nakane explains the character of group consciousness in the society
based on 'Ketsuen' and 'Jien' as follows: 'The character of group consciousness is already indicated when Japanese people signify their work
place, company, office, school, and party as 'mine' and those of partners as
'theirs'. In this expression it is symbolic that the company is not considered
as a business organization with which an individual has a specific contract.

It is not seen as a free-standing object, but is instead considered to be related to the individual directly' (Nakane 1989:175). This kind of specific group consciousness results from the common conception, i.e., house or house-hold which has determined Japanese society as a whole.

As an example, a group called, 'Batsu' could be created, composed of members of the same schools and universities. According to Kishida Junnosuke, Chairman of Japanese Research Institutes, 'Batsu' played an important role for economic reconstruction after the Second World War (Kishida 1987:242).

In order to recognize individuals in different 'Ketsuen' and 'Jien' as members of the same group, group consciousness is always stressed and the close emotional link between the members in the group is given a prominent place. The constant human contact creates a feeling of homogeneity in the group and the principle of group consciousness influences not only the action of an individual, but also his or her ideas and even way of thinking. The feeling of homogeneity in a group is based on an emotional participation that fully excludes other groups. A family and company tradition of emotional participation is continuously emphasized to support the building of the group and to create a basis for assembling groups.

With the principle of group consciousness Japan has developed a vertical system for human relationships. It represents a relationship from A to B that is not an equal social rank. In contrast, a horizontal relationship exists in an equal social rank. Strength of precedence plays an important role in Japan. Normally, the order of precedence between employees if they have the same education is determined by their admittance dates.

In many companies consolidations of employees are built consisting of members admitted in the same year. These groups distinguish the order of precedence between senior and junior clearly, and it is automatically verticalized as a relationship between superior and subordinate. Through the verticalization an intimate connection between 'Oyabun' and 'Kobun', superior and subordinate is set up. Horizontal relationships stimulate strong competition within ranked groups. These basic principles function in politics as well.

The mechanism of different elements

In the 'Meiji Constitution' of 1889 Japanese society was built up in a 'Tennô-System'. The smallest unit was a hamlet, a traditional rural community which was built in the premodern period. It consisted of a village, the smallest legal administrative unit. It was controlled by a prefecture which was an administrative unit on the national level. Thus, the 'Tennô-System' contains a continuous line of power and authority delegations.

In the 1920s and 1930s social differenciation emerged from industrialization. Diversified interests in modern society created distinct interests that denied the mechanism of the 'Tennô-System'. To stabilize the system, a relative differenciation on the middle level was allowed, while it assured a strict integration of top and bottom levels. At the time, two different basic units for it existed: One was an existing hamlet which consisted of different functional organizations based on farmer, veteran, youth etc. The other was the workshop hall which was built through urbanization in the city areas. Factory workers could experience group consciousness.

In spite of the modified form of social integration, two difficulties for the continuation of the 'Tennô-System' emerged: tenant and worker conflicts in the 1920s, and the communist movement. These conflicts split basic elements of the hamlet and the workshop hall, and for the first time in Japanese history the communists demanded an abolition of the system. The government responded to the communists by exercising suppresion, and then launched a political attempt to solve the problems of the Tennô-System.

With the five year plan for the regeneration of rural communities and the establishment of 'Sanpô' (Union for Service to the Country through Industry) the government succeeded in restoring the two basic elements, hamlet and workshop hall. In order to avoid conflicts between tenants and workers, it supported farmers and built a labour union to replace 'Sanpô'. The labour union was however only used to hinder workers' movements (Ishida 1989:122).

After the severe oppression of the left wing movement a danger from the extreme right wing appeared. The threat from the right wing was not simply the way it used force, but also the way it demanded a fundamental reformation of the basic structure of the political system. The right wing attempted to bring a new principle, national political order, into the traditional authority. This was not however accepted by anyone in a subordinate position within the social hierarchy. The new principle was massively criticized by the government and ruling elite groups. Finally, the violent revolt of rightist groups ended in February 1936 when the military coup was crushed.

In 1940 the Society for Supporting Imperial Power (SSIP) was established to move the nation in the right direction in an institutionalized way. It aimed at rehabilitating a concentrated relationship between different groups based on the hamlet and workshop hall, and at initiating leadership. The initiation of leadership contributed to rebuilding the authority of the government. SSIP stressed national unity, and the government emphasized it as an instrument for avoiding conflicts inside the nation. Logically, distrust and hatred against foreign countries was mobilized.

After the Second World War, SSIP was united officially by the American military regime. In spite of the official disbandment of the Tennô-System, the SSIP shared similar characteristics with it. Labour unions were organized by workers' organizations which were set up in every factory as branches of the SSIP, even though the American military regime encouraged an expansion of labour unions. Thus, employers or foremen instead of the simple worker could influence the formation of labour unions (Ishida 1989:126-27).

During the first year after World War II Japanese city dwellers moved to the countryside because many cities were destroyed by massive bomb raids. In the 1960s Japan achieved a rapid economic growth and therefore required a larger labour force. Consequently, the economic boom caused a rural exodus.

With the economic upswing in the 1960s the average level of income increased rapidly. High school and university education standards were brought up to international levels. In short, no strong demand stimulus was apparent until the end of the 1970s. This was due to the fact that, even with expectations of increasing incomes, most people preferred to save rather than consume. Low purchasing power gradually contributed to equalizing the economic lead of Western countries.

One a problem in the social sector however, was the increasing portion of elderly people. Given the early forcasts, the number of 45-54 year olds, and the age group older than 55 years, would increase to about 29.9% and 58.6% of the entire population between 1975 and 1990 (Heinichen 1980:40). However, in reality, the proportion of people in those age groups has risen 30.1% and 64.7% respectively. According to the revised statistics from 1992, they have increased 32.7% and 75.4% respectively (Statistics Bureau Management and Coordination Agency 1993:48-85).

This phenomenon seems to be a common social development in post-industrial society. The increase of employees in older age groups burdens the national economy because wages based on the principle of seniority rise with an uninterrupted service term. At the same time the political leaning of the older generation tends to be conservative or oriented towards nationalism.

Japanese style democracy in the Asian context

Western societies can be characterized as individualistic societies which emphasize 'I' consciousness, autonomy, emotional independence, individual initiative, right to privacy, financial security, and universalism, while Asian societies may be regarded as collectivistic societies which pursue 'we' consciousness, collective identity, emotional dependence, group solidity, duties and obligations, group decision, and particularism (Kim 1991:3). In addition, the independent view and interdependent view may also explain the different characters of Western and Asian societies: The former is described as being egocentric, separate, idiocentric, and self-contained, while the latter focuses on being sociocentric, holistic, collective, allocentric, ensembled, and relational (Markus and Kitayama 1991:226-27).

Japan as an Asian country shares the above implied values of the Asian societies. These include ingroup favoritism, factionalism, localism (regionalism) which result in conformity and competition on the one hand, and prevent the promotion of principles, rules and laws on the other hand. Thus Japanese politics' emphasis on particularism rather than universalism is based on a typical Asian cultural background (Kim 1991:11). For instance, core elements such as human-relatedness remain strong in this society, although many external features of Japanese culture have changed through industrialization and urbanization.

Against this cultural background, a dominant party system has emerged which is based on the Confucian values of consensus and stability. Harmony and cooperation practiced in the dominant party system are more preferred values than competition and the majority principle. In fact, the values of personalism, authority, and dominant parties strengthen the importance of the other (Neher 1994:955).

As another factor for Japanese style democracy, the role of a strong state can be mentioned. A strong government enabled rapid economic development based on government-led economic policies. Moreover, it could move in needed directions without facing any significant resistance of societal groups.

In short, Japanese style democracy emphasizes not only a productive and sustainable political democracy that ought first of all to provide for the welfare of the people, but also the widest possible national consensus building which is superior to Western style democracy based on the majority principle (Commission for a New Asia 1994:34). Thus, political perceptions of democracy in Japan are based on productivity and sustainability of politics and national consensus building. In addition, these are seen to stress the responsibilities and duties of citizens while Western democracy focuses on individual freedoms and rights.

Traditionally, Confucianism stresses a duty conception instead of a right conception. The Emperor has his own duty to rule which is the 'mandate of heaven'. Politicians are committed to serve the people and people have a duty to serve the nation. The relationship between the different categories ought to function harmoniously. If one of these does not fulfil its duty, the mandate of heaven breaks and the nation will face political turmoil.

This basic political conception is still dominant in Japan. For example, Hashimoto Ryûtarô, the new LDP leader, stressed during an interview, his duty to restore credible politics to the Japanese people.

Critique of Japanese style democracy

As mentioned earlier, the dominant party system has resulted in a close linkage between politicians and industrialists that contributed to rapid economic growth on the one hand, and caused political corruption based on money politics on the other. Additionally, factionalism does not reflect the will of the people, although Japanese style democracy tries to build a national consensus as widely as possible. For example, the Former Prime Minister Kaifu Toshiki had to resign even though his electoral reform bills were supported by the majority of people before the general election in 1993, the reason that his faction belonged to the minority group in the LDP, and he was therefore uable to influence other factions.

Following the passage of the political reform bills, opposition parties, including Shinseito, Komeito and the Democratic Socialist Party, built a new opposition party, the New Frontier Party, on November 24th 1994. By contrast, the ruling coalition consisted of Murayama's Social Democratic Party, the LDP and New Party Sakigake, a small LDP splinter party.

Even after political reform, public views on current politics are rather critical because of chronic factionalism and personalism. The common view is that the formation of new parties is only for tactical reasons — how to win the next election in order to expand their factional interests — and that politicians should pay attention to long term visions instead of dealing with day-to-day issues and other short-term concerns.

Conclusions

The history of Japanese democracy is not so old if we define the term 'democracy' as a Western conception. During the Meiji Restoration (1868-

1912) Japan attempted to transform its political system from the feudalistic to the Western democratic system, although the Tennô-System has always held the prerogative. It has been Japan's unique political and social system.

After the Second World War, Japanese politics was influenced by the American political system. A political system is a social product which stems from a cultural background. Japan has already spent longer than one half century in order to harmonize Western democracy, pursuing individual freedom and human rights, with its own cultural background. In reality, however, we still see some ambiguous phenomena in Japanese politics. Some Western political analysts have argued that the Japanese political system is not really democratic. Is this true? I must say that it is not true if we consider the different cultural background. As a national economy obtains its own cycle, a political system needs to adopt its own pathway in its society. Japan has gained much experience from its history. When the government in the Nara Period (710-94) imported the Chinese bureaucratic system without any consideration to Japanese social conditions of the time, it collapsed, and the nation faced political turmoil (Bito and Watanabe 1993:5-6). Hence, Japan should struggle for its institutional reformation in politics and society.

However, it is also true that Japanese democracy to some extent is still weak in terms of principle, rule and law. In order to improve these elements and at the same time to keep its cultural virtues, Japan is obliged to show us its new visions and future-oriented political and social systems.

References

Abe, Hitoshi/Shindo, Muneyuki/Kawato, Sadafumi. 1994. *The Government and Politics of Japan.* Tokyo: University of Tokyo Press.

Bito, Masahida/Watanabe, Akio. 1993. *Chronologie der japanischen Geschichte.* Tokyo: Munbusho.

Commission for New Asia. 1994. *Towards a New Asia. A Report of the Commission for A New Asia 1994.* Singapore.

Choi, Sang-Yong. 1983. The Japanese Political Culture and Foreign Policy. *Modern Japan (in Korean),* ed. by Han, Bae-Ho, 131-222. Seoul: Hangilsa.

Eo, So-Young. 1986. *Modern Japanese Politics* (in Korean). Seoul: Bupmunsa.

Flanagan, Scott C. 1968. Voting Behavior in Japan: The Persistance of Traditional Patterns. *Comparative Political Studies,* Vol. 1, 391-410.

Fukui, Haruhiro. 1970. Japan: Factionalism in a Dominant Party System. Faction Politics: Political Parties and Factionalism. *Comparative Perspective,* ed. by Frank P. Bellon/Dennis C. Beller, 46-66. Santa Barbara: American Bibliographical Center, Clio Press.

Hall, John Whitney. 1992. *Japan: From Prehistory to Modern Times*. Tokyo: Tuttle.

Hendry, Joy. 1995. *Understanding Japanese Society*. London: Routledge.

Heise, Jens. 1989. Nihonron-Materialien zur Kulturhermeneutik. *Im Schatten des Siegers: Japan*, ed. by Ulrich Menzel, Band 1. 76-97. Frankfurt: Suhrkamp.

Heinichen, Otto Raban. 1980. Japans Wirtschaft. *Wirtschaftspartner Japan*, ed. byInstitut für Asienkunde Hamburg, 29-45. Hamburg: Institut für Asienkunde.

Ishida, Takeshi. 1971. *Japanese Society*. New York: Random House

Ishida, Takeshi. 1989. Konflikte und ihre Beilegung: Omote-ura-und Uchi-soto Beziehungen' *Im Schatten des Siegers: Japan*, ed. by Ulrich Menzel, Band 1., 111-39. Frankfurt: Suhrkamp.

Ishida, Takeshi. 1989. Die Integration von Konformität und Konkurrenz. *Im Schatten des Siegers: Japan*, ed. by Ulrich Menzel, Band 1., 140-70. Frankfurt: Suhrkamp.

Journal of Japanese Trade & Industry. 1995. No. 1.

Kim, Uichol. 1991. Introduction to Individualism and Collectivism: Conceptual Clarification and Elaboration. Working Draft. University of Hawaii.

Kishida, Junnosuke. 1987. Marketable Technology, Key to Postwar Success. *Japan Quarterly*, July/Sep. 242-50.

Kobayashi, Hiroaki. 1987. *Wirtschaftsmacht Japan*. Köln: Sigma.

Look Japan. 1989. March 10.

Markus, H./Kitayama, S. 1991. Culture and Self: Implications for Cognition, Emotion, and Motivation. *Psychological Review* 98, 224-53.

Nakane, Chie. 1989. Die japanische Sozialstruktur: Theorie der unilateralen Gesell-schaft. *Im Schatten des Siegers: Japan*, ed. by Ulrich Menzel, vol. 1, 171-207. Frankfurt: Suhrkamp.

Neher, Clark D. 1994. Asian Style Democracy. *Asian Survey* vol. 36, No. 11. 949-61.

Pohl, Manfred. 1985. Demokratie auf japanisch. *Der Bürger im Staat*, ed. by Landes-zentrale für Politische Bildung, Baden-Württemberg, vol. 35, 26-32.

Pohl, Manfred. 1980. Politik und Gesellschaft. *Wirtschaftspartner Japan*, ed. by Institut für Asienkunde Hamburg, 11-27. Hamburg: Institut für Asienkunde.

Richardson, Bradley M. 1974. *The Political Culture of Japan*. Berkeley: University of California Press.

Statistics Bureau Management and Coordination Agency. 1993. *Japan Statistical Yearbook* 1993/1994. Tokyo: SBMCA.

The Economist. 1993. June 26-July 02.

Thayer, Nathaniel E. 1969. *How the Conservatives Rule Japan*. Princeton: Princeton University Press.

The Unique, the Ordinary, and General Lessons from Tokyo Urbanism[1]

Leif Selstad

Claims as to what is unique and ordinary in urban life in Japan have been represented in different but overlapping ways by researchers. A number of perspectives have been used to portray city life in the Tokyo metropolis, with implications for how it may be understood in relation to urban conditions elsewhere in Japan and in other parts of the World. While the literature on urban social life in Tokyo is quite extensive, and can only be scratched at here, few attempts have been made to discuss it in terms of views on urbanism in general (cf. Hannerz 1980). The contributions may become somewhat oblique when considering themes in urban history such as complexity of scale, markets, interest formation, class conflict, and social networks. While there are exceptions to this trend, claims that are made, whether of spatial disorder or planning, oppressive control or human warmth, tend to see Japanese urban life as somehow different, without always specifying the distinction (Iwatake 1993:104). In many ways Tokyo is a world unto itself, and is so beheld by the people who live and act within it.

The theme of what is distinct or common, may provide an intake to a more general understanding of the intricacies of social life in general and urban life in particular. Whereas studies about social life in Japan often have statements of what is unique or ordinary, few attempts have been made to clarify the ways in which such claims are made, or to relate them to wider generalizations of social forms or discourses. One such area of discourse concerns the interplay between local and large scale, metropolitan areas of social life. Images like those of Tokyo as a 'congeries of villages' (Dore 1968:386) are both alluring and disturbing. On the one hand, one should not under-

1. For comments on this paper I would like to thank my colleague at Finnmark College, Tore Nesheim. Critical comments and suggestions were also received from participants at the Fourth Nordic Symposium on Japanese and Korean Studies, Aarhus.

estimate the scale and complexity of Tokyo as a metropolis. A huge and bustling infrastructure, with government and business conglomerations involved in large scale economics, leave their mark on the city. On the other hand, an oversimplified view of local organization and interests, is bound to be detrimental to a deeper understanding of the city. Local life interweaves with wider social developments in Tokyo in manifold and intriguing ways.

It is this latter issue of the local in the urban that will be focused on here. An attempt will be made to show that the ordinary and the unique often form part of the same phenomena, that may be reduced to general areas of concern, such as the coexistence of traditional and modern areas of social life. The interpenetration of what may be held to be distinctive areas of acting and performing, traditional and modern, local and urban, entails that a wide and composite perspective on social complexity may be of use. This should reflect on how social conditions have an impact on people's lives, and how people try to manage their existence within multiple and often contradictory fields of social involvement.

An urban village in Tokyo

As a starting point, my own research in a locality near downtown Tokyo may be referred to. The place in question, Tsukuda or Tsukudajima, is small and well delimited, with 900 residents (in 1985), and would appear in many ways to be in some sense 'unique', an 'urban village' (Gans 1962:4). The conditions that may be referred to, include the historical background of Tsukuda as a fishing village, but also continuing, substantive traits like economy, where nearly half the local men are engaged in fishing related occupations, in particular at the Tokyo Central Fish Market. Another such trait is the strong emphasis on kinship locally, where roughly 85 percent of local residents were either locally born or married to a native (Selstad 1994:5). This is a very high figure, even when compared with traditional, isolated fishing villages.Furthermore, a number of local organizations and associations have defined the village area as their jurisdiction. In particular this concerns the Local Association (*chôkai*) and the Shrine Association (*Sumiyoshi-kô*), each with its own leadership and organization embracing the whole village. The latter manages the local festivals, which give life and meaning to local units of organization such as the village sections (*bu*) and men's age grades. Ritual life culminates in the Great Festival, which is performed every third year, and which epitomizes much of local traditions and ritual life, attracting huge crowds of visiting spectators. By considering these and other substantive and symbolic features, an image may be presented of Tsukuda as still a form of rural village, that in some respects would be more traditional than even out-lying fishing localities in Japan.

At the same time, Tsukudajima is part of the Tokyo metropolis, located less than two kilometers from the center of the supercity. For more than 400 years, local people have taken part in city life, and this is reflected in several ways locally. Only a handful of men are engaged as fishermen today, the tra-ditionally caught fish, whitebait (*shirauo*), having been exterminated by pol-lution. Nearly 70 percent of the labor force, notably women, are engaged in more city related occupations like office work and services. Residents par-ticipate in urban life in numerous ways, such as through shopping, re-creation, and contacts with public administration. In spite of the markedly traditional image of many facets of local life, and the place itself, its low, mostly wooden houses, its alleys, and the fishing boats in the canal, it be-comes apparent that local people continually take part in modern life. What is more, they seem not to envisage any clearcut opposition between tra-ditional and modern involvements, but may rather claim that it is possible to combine 'old traditions and new techniques'.

In order to approach this contrast between Tsukuda as a traditional vil-lage and the locality's immersion in an urban environment, several modes of explanation could be adopted. Rather than resorting to a simplistic or in-strumentalist model, an attempt will be made to show that a broadly based description of local conditions will help clarify local conditions of persistence and change. An investigation of Tsukudajima as a local community, then, would have to rely on a wide or thick description of social life, where tra-ditional and modern nuances can be included in ongoing social discourses (Geertz 1973:6). It is through a description of this kind, that the coexistence of traditional and modern involvements may be accounted for, and the 'uniqueness' of Tsukuda may be elucidated.[2] We will return to the issue of traditionalism shortly, but first a contrasting example of urban life may be presented.

2. When entering the debated theme of uniqueness, it seems necessary to mention some possibilities of misrepresentation. This concerns the closed discourse on Japanese nationalism and 'Japaneseness' (*nihonjinron*) (Befu 1992). The same applies to some extent to the image of ordinary (*futsû*), which also becomes part of nationalist discourse. Emphasis should be made, that what is discussed as unique or ordinary are not absolute attributes, but obtain significance only in relation to a wider discussion of social and human conditions. At one level of discourse, as that of nationalism, confusion is bound to remain, irrespective of clarification.

The ordinary and the distinctive in an urban locale

In such a project of describing the compositeness of social life, the existence of numerous other local studies from Tokyo helps broaden the perspective for such a description, since they generally provide a broad and pervasive image of local conditions. One common observation is that parts of the traditional ethos, dealing with bonds of obligation and group solidarity, persist within the social life of the modernizing urban milieu. For the suburbs, both Vogel (1971) and Allinson (1979) discuss the persistence of personal bonds of obligation and loyalties based on a group ethos. Closer to the Old Downtown (*Shitamachi*) area, Dore (1958:249) writes of the ambiguity of the traditional-modern distinction, crosscut by considerations of income, class, education, and 'celebratiousness'.

In one local study, the 'ordinary' nature of the local setting is accentuated (Bestor 1989:7). The locality in question, 'Miyamoto', is located only 8 kilometers from Tsukudajima, and similarly has a small population and a well defined territory; yet its description is strikingly contrastive. In describing it as ordinary and average, Bestor is referring to the place as fairly nondescript, with mixed residential and commercial neighborhoods. The mixture of shops and homes, schools and service institutions, are among the many facets that make Miyamoto resemble many other localities in the city. The image of being ordinary also has an ideological dimension, in showing what is passable. Hence it becomes notable that parts of the political and social life in Miyamoto seem both distinctive and challenging. One main area of interest in the study is the political life of the local association (*chôkai*), where Bestor was allowed to attend meetings and make observations.[3] This becomes remarkable, when considering the semi-official status of the association, due to its being reckoned a main unit in the nationalistic and militaristic mobilization of the population in Japan during World War II (*ibid.*:75). The special position of the local association, somewhat compromised and sensitive, becomes a meta-discourse in the outline of the ordinary. That its organization remains basically the same today as before the war, would appear from the description of its constituent units, down to the more quaint information on the fixed ranking of seats at association meetings. Even more exceptional is the election of a local leader. The candidate for local leader is appointed, or appoints himself, beforehand. He is then nominated as an only candidate, and finally is elected 'by acclaim', that is, without elections taking

---

3. In Tsukuda I could not attend the main meetings of the local association, but could visit those of the shrine association.

place at all (*ibid*.:188-90). In local politics, at least, Miyamoto does not seem to be so ordinary. Generally speaking, there is considerable variation in the way political representation is organized in different localities in the city; in Tsukuda leaders tend to be appointed for life, there having been only three leaders since 1945, while nominal but actual elections are held every other year. At the same time, Bestor is able to show that localities form an important power block for almost all seats in the Metropolitan Government and its sub-units (*ibid*.:88).

The variability and dynamics of local social life in Tokyo extend to other areas than politics, such as religion, or the ways in which traditional and modern involvements are negotiated. The ordinary and the unique become commentaries on such negotiations, parts of ongoing social discourses within the dynamics of social life. The challenge is how to deal with this interchangeability of general and special viewpoints. When dealing with politics, Miyamoto is in some sense more unique or particular than may be the case in Tsukuda. The locality itself, on the other hand, may be more anonymous or nondescript, and is not a touristically famous spot as is Tsukuda. If we are not to be caught up in an understanding of the particular, we need to consider the wider, underlying social conditions that go into the situation we are trying to describe. Our task is, in other words, to find, if not what is universal, then at least something general in the special, rather than proclaiming places, situations, or circumstances to be 'unique' or 'ordinary'. Our next task will be to take description one step further, in trying to extract some general lessons from the material under presentation.

Traditional and modern as part of urban discourse

Contributions to urban studies in Tokyo often touch upon the exciting and scholarly challenging coexistence of modern and traditional social forms in the Japanese urban environment. A belief in progress can go along with the upkeep of neighborhood shrines and festivals (Vogel 1971), or modern police surveillance may be combined with links of patronizing and gratuity (Ames 1981). Incidentally, one tantalizing observation is of the consumption of international, 'global' goods being appropriated for local identity discourses on gender, class, and power, through the inherent ambiguity of goods in symbolizing identity (Clammer 1994). How does one account for the persistence of a traditional ethos in modern settings?

It is not possible to give a straightforward answer to why traditions are maintained. In the monograph on Miyamoto, a main concern is what role cultural traditions play in the persistence of a 'typical' urban milieu in Tokyo

(Bestor 1989:10). In his analysis, Bestor relates the phenomenon of traditionalism directly to local organization and integration, by indicating that it is concerned with local strategies of maintenance. Focusing on the old middle class in the towns, the merchant class, he states that this group employs traditions both to preserve the milieu and to ensure continued influence and political clout (*ibid.*:264). There is considerable reason in this, but it begs a number of question, such as why other people, not members of the bourgeoisie, are supportive of local traditions. For most people no simple, rational intention or explanation may be given for taking part in traditional life. A further problem arises, when tradition is discussed in terms of a few, easily recognizable ritual and social performances, such as a local festival; traditions that may be viewed as harmless, politically speaking. Whereas a focus of interest in the Miyamoto study is the local association, and it is here we find some of the strongest and more controversial traditions, as when avowed elections are made through acclaim. In such political traditions one finds some of the exiting material in Bestor's account, which becomes backgrounded in favor of the less controversial ritual traditions.

The coexistence of seemingly contradictory practices links up with the often discussed issue of syncretism in Japanese thought, that is, the adoption and mixture of elements from two or more religious systems or areas of thought. Syncretism is described most often in relation to the coexistence of Shinto and Buddhist beliefs in the performances and practices of popular religiosity (cf. Befu 1975; Hori 1968). While the concept is debated, one sense in which syncretism may be understood is as the local appropriation of symbolic forms, linked with locally based performance rather than externally established dogma.

One predominant way in which syncretic forms are localized in Tsukuda is through ritual life and festivals. During the Great Festival, above, the considerable time and effort spent serves to transform the locality completely, and inaugurates a period of 'festival life'. During this period some intense symbolic activity takes place, including the carrying of wooden lion heads (*shishi*), which serve to ritually purify the local area for the subsequent carrying of the local shrine's god cart or portable shrine (*mikoshi*). The carrying of lion heads includes series of ritual 'fights' (*kenka*), that through the form and vigor of their enactment come to symbolize the vitality of the local community. These fights are encompassed by a parade, an ordering event. Through ritually opposing and bringing together festival performers in a wide variety of ritual events, the overall effect is one of creating a spirit of inclusion for the festival as a whole. Celebrations become a social drama, an opportunity for people to get together in contexts detached from everyday concerns and limitations, providing experiences of togetherness or 'communitas' (Turner 1969).

Instead of reducing this contextual feeling of community to a question of structure and anti-structure (*op. cit.*), festival life may be seen as part of a social discourse, that is to say, the dialogues and negotiations that take place between categories of social actors in different situations and arenas. Festival life is not only symbolically productive, it is linked up more or less directly with social life locally, such as through kinship, marriage, and social ranking. As a case in point, women mentioned a husband's refusal to take part in the festival as grounds for divorce (Selstad 1994:22). Negotiations take place between women and men during the festival, that become commentaries on everyday negotiations inside and outside the local community. In numerous ways, ritual life is intertwined with local life, and this becomes one way of understanding local support for the festivals. Fishing related activities, local kinship ties, associations, and leadership, are all tied up with the cycle of celebrations in Tsukuda, in what may be termed a social field of tradition (cf. Grønhaug 1978:47). Local traditionalism in Tsukudajima is characterized precisely by its local embeddedness. Rather than viewing it as an explicit ideology or strategy, one may envision it as a discourse on tradition, that through people's activities interrelates with discourses in other social fields, such as their involvements in modern urban life, without social life being predetermined by such interconnections.

A point to start from in outlining social discourses would be an investigation of individual careers and identities. In Tsukuda, a preponderant majority of residents indicate that they are supportive of the local milieu and its special traditions, but also indicate an overall support for living in an urban environment, and there is considerable variation in responses depending on gender, age, occupation, and individuality (Selstad 1994:34). These individual variations and dispositions might be viewed against persons' life experiences or habitus (Bourdieu 1977), but in order to avoid possible deterministic implications, must also be interpreted widely within the overall contexts of social life and discourses (Geertz 1973). There are impulses of both dependence and self-sacrifice, and aspirations of personal freedom, security, and self- reliance, in people's responses and attitudes to social life (cf. Doi 1973; Dore 1958). Such contrasting attitudes need to be taken into account without locking our perspectives on human action. A narrowly strategic or instrumental view, might for instance contend that people in Tsukuda adhere to traditions in order to preserve their locality or obtain some recognition from the urban authorities. Against such simplification it may be observed that local people generally do not express any opposition between traditional and modern involvements.

The clearest instance of this was the lack of any overt expression of opposition among local people to the city's recent plans of urban development in the near region. Several high rise buildings are being constructed in an area adjacent to the village, and also including the razing of a few sheds and houses in Tsukuda itself. As construction was under way, during a local festival the leader of the local association came over to a group of men at an outdoor party and proceeded to talk about his involvement in the project; noting that one would be able to look down at the clouds from the tallest building. Instead of picking up on the subject of local razing and the high rise project, the local men simply turned away and continued talking about other things. While there may be different reasons for avoiding this subject, including lack of information about the project, it seemed clear that no direct link was drawn between the urban development and the ongoing, local traditional performances.

This lack of expressing opposition between traditional and modern engagements becomes part of an argument about the embeddedness of social life. When local people do not see urban development in juxtaposition to their engagement in traditional life, it would appear meaningful to view local traditionalism in Tsukuda as a broadly delimited and extensive set of social circumstances and occasions, as a loosely delimited area of social discourse. Much of what can be described as local traditonal life may then be seen as set aside in a social field attached to 'festival life', embracing ritual performances and rewritings of everyday life. An understanding of such interconnections would depend on a broad and wide ranging description of local life, which would also take into consideration people's engagements in non-local arenas and settings. Such a synthetic approach would entail that different areas of people's life world, local and urban, traditional and modern, must somehow be accounted for as distinct, and yet interrelated. The complexities of human goals and experiences should be descriptively interlinked with the composite dynamics of urban social life.

Aspects of Tokyo urbanism

This compositeness can perhaps best be examplified by the interests involved in modern urban developments. The project noted above, called River City 21, is part of a massive and conglomerative urban development scheme, involving the Tokyo Metropolitan Government and the Mitsui Corporation as the main developers. In this context, the interests of the local leader places him in a curious double bind situation (Bateson 1972:201). While consulted by the urban developers and receiving some returns for his assistance, he at the same time singlehandedly contacted the developing company when plans for extensive local razing in Tsukudajima were brought to his attention. It was claimed that he managed to convince the developers to leave the local area nearly intact. As both a local leader and a leader of festival events, through the Shrine Association, he supports both tradition and modernization, and an explanation of his role as one of schismogenesis, a person divided within himself, might seem tempting (*ibid.*; cf. Barth 1971:65). The modification and divergence of planning itself, however, entails that personal conflicts are part and parcel of the wider social settings and dynamics of ongoing urban life.

The development project itself becomes composite and 'context dependent' in its design and implementation (cf. Iwatake, *op. cit.*). Its constituent parts comprise museums and cultural programs besides gigantic high rise plots; it aims at upgrading the capacity of the urban center, as well as suggesting decentralized and poly-nucleated developments.[4] While trying to present a more urban, '21st century' image of the city, there are also program statements for a traditional, 'hometown' renaissance. The efforts of the local leader and the developing agents become part of this composite process. The local leader finds his backing in the local sphere, which is tied up with his engagement in traditional events, and in turn links him to a wider system of political brokerage in the urban polity. As noted above, the backing of a local power base is directly linked with ties of political patronage in governing bodies within the Tokyo Metropolis (Bestor 1989). Through cross cutting links of this sort it may be claimed that modernization and urban development in Japan, while massive in appearance, may still be modified and partially lenient in its implementation. More generally, crossing loyalties are part of the wider society, and dilemmas experienced by local people become constituent aspects of the more general dynamics of living in composite, multifaceted, and seemingly contradictory social spheres. In this way, contrasting involvements and conflicting demands can be seen to be handled in discourses within distinctive but interrelated sets of social arenas, or social fields. Compositeness in urban developments makes it possible for people to continue engaging in traditional and modern events, and to find room for unique expressions in the ordinary events of social life.

---

4. The contrast between centralized and 'non-focused' modes of urban planning, and their joint implications, have been discussed by Suzuki and Watanabe (1994).

Urban studies in Japan are often concerned with understanding how people cope in the urban setting, trying to create viable identities and communities (cf. Katô 1982; Arisue 1985). These studies may be viewed against recent theories on modernization and urbanisation, where forces such as markets, mass production and individuation should be accounted for (Hannerz 1980). Such structural aspects, if treated too deterministically, may obscure the complexities involved in large scale developments. Thus some contributions have attempted to account for the distinctive social life in Tsukuda by reducing it to a question of religious fervency or political conservatism (Sawara 1972:307f; Kawai 1982). Conversely, acknowledgements of complexity may revert to explanations of sentiment, viewing 'hometown' feelings as inherent or natural, local folkways as part of 'the dynamics of a Japanese disposition' (Katô 1982; Arisue 1983:51). In order to avoid over-simplifying peoples' motives and actions, it has been suggested here that one might consider them in relation to wider discourses of social life that overlap and interpenetrate within the multiple levels of social fields in the cityscape.

Through a wide, descriptive approach, linking the singular experiences of living with wider areas of discourse and social engagements, one may avoid reducing people's often vague or inarticulate motives to simple explanations of instrumental strategies. Generalizations concern not so much the existence of phenomena like 'urban village', 'festivals', 'traditions', or 'ordinary places'. Rather it is concerned with suggesting widely angled approaches to societal and human conditions, that may convey intakes to the intricacies of social life. Our analyses should help expand our knowledge about the experiences people have, such as that of living in an urban world that is both complex and composite, which reflect on the multiple levels of involvement that give the city its multifaceted and challenging appearance. The unique and the ordinary are not definitive attributes of a situation, but make sense only when discussed in relation to the intricacies of urban life. In the end we may hope to learn something about the ways in which people manage to live their lives in a world as intriguing and tantalizing as that of Tokyo urbanism.

References

Allinson, Gary D. 1979. *Suburban Tokyo*. Berkeley: University of California Press.

Ames, Walter L. 1981. *Police and Community in Japan*. Berkeley: University of California Press.

Arisue, Ken. 1985. Innaa-shiti mondai to rekishiteki seikatsu kankyoo. *Hôgaku kenkyû* 58:167-95.

Barth, Fredrik. 1971. Minoritetsproblem från socialantropologisk synpunkt. *Identitet och minoritet*. Stockholm: Almquist & Wiksell.

Bateson, Gregory. 1972. *Steps to an Ecology of Mind*. Toronto: Random House.

Befu, Harumi. 1971. *Japan: An Anthropological Introduction*. New York: Chandler.

Befu, Harumi. 1992. *Japan's national identity*. (NAJAKS Symposium). Tampere.

Bestor, Theodore C. 1989. *Neighborhood Tokyo*. Tokyo: Kodansha.

Bourdieu, Pierre. 1977. *Outline of a Theory of Practice*. Cambridge: Cambridge University Press.

Clammer, John. 1994. *The global and the local*. (EAJS Paper). Copenhagen.

Doi, Takeo. 1973. *The Anatomy of Dependence*. Tokyo: Kodansha.

Dore, Ronald P. 1958. *City Life in Japan*. Berkeley: University of California Press.

Dore, Ronald P. 1968. Introduction to H. Nakamura: Urban ward associations in Japan. *Readings in Urban Sociology*, ed. by R.E. Pahl. Oxford: Pergamon.

Gans, Herbert. 1962. *The Urban Villagers*. Toronto: Free Press.

Geertz, Clifford. 1973. *The Interpretation of Cultures*. New York: Basic Books.

Grønhaug, Reidar. Scale as a variable in analysis. *Scale and Social Organization*, ed. by F. Barth. Oslo: Universitetsforlaget.

Hannerz, Ulf. 1980. *Exploring the City*. New York: Columbia University Press.

Hori, Ichiro. 1968. *Folk Religion in Japan*. Chicago: University of Chicago Press.

Iwatake, Mikako. 1993. Tokyo in the postmodern world order. *Modulations in Tradition*, ed. by J. Kivistö et al. Tampere: University of Tampere.

Katô, Hidetoshi. 1982. *'Tokyo' no shakaigaku*. Tokyo.

Kawai, Takao (ed). 1982. *Daitoshi ni okeru shakai-idô to chiiki-seikatsu no henka: Tsukishima chiku; shakai-chôsa-hen*. Tokyo.

Selstad, Leif. 1993. Tsukuda matsuri. *Modulations in Tradition*, ed. by J. Kivistö et al. Tampere: University of Tampere.

Selstad, Leif. 1994. *En 'storbylandsby' i Japan*. Alta: Høgskolen i Finnmark.

Suzuki, Takashi, and Watanabe Sadao. 1994. *Structure and planning of the Tokyo metropolitan area*. (EAJS Paper). Copenhagen.

Turner, Victor W. 1969. *The Ritual Process*. Chicago: University of Chicago Press.

Vogel, Ezra F. 1971. *Japan's New Middle Class*. Berkeley: University of California Press.

Applying Hermeneutics to the Studies of Discourses on Welfare: The Case of Japanese Welfare Discourses

Takahashi Mutsuko

This paper aims to study the social makings of the Japanese welfare society by analyzing those discourses that concern welfare and express the understanding of it in Japan. In studying welfare discourses in post-1945 Japan, we are immediately faced with the multiple meanings of welfare and with various modes of manifestation of these meanings in Japanese society. The question is not only how the term *fukushi* has found its regular place in discourses despite the fact that *fukushi* was created as a Japanese translation of the English word 'welfare'. I do not aim to treat the term *fukushi* merely as a translated word responding to a translated concept. In the case that the scope of discussions is fixed on the *emic-etic* distinction at the superficial level of words by dividing *fukushi* (welfare) as *emic*, welfare as *etic*, there is the risk of just going round in circles of *emic-etic* dichotomy without clarifying further the social constructs of discourses of welfare.[1] To discuss the nature of the *emic-etic* distinction should not be limited to the effort to make a contrast of different meanings between a pair of translated words, for example, by consulting dictionaries (cf. Befu 1989:335-37).

I am not going to just give fixed definitions to the term *fukushi* (welfare) apart from the social context in which the concept is involved in discourses. In order to display the dynamics in changes with the meaning of the *emic* term *fukushi* (welfare) and its use in longer terms of several decades in the post-1945 period, it is essential to widen the scope of my discussion to 'discourses'. Diane Macdonell points out that 'work on discourses indicates that, within a 'language' (for example, within English or French) the words used and the meanings of the words used alter from one discourse to another'

---

1. On the discussions about *emic-etic* distinction, see also Takahashi 1995:8-10.

(Macdonell 1986:8).[2] In the development of the Japanese discourses of 'welfare society' I shall pay special attention to what is excluded; as George V. Zito states:

just as *parole* operates by exclusion, so Foucault says discourses operate by exclusion, by purposively omitting relevant cases (Zito 1984:102).

In other words, my study is of the *emic* approach not with attention just on the term *fukushi* (welfare) but rather with focus on the discourses which have manifested understanding of welfare inside Japanese society. At the same time, this study includes *etic* features in that the social environment of those discourses and its change reflect factors of globalization[3] in which Japanese society has been involved. In brief, to focus on the Japanese welfare discourses does not necessarily mean that a researcher closes her/his eyes to the rest of the world outside Japanese society.

Beyond the quantitative measuring of welfare states

My research does not aim to explore, as some researchers have done, whether there actually exists such a unique 'Japanese-style/model welfare society' that may correspond, in some way, to other Western models of welfare states (see e.g. Watanuki 1986; Campbell 1992). For those who prefer simple and clear-cut answers to multilayered analysis of 'inside stories', I can state here already that among those who have taken the above-mentioned approach the answer to this question is mostly 'No'. They take for their studies a quantitative approach, literally 'measuring' the development of the public welfare sector in post-war Japan. In my research, however, the research problem is not articulated as whether it is possible to argue that the

2. See Macdonell 1986:1: discourse, including all speech and writing, is social and differs with the kinds of institutions and social practices in which they take shape, and with the positions of those who speak and those whom they address.

3. Here, globalization basically refers to 'the rapid developments in communications technology, transport and information which bring the remote parts of the world within easy reach.' See e.g. Giddens 1990:64. See also Giddens 1995:4-5: 'globlization does not only concern the creation of large-scale systems, but also the transformation of local, and even personal, contexts of social experience'. See *ibid*.:5: 'globalization is not a single process but a complex mixture of processes, which often act in contradictory ways'.

Japanese-model welfare society exists in any such sense that we could simply measure its size and the degree of maturity of its social security system by just collecting data.

In the light of the comparative approaches to welfare states, attempts have been made to categorize different types of welfare states. For example, Gøsta Esping-Andersen presents the three welfare-state regimes of liberal, corporativist and social democratic (Esping-Andersen 1990:26-33). Esping-Andersen seems to take a 'broader approach' by regarding as too narrow the conventional concept of the welfare state associated with social amelioration policies (*ibid.*:2). Norman Ginsburg, admiring greatly Esping- Andersen's study, appreciates *the politics matters* approach with a theme that political forces of agency like party politics have had a predominant influence over welfare state development and that therefore comparative political differences account in large measure for differences in welfare expenditure (Ginsburg 1992:20).

Indeed, as Ginsburg states, we notice that 'politics does matter' in studying the development of welfare state policy in a given society. However, the political differences between countries may not be any fixed and static state. The politics of each targeted country may have the tendency that at least partly responds to the assumption of 'political regimes'. However, while taking a categorization of the regimes as a point of departure for discussions, little attention is paid to the question of how well the categorization of these regimes makes sense in the specific context of each society, or the question of which way the regimes make sense in each society. While categorizing the political regimes, we tend to miss a large part of the dynamism of social activities that has had much effect on the development of welfare policy in a society.

According to this categorization of three regimes, Japan finds her place in the liberalist regime, which is in a contrast to the social democratic regimes, including the Nordic countries. On the other hand, what I miss in the three-regimes-approach by Esping-Andersen is the studies of the process of establishing a certain political regime in a given society and the analysis of the social makings of welfare politics. Even among the Nordic countries it is clear that the social democratic regime has a different connotation in each of these countries. For example, in Finland the Social Democrats as a political party[4] has never enjoyed so a dominant position in the domestic political

---

4. In creating cabinets in Finland it is the 'coalition' of several political parties that has been the most common alternative. In contrast, as Ginsburg (1993:173) states, 'the SAP (Social Democratic Party) dominated Swedish national governments throughout the

arena as could be seen in Sweden. In comparison with other industrial countries, these two Nordic countries have given a considerably large share to the public sector, which seems to let these two cases represent 'social-democratic regimes' in a sense. As the Swedish welfare state usually re-presents the 'Social-Democratic case' (Ginsburg 1993:173-75), the 'social-democratic' implication in its political tendency is based on the Swedish experience of the welfare state. Without knowing the Swedish case, the 'social- democratic regime' or any other regime cannot be made sense of in a broader discussion targeting other welfare states. In brief, the divisions of these regimes of welfare states cannot be given 'objectively'. Even though objectivity is sought in handling cross-sectional data of various welfare states, little discussion is made as to the question of how these words used for naming the regimes can be made sense of in a given society.

In fact, what the three regimes of welfare state implies is the assumption that by focusing on the tendency both in the political 'tendency' and in the budgets some characteristics can be pointed out so as to categorize the wel-fare states in one way or another. What I am going to do is not to endorse this assumption but to study the social makings of welfare state policy by examining the welfare discourses. I will not re-call Japan's case *liberalist* by pointing again to the smaller share of welfare expenditure in comparison with other 'welfare states'. Rather, I am most interested in what has brought such consequences to Japan; what has prevented Japan from becoming a wel-fare state in the mode prevailing elsewhere — as in the Nordic countries. The 'hermeneutical approach' seems to be remote from the mainstreams of welfare studies that aim for quantitative cross-sectional measuring of the de-velopment of welfare states, mainly in the OECD countries. I do not mean to undermine the significance of 'social measuring', which offers us im-portant data and descriptions concerning well-being in societies. However, those approaches, often aiming 'to formulate laws of societal motion' (Esping-Andersen 1990:3), imply support for the positivism whose on-tological and epistemological assumptions have already been faced with severe attacks. Criticism of the neutrality or objectivity of positivistic ob-servation is largely based on the grounds that science is conducted by people, and people cannot divorce themselves from their prior knowledge and expectations.[5]

period in which the welfare state was constructed — indeed from 1932 to 1991 with only brief exceptions in 1936 and 1976-82'.

5. Cook (1985:23-27) also points out that positivists assume the existence of the world

Any scholar has implicitly or explicitly her/his own involvement in 'understanding' of the world in which she/he conducts research. For example, Sohail Inayatullah points out that the assertion that a way of knowing is is simply an attempt to privilege one's ideological system over others: to stress objectivity in search of universalistic frameworks, rules or models almighty for each society tends to simplify understanding of the nature of social change (Inayatullah 1990:119). Moreover, in connection with my approach, I feel attracted by Paul Ricoeur's statement that 'hermeneutics itself puts us on guard against the illusion or pretension of neutrality' (Ricoeur 1982:43). The hermeneutical approach means to explicitly admit that it is no one but 'I' who am the interpreter of the meanings in the transient world. 'I' cannot hide from the cultural biases 'I' have already got from the social environment. Each time when we move in the world of meanings, we deal with the world of the mind of human beings rather than the natural scientific world. We are by no means free from his/her cultural biases or from the Gadamerian preunderstanding (Gadamer 1985:351-52), either.

I try to focus on the question of what has brought such a situation in Japan that warrants its being labeled as a country with liberalist politics in the field of welfare. For this question we cannot say that it is because Japan belongs to the liberalist regime. Such categorization does not help us much when we want to know how the politics in a country has developed in a way closed to the assumptions of a liberalist regime. Instead, I shall study how the discourses on welfare have been created on various levels in Japan and how those welfare discourses have had impacts on the development of welfare policy. I shall try to show what kind of impacts the cultural biases have had on the world view under which social discourses are created.

Deconstructing the Japanese-model welfare society

It was at the end of the 1970s that the Japanese-model welfare society (*Nihon-gata fukushi shakai*) was most actively discussed at the initiative of the LDP. The LDP and a group of scholars close to the LDP opposed the idea of developing a public-sector-oriented welfare state in Japan by describing the examples of British or Swedish welfare states simply as failures. In the LDP study report published in 1979 these two cases of the British and Swedish welfare states were said to have only caused problems rather than improved citizens' well-being. The failure mainly meant economic stagnation, failed

outside of the mind: they further assume that this world is lawfully ordered and that the task of science is to describe this order.

state finance, chronic strikes and an unstable political situation, which was expressed for example as *Eikoku-byô* (British disease).[6] *Suêden-byô* (Swedish disease) is mostly characterized by the collapsed state economy and also by discontent about the state and society among citizens: heavy burdens of citizens due to the taxation system, dissolving family and kin ties, solitude in later life, and so forth (see e.g. Ryûen 1981).[7]

However, the LDP's criticism of Western welfare states in the late 1970s was not concentrated only on the Western models of the welfare state. Rather, it was an indirect attack on the welfare policy of the non-LDP local governments. In the political arena, in the late 1970s, the non-LDP parties were losing their offices as prefectural governors after their glorious era. The financial crisis of the Tôkyô Metropolitan Government, led by the Socialist Governor Minobe Ryôkichi from April 1967 to March 1979, happened to allow the LDP to open fire on the policy by 'progressive local government' (*kakusin jichitai*) of developing the welfare state in its official initiatives. In a sense, the discourse of the Japanese-model welfare society in the circle of the LDP and its fellows targeted both the Western welfare states and the welfare policy the non-LDP local governments actively developed in the 1970s.

Ichibangase Yasuko argues incisively that political discourse on the Japanese-model welfare society in the late 1970s fundamentally delayed proper preparation in Japanese society for the ageing of society. The Japanese family was often glorified as an indispensable fortune for Japanese society, but serious discussion on how to support family life and to cope with chal-

6. According to Kanbara (1986:134), in addition, there also appeared terms for some other European countries like *Hokuô fukushi kokka-byô* (disease of Nordic welfare states), *Furansu-byô* (French disease) or *Itaria-byô* (Italian disease) with a common feature of workers who no longer diligently work thanks to the benefits offered by the welfare state. At the end of the 1970s these 'diseases' were then integrated into another term *Yôroppa-byô* (European disease) that then became synonymous with *senshinkoku-byô* (disease of the advanced countries). See also Miyajima (1992:17, 290) who points out that in Japan Sweden is often referred to as an example of a 'welfare society without vitality' (*katsuryoku naki fukushi shakai*), even though the case of Sweden, especially the Swedish economy, is not always sufficiently studied in Japan.

7. For a recent discussion about Swedish welfare society from a Japanese perspective, see also Kurube 1991. However, I do not agree with the holistic approach to Swedish society on the basis of the implications of the 'ethnic purity of Swedes' (Kurube 1991: 21) which is embodied in Kurube's framework and setting of the question as it is already revealed by the title of this book *Suêdenjin wa ima shiawase ka?* [Are Swedes happy now?]. For example, this book does not contain any discussion about ethnic minorities in contemporary Sweden, as its point of departure seems to be based on the contrast between Swedes and Japanese.

lenges of the ageing of society tends to be lacking on the level of policy-making after the late 1970s (Ichibangase 1992:83). Moreover, the discursive structure of the Japanese-model welfare society covers not only ideological features in the domestic political arena but also the nationalistic reactions to the Western models of social development. Discourse on Japanese-model welfare society tends to borrow some convenient elements from the mainstream of discourse on Japanese culture, because naturally it is necessary to point out successful and positive features in Japanese social systems while justifying the effort to escape from the West instead of catching up with the West.

Versions of 'Japanese-model welfare society'

Because 'Japanese-model welfare society' was discussed in the late 1970s mainly by the LDP or those scholars who implicitly served the LDP, it tends to be regarded as only representing the LDP view. In point of fact, the discourse on Japanese-model welfare society contains different versions which were presented from the late 1970s to the early 1980s by some scholars with no explicit political affiliation but with a keen interest in the nature of welfare society in a Japanese social context. The following is an attempt to analyze what kind of characteristics some scholars of welfare studies have underlined in studying Japanese welfare society. In the following I concentrate on the discussions presented by Professors Baba Keinosuke and Maruo Naomi who are both the best known and the best respected scholars of welfare economics.

Baba Keinosuke published a book entitled *Fukushi shukai no Nihon-teki keitai* (Japanese form of welfare society) in 1980, which consists of several articles published in the late 1970s. Baba starts with a hypothesis on the transition from industrial society to welfare society: in industrial society, members of society act pursuing achievements on the basis of equal opportunities and are ready to accept whatever results from their acts; in welfare society, according to the idea of solidarity, adjustment is made to uneven results for securing a similar living for all members of society (Baba 1980:112). Baba argues that welfare society is a complex society with co-existence and integration of achievements and solidarity (*Ibid.*:112). Regarding the significance of Japanese modernization as being tripartite and including modernization, industrialization and, Baba points to the Japanese — non-Western — essence which distinguishes Japan from the West: he refers to *chûkan shûdanshugi* (groupism of medium groups) as a distinctive and unique feature of Japanese social structure (*ibid.*:136). According to Baba, *chûkan shûdanshugi* means that in social structure the focus is placed on those organizational bodies — such as companies[8] — which are located between the state and individuals/families: an individual finds his/her meaning in life and has a deep sense of belonging by becoming a member of a certain 'medium group' (*chûkan shûdan*), although the group itself is based on functional purposes. The individual attempts achievements in order to win in competitions with other group(s): within the group one belongs to, he/she behaves collectively, whereas one behaves individualistically (*kojinshugi-teki ni*) outside the group (*ibid.*:137). Industrial society, which Western countries built up according to individualism, was introduced to Japan on the basis of the groupism of medium groups, which implies the Japanese form of modernization (*ibid.*:137).

Baba insightfully points to the fact that as Japanese society is ageing at a rapid pace, the transition to welfare society should be required in order not to let the family alone respond to the increase of burdens in taking care of the aged population (*ibid.*:138). In other words, even though Baba takes the view that coresidence of three generations within a household is distinctive for Japanese society, he proposes the secured national minimum income, fair competition and positive discrimination in order to modify the principle of industrial society with emphasis on achievements and to make it possible for Japanese society to shift to welfare society with solidarity (*ibid.*:139). Being aware of the imbalance in the development of achievement-oriented industrial society, Baba argues that it is essential to reorganize the sphere of daily life (*nichijô seikatsu-ken*), which tends to remain peripheral in a society of groupism of medium-groups, so as to correspond to challenges of the ageing of society (*ibid.*:140). In stating that the reorganization of the sphere of daily life as a creation of *komyuniti* (community) should aim at providing networks of services that would partly compensate functions of the family in the care of aged people, (*ibid.*:157) Baba presents his own view of Japanese welfare society that is clearly in conflict to that given in the LDP's report where the Japanese family was merely admired.

Moreover, Maruo Naomi published a book under the title of *Nihon-gata fukushi shakai* [Japanese-model welfare society] in 1984.[9] His intention seemed to be to present an expert's discussion but not necessarily to add support to

8. In this discussion, Baba seems to mean mainly large-scale companies in referring to 'company'.
9. See Maruo 1993. See also Maruo 1979 (first published in 1967), 22: by 'welfare state' (*fukushi kokka*), Maruo himself means a certain ideal model 'to be pursued for responding to the understanding of the concept of welfare (*fukushi*).

'the political ideology of the LDP. Contrary to the LDP study report with the same title, Maruo clarifies that Japan still has much to learn from the Nordic or British welfare states particularly in the two points of 'normalization' (*nômaraizêshon*)[10] and 'amenity' (*ameniti*) (Maruo 1993:5). In Japan these concepts of normalisation and amenity have been discussed mainly by welfare experts since the 1970s, as community care gained much attention. Maruo defines a new welfare society as 'the society in which all persons including the elderly or the handicapped can enjoy their ordinary lives in an attractive living environment and a comfortable working environment fully using their personal capacities': it is characterized by safety, amenity and community. In this connection, Maruo specifies problems with the British and Swedish cases by stating that Sweden has too much emphasized the role of the government in supply of welfare and redistribution of income so that the informal sector has remained rather undeveloped; Britain has been left behind in innovation of economy and technology (*ibid.*: 170-71).

Still, Maruo does not confuse his readers by suggesting, on one hand, the Japanese model as an alternative for the future and, on the other, that such an ideal has not yet been achieved in contemporary Japan. Nor in Maruo's discussion is the Japanese sense of solidarity towards family, working place and local community regarded as Japanese traditional good manners (*ibid.*: 173). The clear distinction seems important in having a constructive discussion. As for the market, which is one of the essential areas for Maruo's idea, so-called Japanese management is regarded as advantageous due to its economic efficiency achieved by paying attention to communication in the workplace, whereas the sense of groupism can be a demerit as women, the handicapped and the elderly in particular tend to be left without the benefits of Japanese management (*ibid.*: 166-67). Maruo also names this Japanese model 'participation-oriented' (*sanka-gata*), meaning that decision-making and solutions are achieved by smoothing communication and sharing common information and understanding on issues among participants. As for the informal sector of family and community, Maruo admits that the contemporary Japanese family cannot alone undertake all the burdens derived from the ageing of society without arranging any new network in the community, including promotion of voluntary work as a mode of 'participation' (*ibid.*: 189-94).

The discourse on Japanese-model welfare society has the tendency to understand 'society' rather mechanically as a composition of the market and the informal sector excluding literally the 'state' from its main scope of dis-

10. In Japanese 'normalisation' is also rendered *nômarizêshon*.

cussion. Maruo Naomi argues that because the 'Japanese-model' (*Nihon-gata*) focuses on both the market and the informal sector as the supply-side of welfare, it is more apt to call it 'welfare society' rather than 'welfare state'. (*Ibid.*: 173) Sahara Yô, welfare economist, points out that it was the publisher — but not Professor Maruo — who finally named this book Japanese-model welfare society: Sahara heard this directly from Maruo himself. Sahara argues that Maruo does not seem to regard the naming of 'Japanese-model' as important and that the expression 'Japanese-model' thus remains rather journalistic (Sahara 1989:11). However, it may not be right to judge the 'Japanese-model' as merely journalistic. Instead, it seems interesting to discuss what made this 'Japanese-model' so attractive for the publisher or for journalism in general, as it is natural for publishers to feel concern about the market value of books they produce. Maruo's argument on Japanese-model is not as afflicted with obvious political ideology as is the LDP's *Japanese-model Welfare Society*, although he does not explicitly express disassociation from the LDP report, either. Moreover, in the sense that Maruo's idea is based on an appreciation of Japanese management and on concerns about the informal sector of family and community, his discussion is by no means free from another series of discourse, that is to say, the discourse on Japanese culture (*Nihon bunka-ron*) that has been getting more publicity than ever in Japan since the 1970s.

'Vital welfare society'

Until 1979 the Japanese economy achieved its adjustment to the era of low economic growth by overcoming the stagflation of the mid 1970s. It was in such a social environment that the reform of administration was launched in 1980. 'Japanese-model' gained the connotation that it aimed to justify the review and reduction of social expenditure in general. In this sense, the LDP failed to create a positive image for 'Japanese model' (*Nihon-gata*) by admiring Japan's good traditions in contrast to the West. Here seems to be a reason to advertise Japanese welfare *society* — instead of Japanese welfare *state* — in another expression like 'vital welfare society' (*katsuryoku-aru fukushi shakai*), which has been used since the early 1980s. However, simply because the Japanese model is no longer mentioned in public, it does not necessarily mean that the conceptual framework derived from that 'model' has already lost its meaning in Japanese discourse on welfare society.

The two main pillars proposed by the Second *ad hoc* Commission[11] for the

---

11. As to this Commision, see eg. Takahashi 1995:192-98.

Reform of Administration (called 'Commission' in the following) were the realization of 'vital welfare society' and the promotion of 'Japan's contribution to the international community'. Whereas the 'vital welfare society' was based on a similar idea to the 'Japanese-model welfare society' of 1979, due to the too strong connotation of the LDP, the expression 'Japanese model' has no longer been explicitly used in Japan since the reform of administration started in the early 1980s. The reform of administration (*gyôsei kaikaku*) has succeeded in touching the fundamental frameworks of policies in broad areas by appealing to the inescapable necessity to make changes, particularly in administration. The Commission worked by appealing to the common sense of taxpayers that no waste should be allowed in the bureaucracy. The Commission's proposal for 'vital welfare society' encouraged the state not to undertake too many responsibilities for citizens' welfare. However, it was hard to argue against the vitality which had just been achieved by the adjustment to low economic growth in the late 1970s. In other words, in the late 1970s and early 1980s it was hard to justify a welfare state policy that would expand the public sector in the eyes of those taxpayers who were also voters in the elections. The Reform of Administration in the early 1980s succeeded in labeling the public sector 'inefficient' as a whole and in carrying out a cutback of state support to the social welfare sector, although the Commission did not include welfare experts as its members.

The 'vital welfare society' (*Katsuryoku-aru fukushi shakai*) as a catch-phrase of welfare policy was presented to the public in the early 1980s together with another catch-phrase: Japan's contribution to the international community (*Nihon no kokusai kôken*), with emphasis on Japan's 'internationalization' (*kokusaika*) in the reports of the Commission. According to Ishida Takeshi, the reform of administration since the early 1980s supported a small-scale welfare state (*fukushi shôkoku*) and, at the same time, a large-scale military state (*gunji taikoku*) in terms of undertaking more responsibilities at the level of international politics (Ishida 1990:9). In referring to the movement towards the military state, Ishida implies that, especially during the cabinets of Prime Minister Nakasone Yasuhiro Japan's contribution to the international community gained more attention in public discourses on Japan's internationalization. In other words, the more Japan achieved economic power, the more attention was paid to her new role in the international community in general.

Since Prime Minister Nakasone declared he would make 'the total closing of accounts of post-war politics' (*sengo seiji no sôkessan*) one of his main political goals, it may be reasonable for not a few peace researchers, including Ishida, to express deep concern about the peace-oriented Japanese Constitution created for post-1945 Japan. In this sense, to let the national defence-force budgets exceed one per cent of the GNP had a symbolic meaning as an explicit challenge to the principle closely linked to the basic framework of post-war Japanese political culture. To limit the defence (*de facto* military) budgets to one per cent of GNP was long one of the political agreements under the post-war peace-oriented Constitution. By appealing strongly to the importance of Japan's new role as a leading economic power in the international community, it was argued that it was meaningless to stick to this limit. However, it may be a slight exaggeration to call contemporary Japan a 'large-scale military state', simply because it has made the defence budget slightly over one per cent of GNP. In practice, it is not the armed forces but Official Development Assistance (ODA) that has been vastly developed since the early 1980s.[12]

The discourse on Japan's internationalization gave good reason to challenge the peace-oriented principle in politics. It is noteworthy that this challenge was made without voicing any militaristic or invasive motives for aggression towards other countries contrary to what the term 'militarism' may usually imply. Rather, by arguing that Japan should take more responsibility for self-defence instead of relying on a 'free-ride' on the U.S. army, an attempt was made to 'review' the peace-oriented principle of post-war Japanese politics. In light of the argument for making Japan more 'independent', to stick to the peace-oriented principle was regarded as a fairly out-moded idea unsuitable for contemporary Japan.

The two main pillars — Japan's contribution to the international community and the vital welfare society — presented by the Commission in 1983 made manifest the search for a new framework replacing the framework developed in 'post-1945' — or, 'post-war' (*sengo*) — Japanese political culture. This post-war framework, which was then faced with a fundamental review in the 1980s, included principles of welfare policy. It is in this context of discourses that explicit suspicion was expressed about the 'principle' of state responsibilities for the social welfare system established since the late 1940s as inflexible and out-dated. For example, Miura Fumio, one of the leading experts in preparing reforms of the social welfare system since the mid 1970s, takes the view that the post-war social welfare system on the basis of state responsibility was developed in a social environment which was unique to

---

12. The Japanese Government has increased its ODA at a fast pace. According to the governmental plan to assist developing countries with a contribution of fifty billion dollars in five years between 1988 and 1992, the amount of Japanese ODA has exceeded that of the United States.

Japanese society of the late 1940s in the light of cross-national comparative studies on the development of social welfare. According to Miura, thanks to high economic growth in the 1960s and early 1970s, the social welfare system under state responsibility remained basically unchanged without displaying its limits until the mid 1970s (Miura 1991 (1987):298-301).[13]

Miura seems to mean that the social welfare system which developed in post-war Japan was just a product of unique historical events — the Occupation period following the defeat — and that therefore such a social welfare system may not suit contemporary Japan. In a word, it seems natural that a social welfare service develops under a given social and political environment which is always unique. Miura's argument implicitly supports the 'total closing of accounts of post-war politics' in the welfare sector. However, it is not clarified which research work is concretely meant when Miura refers to 'cross-national comparative studies on the development of social welfare' (*ibid.*:299). Because it may not be possible to find one universal model in the development of social welfare service in a given society, to refer to 'comparative studies' in this context ends up emphasizing the uniqueness of the Japanese case, implying that this case was 'internationally unique'. An attempt is made to intentionally emphasize this uniqueness as a way of arguing for the invalidity of the 'post-war' Japanese welfare system, being challenged by the ageing of society towards the early decades of the next century. In regarding the post-war welfare system as out-dated, the three decades tend to be treated as merely a time past, without taking into account the impacts of those various movements on the development of welfare policy which are discussed in the previous chapters of this volume. Despite such controversies about the significance of the post-war welfare system in Japan, such an interpretation seems to have prevailed in official visions and ideas of the 'Japanese-model welfare society'.

The 1990s — the era of voluntary work

Since the early 1990s to speak of voluntary work in relation to the ageing of society has become a fashion especially in the field of social welfare in Japan. In the light of demographic development the era of the aged society is truly approaching Japan. On the other hand, it is not self-evident why the main focus is placed on voluntary work in the Japanese discourse of welfare. The

13. See also Miura 1991 (1987): which also casts doubt on whether such a solution of placing the responsibility for social welfare with the state (government) is really common in other industrialised countries.

effort of officialdom[14] for newly establishing networks of 'voluntary activities' in contemporary Japan does not mean that the network relies solely on old systems like *minsei iin seido* (community welfare commissioner system) which is already tainted with its historical background of the era of the Relief Law in pre-war Japan. It does indeed exist and function in contemporary Japan as the semi-official volunteers appointed by the prefectural governors with delegated capacity from the Ministry of Health and Welfare. Yet, the *minsei iin* are not those volunteers(-to-be) who are now particularly expected to 'participate in establishing the vital longevity welfare society in the near future'.[15] To underline 'voluntary' work does not mean to draw Japanese society back to the past when much in social welfare relied on the good-will of semi-amateur district commissioners.[16] However, since public sector-oriented welfare in Japan has been faced with bitter criticism and reviews since the mid 1970s, what is meant by the non-public sector comes to cover not only such a purely enterprise-oriented sector but also the voluntary work that stands on the border between the enterprise-oriented and something else such as 'good-will'. Furthermore, what seems rather typical for the discourses on 'community care' or on 'voluntary work' in social welfare is that the scope of these discourses tends to remain closed within the assumption of Japanese homogeneity without explicitly questioning who would be members of communities in contemporary Japan.

One of the reasons for this tendency in welfare discourses may be that the transient state of 'community life' and its diversity are not necessarily taken into account in discussing 'welfare society', although the community is often the space where individuals can see changes at the transnational —

14. The welfare society seems to have been given a new expression of 'participation-oriented welfare society' (*sanka-gata fukushi shakai*), as the leading experts and official-dom of social welfare began to use this expression in 1993. For example, the Ministry of Health and Welfare published in April 1993 a 'basic guidance concerning measures for promoting the participation of the people in social welfare'.

15. For example Lee Hye Kyung (1987:260) introduces *minsei iin* as an essential part of the Japanese social welfare service system. Basically there is nothing wrong with Lee's description of the *minsei iin* system in contemporary Japan, but the issue here is how we understand its significance in relation to the broad vision of welfare in Japan. Since this system is distinctive, it tends to be understood as the core of the whole social welfare service in contemporary Japan. See also Gould 1993; Jones 1993.

16. Still, I do not mean to neglect the significance of *minsei iin* (community welfare commissioner) in contemporary Japan. Today, there are about 20,000 *minsei 'in* nationwide. See e.g. Hashimoto and Takahashi 1996. See also Ben-Ari 1991:147-60, who discusses how *minsei iin* functions well at a small village named *Hieidaira* located between the cities of Kyôto and Ôtsu.

rather than *inter*national — level, beyond the borders of nation states. With the Japanese word *kokusaika* it is not easy to distinguish the globalization of the living environment at the level of daily life, which is then close to the transnational level, and the increase of contacts on the *inter*national level between nation states represented by their respective governments. Besides, the transient state and diversity of community life can be seen in the fact that members of the community in contemporary Japan differ in the duration for which they live at the same address to different degrees nationwide. The discussion of 'participation-oriented welfare society' from the perspective of administrations tends to regard 'expected participants' as the people (*kokumin*) as a whole, regardless of social attributes like gender and ethnicity .

In the meantime, the Great Kôbe[17] Earthquake, which took place on 17 January 1995, killing more than five thousand and making about 320 thousand homeless, also provided valuable lessons for the welfare society. For instance:

One of the myths which collapsed in the quake was that volunteerism will never take root in Japan because the young are self-centered and reluctant to show empathy with the disadvantaged (Nishimura and Chiba 1995:6).

In fact, there appeared a boom of voluntary work. This implies that not a few are willing and really ready to do something for others who are basically strangers — not relatives — yet are in trouble, and that this free service and good will becomes visible especially in such an urgent and tangible case as the catastrophe caused by the earthquake.

On the other hand, the earthquake unveiled the ineptitude of the public sector — both local administrations of cities and prefectures and the central government — in coordinating between the public sector and those reserves of voluntary activities and the organization of the reserves. It is pointed out that the aftermath of this earthquake showed that voluntary activities were regarded as being supplementary to the public sector and that non-government organizations (NGOs) as an essential source of voluntary activities are not yet autonomous enough. The case of the Kôbe earthquake shed light on the ambiguity in status and role of voluntary activities and of those who participate in them as individuals or groups. In other words, the ministerial level has long ceased to discuss explicitly and seriously what kind of relationship — supervisor, advisor, teacher, observer, colleague, and so

---

17. In addition to Kôbe city (c. 1,477,000 residents in 1990) and Awajishima Island, this earthquake also caused severe damage in neighbouring cities like Ashiya, Takarazuka, Toyokana, and so on.

forth — it wishes to have with individuals and non-governmental groups in relation to community-oriented social welfare, while concentrating on the single question concerning welfare management: how to match welfare supply and demand. However, when citizens as *borantia* (volunteers) do only what the public authority wishes, it is no longer voluntarism but only passivity waiting for orders and guidance from above, which may end up in causing stagnation in what is far from being a vital 'welfare society'.

The case of the Kôbe earthquake demonstrates the potential for voluntary activities in Japan, which is partly indicated by the official opinion surveys. However, a boom in voluntary activities (*borantarî bûmu*) in an emergency cannot be generalized too far. The aftermath of the Kôbe quake reveals that there is obviously a conceptual gap in understanding what community is: officialdom was faced with its own problems of vertical structure in administrative organization on the level of municipalities that are usually thought to respond to 'community level', whereas non-governmental groups had mobility in acting on 'community level' beyond administrative boundaries and hierarchy. In the light of a flexible reaction to changes and of the capacity to collect information from 'local knowledge', it is questionable whether the public authority is the most competent in comparison to non-governmental groups with nationwide and global networks. It is in this connection that the autonomy of non-governmental groups is the issue in the 'participation-oriented welfare society'. The public authority, which includes prefectural and municipal levels, still has interests in governing, whereas the globalizing social and economic environment surrounding the community does not necessarily stay within administrative borders drawn mechanically on area maps regardless of real communal maps — the sphere of living — where life goes on. The 'participation-oriented welfare society' needs to be modified by reviewing the preunderstanding on community level of the public authority. Without this review, probably it is not possible to popularize 'community participation' on the initiatives of public authority which has its own limits on the communal level due to organizational rigidity and hangs on with difficulty in the changing social environment.

Concluding remarks

As discussed above, the Japanese welfare discourses have been responding to the development of welfare politics for decades. In a sense, attempts have been made to decline 'state' commitment to issues related to citizens' wellbeing by labeling the public sector in general as inefficient. However, only little has been discussed about the question of what is meant by 'society' in 'welfare society'. The discourses of Japanese-model welfare society — particularly in the political arena — tend to have devoted themselves to 'excluding' this core point from the discussion. Once main attention was paid to the welfare society instead of the welfare state, the welfare discourses have become the discourses of welfare society. Indeed, any word referential to the state or the welfare state seems to have regularly been omitted from the scope of the welfare discourse by officialdom, political leaders and some of the influential opinion leaders and welfare experts.

The discourses of Japanese-model welfare society in the late 1970s had a strong impact on the directions of welfare policy from the 1980s even up to today. Although the name 'Japanese-model' took on a negative political implication for the public already in the early 1980s, state responsibility, which was made referential to the inefficient public sector, was prevented from expansion. While the state and central bureaucracy were decreasing their commitment to the adventure of coping with the ageing of society, the focus tended to be placed on the 'mutual help' and 'self reliance' of citizens within communities and families. However, it is unlikely that there were active discussions on how the sense of solidarity can be developed in a social environment in which it is becoming harder than ever to have family and kin ties in an urbanized context of life, so different from the illusory traditionalist image of family in the good old days.

In the 1990s community residents — no matter of what ethnicity — have found themselves in the dense mist of restructuring power relations in domestic political life. Meanwhile, in the field of social welfare community residents seem to be told by officialdom that it is 'your turn' to contribute to the creation of a welfare society, in a Japan faced with the ageing of society, by participating in voluntary activities. However, there has been little discussion about some essential concepts for carrying out the 'participation-oriented welfare society' as a response to the ageing of society. Still, the discussion about whether Japanese society can be regarded as a matured welfare society tends to rely on quantitative indicators and perspectives. Ironically this way of expressing criticism or concerns about the present social environment is based on a similar viewpoint on Japanese identity as found in *Nihonjinron*, because in the discussion of the matured welfare society it is presumed that *'we* Japanese' are concerned about the standard of *our* well-being *in comparison to others* — the West. Regardless of whether Japan has caught up with the West in any sense or not, Japanese discourses on the welfare society are not totally freed from the conventional way of making self-reflections in comparison to the West.

References

Baba, Keinosuke. 1980. *Fukushi shakai no Nihon teki keitai (Japanese form of welfare society)*. Tôkyô: Tôyô keizai shinpôsha.
Befu, Harumi. 1989. The Emic-Etic Distinction and Its Significance for Japanese Studies. *Constructs for Understanding Japan*, ed. Yoshio Sugimoto and Ross Mouer, 323-43. London: Kegan Paul.
Ben-Ari, Eyal. 1991. *Changing Japanese Suburbia. A Study of Two Present-Day Localities*. London: Kegan Paul.
Campbell, John Creighton. 1992. *How Policies Change. The Japanese Government and the Aging Society*. Princeton: Princeton University Press.
Cook, Thomas D. 1985. Postpositivist Critical Multiplism. *Social Science and Social Policy*, ed. by R. Lance Shotland and Mervin M. Mark, 21-62. London: Sage.
Esping-Andersen, Gøsta. 1990. *The Three Worlds of Welfare Capitalism*. Oxford: Polity Press.
Gadamer, Hans-Georg. 1985. *Truth and Method*. New York: Crossroad. (Originally published as *Wahrheit und Methode*. J.C.B. Mohr, Tübingen 1960. The translation was edited by Garret Barden and John Cumming from the second (1965) edition).
Giddens, Anthony. 1990. *The Consequence of Modernity*. Cambridge: Polity Press.
Giddens, Anthony. 1995. *Beyond Left and Right. The Future of Radical Politics*. Cambridge: Polity Press.
Ginsburg, Norman. 1992. *Divisions of Welfare. A Critical Introduction to Comparative Social Policy*. London: Sage.
Ginsburg, Norman. 1993. Sweden: The Social-Democratic Case. *Comparing Welfare States: Britain in International Context*, ed. by Allan Cochrane and John Clarke, 173-203. London: Sage.
Gould, Arthuer. 1993. *Capitalist Welfare Systems: A Comparison of Japan, Britain and Sweden*. London: Longman.
Hashimoto, Raija and Takahashi Mutsuko. 1997. Minsei i'in (welfare commissioner) System: Its Distinctive Features and the Significance in Japanese Social Welfare. *International Social Work* 40/3, 304-13.
Ichibangase, Yasuko. 1992. *Chiiki ni fukushi o kizuku (Creating welfare in local communities)*. Tôkyô: Rôdô junpôsha.
Inayatulla, Sohail. 1990. Deconstructing and reconstructing the future. Predictive, cultural and critical epistemologies. *Futures*, March 1990, 115-41.
Jones, Catherine. 1993. The Pacific Challenge. Confucian Welfare States. *New Perspectives on the Welfare State in Europe*, ed. by Catherine Jones, 198-241. London: Routledge.
Kanbara, Masaru. 1986. *Tenkanki no seiji katei. Rinchô no kiseki to sono kinô (Process of politics in the period of transition. Development of the Ad Hoc Commission for the Reform of Administration and its function)*. Tôkyô: Sôgô rôdô kenkyûsho.

Kurube, Noriko. 1991. *Suêdenjin wa ima shiawase ka (Are Swedes happy now?)* Tôkyô: NHK books.

Lee, Hye Kyung. 1987. The Japanese Welfare State in Transition. *Modern Welfare States. A Comparative View of Trends and Prospects*, ed. by Robert R. Friedmann, et al., 243-63. Sussex: Wheatsheaf.

Macdonell, Diane. 1986. *Theories of Discourse. An Introduction.* Oxford: Basil Blackwell.

Maruo, Naomi. 1979. *Fukushi kokka no hanashi (Discussion on welfare state).* Tôkyô: Nihon keizai shinbunsha (11th impression, first published in 1967).

Maruo, Naomi. 1993. *Nihon gata fukushi shakai (Japanese-model welfare society).* Tôkyô: NHK books 455, Nippon hôsô shuppan kyôkai.

Ministry of Health and Welfare. 1994. Kokumin no shakai fukushi ni kansuru katsudô e no sanka no sokushin o hakaru tame no sochi ni kansuru kihonteki na shishin (Basic guidance concerning measures for promoting the participation of the people in social welfare), April 1993, reprinted in Gekkan fukushi (Monthly: *Welfare*), special issue: *Fukushi kaikaku* V (Sanka-gata fukushi shakai no kôchiku) (*Welfare reforms*, part V (Creating the participation-oriented welfare society)], 154-58.

Miura, Fumio. 1991 (1987) Zôho. *Shakai fukushi seisaku kenkyû. Shakai fukushi keieiron nôto* (Revised edition. *Study on social welfare policy. Writings on management of social welfare*). Tôkyô: Zenkoku shakai fukushi kyôgikai (4th impression of the revised edition first published in 1987).

Miyajima, Hiroshi. 1992. *Kôreika jidai no shakai keizai (Socio-economics for the era of ageing).* Tôkyô: Iwanami shoten.

Nishimura, Kunio and Chiba Hitoshi. 1995. After the Quake. *Look Japan*, Vol. 41, No. 470, May 1995, 4-10.

Ricoeur, Paul. 1982. The Task of Hermeneutics. *Hermeneutics and the Human Sciences*, edited and translated by John B. Thompson, 43-62. Cambridge: Cambridge University Press.

Ryûen, Ekiji. 1981. *Fukushi kokka no byôri. Suêden-byô no kaimei (Pathological symptoms of the welfare state. Discussion about the Swedish disease).* Tôkyô: Mainichi sensho 6, Mainichi shinbunsha.

Sahara, Yô. 1989. *Nihon-teki seijuku shakai-ron. 20-seikimatsu no Nihon to nihonjin no seikatsu (On Japanese mature society. Japan and Japanese people at the end of the 20th century).* Tôkyô: Tôkai daigaku shuppankai.

Takahashi, Mutsuko. 1995. *Japanese Welfare Society. Analysing the Japanese Welfare Discourses.* (Acta Universitatis Tamperensis, ser A vol. 462). Tampere.

Watanuki, Joji. 1986. Is There a Japanese-Type Welfare Society?. *International Sociology*, vol. 1, No. 3, 259-69.

Zito, George V. 1984. *Systems of Discourse. Structures and Semiotics in the Social Sciences.* Connecticut: Greenwood Press.

Biographical Notes

Lars Bonderup Bjørn, Ph.D. from the University of Aarhus (Denmark), is Director's Assistant in Aalborg Industries, Aalborg (Denmark).

Jørgen Bramsen is an M.A. student at the Department of Asian Studies, University of Copenhagen (Denmark).

Bjarke Frellesvig, Ph.D. in Japanese Linguistics from the University of Copenhagen (Denmark), is Associate Professor at the Department of East European and Oriental Studies, University of Oslo (Norway).

Steven Hagers is a Ph.D. student at the University of Leiden (Holland).

Luk Van Haute, Ph.D. in Japanese Literature from the University of Gent (Belgium), is the coordinator of the Japanese Studies Program at the Mercator Institute in Gent.

Mariko Hayashi, Ph.D. in Psychology from the University of Aarhus (Denmark), is Associate Professor at the Institute of East Asian Studies, University of Aarhus (Denmark).

Christian Morimoto Hermansen is a Ph.D. student at the Department of Asian Studies at the University of Copenhagen (Denmark).

Benedicte M. Irgens is a Ph.D. student at the Institute of Linguistics and Comparative Literature at the University of Bergen (Norway).

Olof G. Lidin, emeritus Professor at the Department of Asian Studies, University of Copenhagen (Denmark), received his Ph.D. in Japanese from the University of California, Berkeley (USA).

Mika Merviö Ph.D. in Social Science from the University of Tampere (Finland), is Associate Professor of Political Science at the Miyazaki International College (*Miyazaki kokusai daigaku*) in Miyazaki (Japan).

Yôichi Nagashima, Ph.D. in Japanese Literature from the University of Copenhagen (Denmark), is Associate Professor of Japanese at the University of Copenhagen.

James O'Brien, Ph.D. in Japanese Literature from Indiana University (USA), is Professor of Japanese at the University of Wisconsin (USA).

Onishi Takuichiro graduated from Tohoku University (Japan); he is chief researcher at the National Language Research Institute, Tokyo (Japan).

Sang-Chul Park, Dr.rer.soc. and Dr.ekon., is a research fellow at the Centre for East and Southeast Asian Studies, Göteborg University (Sweden).

Leif Selstad, Ph.D. in Social Anthropology from the University of Bergen (Norway), is Assistant Professor of Cultural Studies at Finnmark College, Alta (Norway).

Reïko Shimamori, Ph.D. in Japanese Linguistics from the University of Sorbonne, Paris (France), is Associate Professor in Japanese at the University of Lyon III (France).

Roy Starrs, Ph.D. in Japanese Literature from the University of British Columbia (Canada), heads Japanese Studies at the University of Otago (New Zealand).

Takahashi Mutsuko, Ph.D. from the Department of Social Policy and Social Work at the University of Tampere (Finland), is Associate Professor of Sociology at the Department of Comparative Culture, Miyazaki International College (*Miyazaki kokusai daigaku*), Miyazaki (Japan).

Lone Takeuchi, Dr.Phil from the University of Copenhagen (Denmark), is a former Lecturer in Japanese at the School of Oriental and African Studies, London (UK).

Noriko Thunman, Ph.D. from Stockholm University (Sweden), is Professor of Japanese at the Department of Oriental Languages, Göteborg University (Sweden).

Yuko Yoshida, Ph.D. in Linguistics from the School of Oriental and African

Studies, University of London (UK), is Assistant Professor at the Institute for Language and Culture, Doshisha University, Kyoto (Japan).

Index of Names